ZHITOMIR,
UKRAINE

ODESSA,
UKRAINE

ALEXANDROVSK-SAKHALINSKY,
SAKHALIN, RUSSIA

ONDINI,
SOUTH AFRICA

NOUMÉA,
NEW CALEDONIA

William Atkins

EXILES

Three Island Journeys

First published in 2022
by Faber & Faber Ltd
Bloomsbury House
74–77 Great Russell Street
London WC1B 3DA

Typeset by Faber & Faber Ltd
Printed and bound by CPI Group (UK) Ltd, Croydon, CR0 4YY

A CIP record for this book
is available from the British Library

ISBN 978–0–571–35298–2

2 4 6 8 10 9 7 5 3 1

For Keith Atkins

Go, book, and bring to the places I loved my greeting –
Ovid, *Tristia*, I.1.15 (translated by Peter Green)

Contents

Prologue

On Homesickness

A book's origins are elusive. Try to follow its roots into the soil of its making and you will find they branch almost infinitely. But two images remain vivid. In the summer of 2016 the news sites were full of photos of life jackets on Greek beaches, thousands of them, discarded by migrants who had crossed the Aegean from Turkey: great moraines of orange, yellow, blue and black. Months earlier, while walking in the desert in Arizona, I had come across heaps of rucksacks left at roadsides and in dry creek beds by migrants from Central America and elsewhere, who had crossed the nearby Mexico border clandestinely. Seven thousand miles apart, those twin accumulations were at once peculiar to our own era and eloquent of a whole history of human displacement.

I began to think I had been wrong: the main cause of our unhappiness was not loneliness, as I had always believed, but a desire to be somewhere *else*. It occurred to me that the lives of an earlier kind of displaced person, political deportees sent to a designated location, could show me things that accounts of migrancy, banishment or confinement alone could not: about the word 'home', and the behaviour of empires, and the conflict between leaving and staying that seems to animate the world.

This form of exile, which can be traced back to Ancient Rome, underwent a revival in the late nineteenth century. We might call it imperial exile, since one of its requirements is that the exiling power controls territory far from its heartland. So it was not a coincidence that the three people who eventually became my subjects lived at a time when European empire-building was at its most rapacious, or that their places of exile were remote islands. A French anarchist named Louise Michel; a Zulu king named Dinuzulu kaCetshwayo; a Ukrainian revolutionary named Lev Shternberg: each sacrificed freedom and home to larger ideas of freedom and home: Michel as a figurehead of the short-lived socialist government known as the Paris Commune, Dinuzulu as an enemy of British colonialism in Zululand, and Shternberg as a militant campaigner for the overthrow of tsarism in Russia.

I was drawn to them because their lives were shaped by three winds that blow strongly today – Nationalism, Autocracy, Imperialism – and because of the way each of them responded to their sentence personally; how they seemed to absorb the fracturing effects of exile, allowing the loss of their homeland to sharpen their sense of duty rather than blunt it. I admired them, especially their ability to keep one eye on the horizon – that is, the future – from the islands to which they were banished: New Caledonia in the South Pacific in Michel's case; St Helena in the South Atlantic in Dinuzulu's; and Sakhalin, off the far-eastern coast of Siberia, in Shternberg's.

Of the three, Michel alone could be described as famous, and even her name isn't often heard outside France. As for their places of exile, only St Helena was at all familiar to me, and purely because of its association with an earlier exile, Napoleon Bonaparte. These three islands appeared to lie far outside the mainstream of history; but in Arizona I'd learnt that the edge was precisely where the power of the metropole – Paris, London, St Petersburg, Washington D.C., Rome – was often most brazenly and revealingly expressed. Go to those three islands, I thought, and you might begin to understand not only what exile meant for your subjects, but something about the nature of displacement itself.

One way of looking at this book is as a collection of stories pieced together, in the field, from lives shattered by exile. But in making the three journeys at its heart, I set out as a biographer only in a limited sense. It was less the life's course I was interested in tracing than the cracks in that life set off by the experience of exile. As I travelled I saw how those cracks intruded, continued to intrude, deep into the lives of others. The people I encountered, the living and the dead, often turned out to be exiles themselves, of one sort or another, sometimes yearning for a belonging that eluded them, sometimes living at peace with their state of unbelonging.

Nearly 2,000 years ago the Roman poet Ovid, whom I came to think of as a guiding spirit overseeing my three journeys, was exiled to the city of Tomis on the Black Sea (the modern-day resort of Constanţa, Romania). Although the reasons for his banishment – 'a poem and an error' – remain hazy, the long, yearning, self-pitying epistolary poems he wrote during those years are among the founding texts of literary exile. Fearing that he will die 'unmourned, unhonoured, in a barbarian land' (in Peter Green's translation), the poet goes so far as to draft his own epitaph:

> I who lie here, sweet Ovid, poet of tender passions,
>   fell victim to my own sharp wit.
> Passer-by, if you've ever been in love, don't grudge me
>   the traditional prayer: 'May Ovid's bones lie soft!'

But Ovid's longing was not unique. Tomis was a troubled settlement; natives of the city were frequently abducted by local bandits, 'driven off, hands tied behind them, gazing back in vain at fields and home'. That last word reminds us that while the victim of banishment is usually forced to leave his world's centre for its periphery, the place to which he is banished is invariably someone else's centre. 'Here, *I'm* the barbarian,' Ovid acknowledges.

By 1914 all of the Pacific and almost all of Africa had been colonised, and one of the tools of that vast occupation was penal expatriation. Whether they were common convicts or political dissidents, exiles were rarely just prisoners; they were at once machines for extracting wealth from foreign soil and flags planted in that soil. Deportation and coerced settlement have always been part of the arsenal of empire – even Ovid, banished to the edge of the Roman world, appreciated that he was not merely an exile but a 'colonist of a troubled frontier post'. Sometimes the colonised and the exiled found common cause. During the 'Kanak Insurrection', for instance, Louise Michel, banished to New Caledonia for life, was able to see the islands' indigenous people as allies with a common foe: a French colonial government that viewed the Communards and the Kanaks alike as different species of barbarian to be tamed.

This book, which was conceived as a reflection on exile, became just as much a book about empire, because the two have always gone hand in hand. It is also, therefore, about the solidarities that formed between those twin victims of empire: the *déporté* and the *indigène*; the banished citizen and the colonised subject.

———

In 1688 a young medical student from Berne named Johannes Hofer wrote a thesis entitled *Dissertatio Medica de Nostalgia, oder Heimwehe* ('a medical dissertation on nostalgia, or homesickness'). In Hofer's sense, nostalgia – a word he coined – did not contain its modern meaning of sentimental longing: it was something far more deadly, and it was in order to pathologise the ailment that he came up with this new name for what he recognised as a peculiar set of symptoms.

'There came to my mind the stories of youths thus afflicted', he wrote, 'that unless they had been brought back to their native land, whether in a fever or consumed by the "wasting disease", they had met their last day on foreign shores.' As if the sundering of the body from its rightful co-ordinates might kill a person as surely as if they had been teleported to an oxygenless planet.

In German, *Heimweh*; in French, *mal du pays* – homesickness; longing for one's homeland – but the condition, Hofer noted, 'lacks a particular name in medicine'. Hence 'nostalgia', from the ancient Greek *nostos*, a homeward journey of the kind made by Odysseus; and the combining form *algos*, denoting pain. The pain of being unable to make the homeward journey. Hofer describes it as 'grief for the lost charm of the native land'. It 'originates by arousing especially the uncommon and ever-present idea of the recalled native land'. He describes the case of a fellow student from Berne, who, having gone to Basel to study, 'suffering from sadness for considerable time, finally fell victim to this disease'. Since he appeared to be dying, it was decided to return him to his home. 'He was scarcely some few miles from our city,' Hofer continues, 'when all the symptoms already abated . . . and he was restored to his whole sane self.'

The condition was temporal as well as spatial; what had been lost was not only the homeland but the life that should have been lived there.

The symptoms: 'Continued sadness, meditation only of the Fatherland, disturbed sleep either wakeful or continuous, decrease of strength, hunger, thirst, senses diminished, and cares or even palpitations of the heart, frequent sighs, also stupidity of the mind – attending to nothing hardly, other than an idea of the Fatherland.' As for an antidote, Hofer suggests 'internal hypnotic emulsions' or 'external cephalic balsams'; but there is really only one sure cure: 'hope of returning to the Fatherland must be given as soon as the strength seems somewhat equal to bearing the annoyances of a return journey'.

In his poems from Tomis, Ovid returns again and again to the effect of his banishment on his health: 'Neither terrain nor water, air nor climate suit me / an unending lassitude seeps through my frame.' Elsewhere he describes his sentence as a kind of dismemberment: 'I felt myself ripped asunder as though I'd lost a limb . . .'

Not for nothing did Hofer describe his repatriated student as having returned to his 'whole' (*integraeque*) self.

———

I suggested that this book could be seen as an attempt to recompose lives shattered by exile. But the journeys I describe, theirs and mine, reminded me that no life, no self, is a unity, however sealed off from history it might appear to be. While I was travelling, my father became ill, and his illness and decline, I realise, have coloured what follows. Though this is not a book about death or grief, every travel book is a kind of allegory. One reason stories of exile move us is that they seem to acknowledge the unhealable ruptures in our own lives – separation and loss, bereavement – even if we ourselves have never left the village of our birth.

I

The Red Flag
Louise Michel

Sometime around 1840 two little girls stand on a rickety homemade stage in a garden in rural France. One of them, skinny and sunburnt, clothes held together by pins, is clasping her hands tightly behind her back, as if she is roped to a stake. The other, her cousin, kneels at her feet, then stands back, wide eyed. As the imaginary flames take hold, the first girl takes a deep breath, then screams at the top of her lungs: '*Vive la République!*'

When I picture Louise Michel, she is either a middle-aged woman in sun-greyed black crêpe, looking out to sea from a Pacific island; or she is *this* Louise – Louisette, as she was known – in the grounds of Chateau Vroncourt, pretending to be, say, the Christian reformer John Hus as he is burnt at the stake.

The chateau, 'between the forest and the plain', in the Haute-Marne, 170 miles east of Paris, was austere grey with a square grey tower at each corner. The villagers of Vroncourt called it *la Tombe* because of its sparsity of windows. 'I am what is known as a bastard,' Michel wrote, 'but those who bestowed upon me the sorry gift of life did so

11

freely; they loved each other.' Her mother, Marianne, was a maid in the Demahis household, where she herself had grown up, and it was with her and M. and Mme Demahis that Louisette spent her childhood. 'My mother was then a blonde, with soft and smiling blue eyes and long, curly hair. She was so fresh and pretty that her friends used to say to her laughingly, "It is impossible for this ugly child to be yours."' Her father seems to have been a wayward Demahis son, Laurent, who paid little attention to his daughter. Marianne, conversely, would remain the most important figure in her life, no matter the distance between them.

Pets: dogs and cats, a tortoise, a boar, an orphaned wolf. In the north tower she set up a study-cum-laboratory, shared with a 'magnificent barn owl with phosphorescent eyes' and 'some darling bats who drank milk like little cats'. 'The devil, if he exists, knows everything I tried there: alchemy, astrology, the summoning of spirits.' In her tower she also wrote verses addressed to her literary hero, Victor Hugo, who was to remain a correspondent, champion – perhaps, briefly, lover – and friend until his death.

Outside, at the end of the courtyard, was a pond framed by rosebushes, on which she sailed toy boats with her grandfather, Etienne-Charles, and where toads bred noisily in the spring. Vroncourt remained her archetypal idyll throughout her life, even if she would one day know another arcadia. 'At the Tomb, near the hazel tree in a bastion of the wall, was a bench where my mother and grandmother used to come during the summer after the heat of the day.'

My mother, to make Grandmother happy, had filled this corner of the garden with all kinds of rosebushes. While the two women talked I leaned on the wall. The garden was cool in the dew of the evening. The perfumes of all the flowers mingled and climbed up to the sky. The honeysuckle, the reseda, the roses, all exhaled sweet perfumes which joined each other.

The chateau was separated from the village of Vroncourt by a grassy plain; to the west were the woods and the hills of Suzerin, while east was the Demahis vineyard, screened by poplars. Even further east, on the road to Bourmont, stood Uncle Georges' mill, with its pond and meadow, and beyond it a range of mountains made blue by distance. Paris, meanwhile, was not yet a dream, and New Caledonia – unheard of, 10,000 miles away – was beyond the frontier even of dreams.

In autumn, with her mother and aunts, she would walk deep into the adjoining forest, and hear the knocking of axes and the snorts of wild boar. Forests and trees remained meaningful for her as emblems of sanctuary throughout her life on both sides of the world, while her love of animals – those owls, and boars, and wolves, later an army of cats – and her contempt for those who ill-treated them were of a part with the disquiet the young Michel increasingly felt about society beyond the chateau grounds.

The children's execution cries echoed out from the courtyard across the expanding ambit of her home: the north tower and the great hall and the bastion-niche where the honeysuckle grew; the vineyard and the forest; the town of Audeloncourt where her mother's family lived; and the mountains in which all were cradled – like the postal address a child will write, beginning with their house and expanding beyond district and nation to continent, planet, solar system, universe . . . but always telescoping back to the address's first line: Chateau Vroncourt.

We learn the meaning of home when we must leave. She claimed she was never homesick for France, only for the dead, for her grandparents and her dear, suffering mother; but Vroncourt would never leave her. It was where she longed for even while she remained in France. Soon it would all be lost, irretrievably. In 1851, aged twenty-one, she heard news from Paris of the bloodshed that followed

Louis-Napoléon's coup: hundreds of protestors killed and thousands more transported to France's colonies in French Guiana and Algeria. Nineteen years later, in 1870, the invading Prussian army, making its way to lay siege to the capital, would tear up her grandmother's vineyard and fell the forest for firewood.

———

Published in 1886, her memoirs are preachy, earnest, mystical, airy in the sense of buoyantly untethered, and unsettling in their symbology of blood, fire, wolves, storms, oak trees and axes (she was a poet at heart if not on paper). The book can be dizzyingly evasive – zooming in on the minutest memory at one moment, only to pull out to an aerial viewpoint the next, often at a time when the action seems most fundamental to our understanding of her life and person.

Its failings are partly a matter of authorial discretion, poor memory and inattention (she was writing it in Saint-Lazare prison, mainly in order to repay a debt to her friend Henri Rochefort). Michel writes at the outset that she will 'leave in the shadows' those who brought her up – her mother and grandparents – but in fact it is the book's later elisions that are conspicuous, as if the weaver's shuttle has been allowed to skip sections of the warp. The years between her arrival in Paris in 1856, aged twenty-six, and the declaration of the radical socialist government known as the Commune in 1871, for instance – the crucial years when the blade of her politics was being sharpened as her influence grew – are granted twenty pages, several of which describe the line-by-line progress of an opera she was writing.

Sometimes it's like reading a collage made out of scraps torn from the political posters she pasted up around Paris – everything declared in red capitals. At other times it's as if she is addressing someone who had been alongside her; one who, knowing the major events, only needs to be filled in on the minutiae. Its most vivid passages, its most lovingly attentive, don't concern the Commune, or her comrades, or politics at all, really, but instead linger on what I see, now, as the twin poles of her life: the Vroncourt of her childhood and the New Caledonia of her exile – specifically another forest, a place she called the Forest of the West.

In 1853 the 23-year-old Michel opened a school in Audeloncourt, her mother's village, a few miles south of Vroncourt. She never forgot her students – Little Mole, Big Rose, Tall Estelle, Lame Aricie, Eudoxie who 'died in my arms during an epidemic' – and their twice-daily rendition of the 'Marseillaise' with its children's refrain, 'We'll take over this course / When our elders are no longer here'. Whenever the village priest led the prayer to the emperor – *Domine, salvum fac Napoleunem* – Michel warned her wards it was a sacrilege to pray for 'that man', Napoleon Bonaparte's nephew, Louis-Napoléon, who had seized power two years earlier. Her ambition to go to Paris having been discovered, the concerned citizens of Audeloncourt denounced her as a republican. And what of it? Summoned by the town prefect, she was accused of insulting the emperor, and threatened with exile to France's penal colony in French Guiana. She would be happy to set up a school there, she replied, and grateful for the fare. The threat went no further.

In 1856, 'the Tomb' having been sold following her grandparents' deaths, she left Vroncourt for Paris, teaching at the school of a Mme Vollier on rue du Château-d'Eau in the 10th arrondissement, until with money Marianne made from the sale of land she had been left by the Demahises, she was able to buy her own day school in Mont-martre. 'The poor woman,' she wrote of her mother's sacrifice, 'how little she got back for that money . . .'

If her memoirs are taken at face value, her arrival in Paris did not mark a political awakening so much as a homecoming: it was where one such as she, with convictions such as hers, belonged. She recognised that Paris was 'at the heart of affairs' but also a portal to the wider world (as it would prove to be, though not perhaps in the way she imagined). She arrived at a city in destitution, in a sort of moral chaos, with more than a third of its population classified as indigent. Understanding that civic planning was a form of civic control, in 1853 the emperor had the old city razed, with 20,000 buildings demolished. The former ramshackle, riddling alleys and streets were replaced by networks of straight boulevards inimical to the building of barricades and broad enough for horse-drawn cannon to move along two abreast. An anti-revolutionary metropolis. The workers, meanwhile, alienated from their capital, were consigned to outlying slums.

It is a mistake to imagine a transforming moment, a single tripwire igniting her 'radicalism', but if we're seeking its roots then Vroncourt is the place. Her grandparents, however peculiar in their crumbling chateau full of feral animals, had hardly been political outliers in Catholic Vroncourt, while Michel's politics only ever bewildered and scared Marianne. It was not that her childhood world was unusual (it was unusual, but not that unusual); just that she was unusually sensitive to injustice, feeling powerfully the pain of other beings, animals particularly. 'The dominant idea of an entire life can come from some random impression,' she would note in her memoirs:

When I was very small, I saw a decapitated goose . . . The goose was walking about stiffly, and where its head had been its neck was a bruised and bloody wound. It was a white goose with its feathers spattered with blood, and it walked like a drunkard while its head, thrown into a corner, lay on the floor with its eyes closed.

When, as an adult, Michel recalled those instances of animal mistreatment she beheld as a child, she found they had accrued an enlarged symbolic weight. Her life's campaign was not 'political' – she had no interest in any kind of office – but simply to oppose the causes of suffering, which could hardly be clearer to her:

> The peasants sow and harvest the grain, but they do not always have bread. One woman told me how during a bad year – that is what they call a year when the monopolists starve the country – neither she, nor her husband, nor their four children were able to eat every day. Owning only the clothes on their backs, they had nothing more to sell. Merchants who had grain gave them no more credit, not even a few oats to make a little bread, and two of their children died.

But it was the image of the blood-spattered, headless goose that haunted her. Blood: her obsession as a poet and a revolutionary. It was the price of freedom; she had seen this even as a teenager. In the years leading up to the Franco-Prussian War of 1870 and the founding of the Commune, she describes a capital beset by increasing paranoia even as it is energised by the prospect of renewal. She is associating with leading republicans and amusing herself by creeping after 'some good bourgeois' late one night, for the fun of scaring him. 'And so here is Louise Michel,' she writes, in an ironic self-portrait. 'She is a menace to society, for she has declared a hundred times that everyone should take part in the banquet of life . . .'

She lived in near-poverty, reliant on her mother and friends for loans. Her school became a menagerie of animals: mice, a tortoise, a grass snake. It would not be the last time she would seek to revive Chateau Vroncourt. The children adored her – her liberalism and kindness. If she yearned for revolution, at this stage, it was for personal revolution, an overthrowing of the spirit of the provinces. It may have been simply living in Paris, in those years of squalor, with the empire seemingly ascendant, that caused her to see that actual

18

revolution was necessary, that the Church of her childhood could not help, and that Napoleon III would not be defeated by even the goriest poetry. She campaigned for women's labour rights, and became secretary of the Democratic Society for Moralisation, an organisation committed to finding jobs for women at a living wage. She was not alone among Parisians in scenting blood on the wind, and understood that equality meant the right to give up one's life, as well as the right to education and a salary: 'If the men hang back when the time comes, women will lead the way. And I'll be there.' When, in 1869, the anti-imperialist Victor Noir, a journalist at one of Henri Rochefort's newspapers, was shot dead by an affronted cousin of the emperor's, Michel took to wearing black; and she would wear it for the rest of her life. She would say it was simply that she never ceased to have something or someone to mourn; but black for Michel was more a uniform than it was a form of widow's weeds – the uniform of her righteousness. It suited her.

Following her maternal grandmother's death in the late 1860s, she was joined in Paris by Marianne, but with 'revolution' imminent she rarely saw her: 'I left her alone during many long evenings. Afterwards it was days, then months, then years. Can the mothers of revolutionaries ever be happy?' For while she taught during the day, by night she and her associates met to discuss revolution. To Victor Hugo, newly returned from Guernsey, where he had been living in exile since publishing a scathing attack on Louis-Napoléon in 1850, she continued to send poem after poem, as she had as a girl; but now, she acknowledged, 'the verses I sent him smelled of gunpowder': 'Do you hear the brazen thunder,' went one, 'Behind the man who takes no side?' Reluctance to take a side was unimaginable to her. As for Louis-Napoléon, that snake, that worm, that spider, as Hugo called him: 'I would have killed my tyrant without any feeling of distress.'

In 1870, fourteen years after Michel's arrival in Paris, the 'tyrant' embarked on a military adventure calculated to bolster support in France at a time when republicanism and socialism were seen as growing challenges to his power. His declaration of war against the North German Federation under Prussia was soon to result in the unification of Germany, disaster for France and disgrace for the emperor. After a calamitous battle with Prussian-German forces at Sedan, on 1 September, 17,000 French soldiers lay dead and Louis-Napoléon was taken prisoner with 100,000 of his troops. The rout wasn't complete. Prussian and German forces far outnumbering their French counterparts burnt their way, sometimes unhindered, across north-eastern France, laying waste to Michel's childhood forest in Vroncourt and finally surrounding a restive Paris whose enmity was soon as much for its own failed government as for the forces be-sieging it. For Michel and her associates, the great destination of their lives was within sight.

Hugo wrote in his journal that a favoured dish in the besieged city was rat pâté: 'It is said to be quite good.' While trying to keep her students fed, Michel joined the so-called Vigilance Committee of the 18th arrondissement, one of a network of socialist community co-operatives that arranged employment, distributed food and cared for the sick. Her associates were 'absolutely devoted to the revolu-tion', she wrote. 'They didn't define duty according to your sex. That stupid question was finally done with.' If the question was not quite done with, Michel did enjoy a growing respect among her group. But it was her willingness to take up arms, when the time came – her seeming blitheness about which end of a carbine's barrel she was looking down – that turned her into a subject deemed worthy of biography.

Louis-Napoléon's Second Empire was overthrown and a provision-
al Government of National Defence established, including Michel's
friends Henri Rochefort and Victor Hugo, only for it to surrender
in January 1871. With Paris still blockaded and most of the regular
French army dead, injured or taken prisoner, the defence of the capital fell to the republican National Guard, a force of some 300,000
untrained men, mostly from working-class Paris neighbourhoods,
who were incensed by the government's capitulation.

In February 1871 a new republican government was elected under
Adolphe Thiers, former prime minister and opponent of Louis-
Napoléon, who signed an armistice with Prussia's Bismarck. A month
later, in a liberated Paris, the Commune was born, backed by the
National Guard and supported by some 80 per cent of the city's elec-
torate. Hugo deemed the Commune 'an admirable thing', albeit 'stu-
pidly compromised' by a spirit of vengeance. This new government
demanded a 'system of communal insurance against all social risk'
and an end to 'pauperism' through the redistribution of wealth. And
it really was a government. Among its first acts were the abolition of
military conscription, child labour and the death penalty, the separation of Church and State, and the adoption of the French Revolutionary Calendar, last used in 1805, with its ten-day week, and
months named after the prevailing weather.

On 18 March – '28 *Ventôse*' – Thiers sent thousands of French
troops into Paris (many of them recently released by their German
captors) to take control of cannon held by the National Guard.
Barricades were constructed and crowds swelled around the troops
attempting to extract the weapons, cutting the horses' harness-
es and pelting the soldiers with bottles. In Montmartre, General
Claude Lecomte commanded his troops to fire on the crowd. The
men refused, and turned the muzzles of their rifles to the ground.
Taken prisoner by the National Guard, Lecomte was marched to

21

their headquarters on rue de Rosiers, with another general, Clément Thomas, who was notorious among socialist Parisians for his involvement in suppressing the uprising of 1848. Recognising both men, a crowd dragged them to a garden at the rear of the building. Michel was present, though the extent of her involvement would be disputed at her trial. Lecomte pleaded for his life – 'I have a wife, children!' – before he and Clément Thomas were shot dead. The latter 'died well', according to Michel. Paris had defended its right to autonomy. 'On this day, the eighteenth of March, the people wakened. If they had not, it would have been the triumph of some king; instead it was a triumph of the people.'

Seeing the shoots emerging of a world she had imagined since childhood, Michel was delirious with excitement, the excitement of the eager martyr. As death loomed she was reborn. She was zealous, and frightening as zealots tend to be when they imagine victory, and seems to have had no fear of pain, let alone of being killed. 'People say I'm brave,' she wrote later. 'Not really. There is no heroism; people are simply entranced by events.' And yet she never seems entranced, only clear-eyed and purposeful.

On 7 April the guillotine on place Voltaire was burnt down to the cheers of a huge crowd. Thiers' new government and army, meanwhile, having decamped to nearby Versailles, proceeded to shell the rebel capital, killing and injuring hundreds.

Michel had been serious about killing Louis-Napoléon. She was only thwarted in attempting to assassinate Thiers because she was unable to get close enough. At first her work was mainly as an *ambulancière*, caring for the wounded, but by mid-April she was fighting with the 61st National Guard battalion at Issy and Clamart, armed with a Remington carbine – a 'good weapon'. At the barricade on rue Perronet in Neuilly, she entered a deserted church. Moments later those outside heard the sound of organ music, which only stopped when a captain burst in and furiously ordered her to stop playing before she drew enemy fire.

'There is an energetic woman fighting in the ranks of the 61st battalion,' ran a report in the Commune's daily journal. 'She has killed several constables and police officers.' Her friend George Clemenceau, having seen her fighting at Issy, noted that she killed only to avoid death herself: 'I have never seen her so calm,' he added, unnerved as much as admiring. 'How she escaped being killed a hundred times over before my eyes I'll never know.' But her survival, during the Commune as in her later life, had less to do with an instinct for self-preservation, and more with that peculiar blitheness with which she apprehended death – not steeliness, exactly, just a simple incapacity to recognise mortality as anything intimate.

On 16 May 1871 came an event that marked the irreversible end of the old order, at the same time as it ushered in the most terrible week the city had ever seen – *la semaine sanglante*. 'Bloody', in this formulation, was not a euphemism.

The Vendôme column, with its statue of Napoleon Bonaparte, represented all that was loathsome about imperial France, according to the Communards: 'a monument to barbarism, a symbol of brute force and false glory, an affirmation of militarism, a negation of international law, a permanent insult to the conquered by the conquerors, and a perpetual attack against one of the three great principles of the French republic, fraternity'. That morning, thousands of Parisians gathered around its base while musicians played songs of revolution. At 2 p.m. cables attached to the column were pulled by a team of horses, only to snap under the strain. It took more than three hours for the cables to be reattached and the column finally to tilt, totter and snap in two as it crashed to the ground. On the rubble-strewn plinth a flagpole was erected and a red flag raised – symbol of the Commune, symbol of liberty. But any mood of jubilance, or hopefulness, was short-lived. In the following week at least 35,000 Parisians were killed by government troops. A familiar scene, an old one: burning homes, bombed homes, collapsing homes, children shrouded in soot. Fire as a weapon, smoke welcomed for masking the smell of putrefaction, smoke that cast the city into such darkness that it 'had the effect of an eclipse', according to one witness; another, Gustave Flaubert, described the atmosphere in the city as 'totally epileptic'. Michel was gruesomely unfazed. 'I love the cannon, the smell of powder, machine-gun bullets in the air.'

In her memoirs she recalled a particular night, soon after the felling of the Vendôme column, when she and a brigade of Communards were defending Montmartre Cemetery. 'Shells tore the air, marking time like a clock,' she remembered; and yet for her 'it was magnificent in the clear night, where the marble statues on the tombs seemed to be alive'. Perhaps that was the source of her fearlessness, to count herself already among the dead. The Versaillais, as the government troops were known, revenged themselves for their humiliation at Sedan on their fellow citizens – some of whom had defended Paris against the same Prussian enemy months earlier. Finding that a Communard captain they were seeking was not at his home, they instead shot his twelve-year-old son. Another boy, suspected of manning a barricade, was found hiding beneath a woman's skirts, dragged out and shot. A funeral cortège of a boy killed in shelling was itself shelled and his family scattered with his body parts. Quartier by quartier, the Commune's barricades were overrun and those defending them (those who survived) taken prisoner, more often shot.

———

At Place Vendôme thirty prisoners were shot in reprisal for the destruction of the column. Communards seeking sanctuary at the Church of the Madeleine were shot, 300 of them. Around the Pantheon, 700. In the Jardin du Luxembourg as many as 3,000. Outside the Théâtre Français on rue Richelieu a ditch was filled with the dead. Blood oozed from tarpaulined heaps in the Tuileries and the courtyard of the Church of the Assumption. Rape and torture were ubiquitous. To be caught with a recoil bruise to the shoulder was as good as a death sentence, but even a working-class accent or a foreign-sounding name sufficed to seal your fate. All across Paris, as the Commune fell, groups of prisoners, men and women and children, were gunned down. The streets were littered with corpses – corners, squares and parks, cemeteries and vacant lots. The killing was on a scale far greater than both the Terror of 1793–4 and the June Days uprising of 1848. Indeed, Paris had seen nothing like it since the anti-Protestant massacres of 1572, and France would not again witness slaughter on such a scale, or of such barbarism, or of such efficiency, until the First World War. The army had become a 'vast execution squad', according to one contemporary commentator. Not that the Communards were innocent of atrocity. On 24 May, six hostages were shot, the Archbishop Darboy and five clerics – the pretext Thiers needed to intensify his attack.

In a speech he gave that day he boasted that his forces had shed blood in 'torrents'. On rue Marcadet, one witness recalled, a stream 'ran with blood as in a street next to the slaughterhouses'. Imagining the scene, the sheer *lavishness* of the slaughter, it seems extraordinary that the city ever recovered, that Michel or anyone else who witnessed the events strolled its boulevards again without collapsing in revulsion.

But for all the blood (every account lingers on it), it's not reds I see when I try to visualise Paris in those days – foaming along the banks of the Seine or darkening in the gutters or coagulating between paving slabs – but white: the smirched white of the powdered quicklime, calcium oxide, that was scattered over the dead to slow decomposition, tonnes of it dusting beards and pavements, caked on people's soles, whipped into plumes by the spring breeze. It haunted Michel. That mantle. Years later she remembered the streets 'dappled white as if by apple blossom'.

Her only injuries, meanwhile, as the Commune fell, were a bullet-grazed ear, a twisted ankle and a hat riddled with carbine holes. Any psychic wounds are harder to assess. How did she close herself to what she had witnessed, not to mention what she faced afterwards? How did she absorb that defeat? Hope was unquenchable in her. It was only after I returned from New Caledonia that I understood that she wasn't heartless, as has often been said (of a part with her 'manliness' and all the other jibes), but on the contrary that the source of her strength and her guts was an overabundance of love. She was the person she had always been, the person who had wept for a trapped wolf in the Vroncourt forest and whose girlhood companion had been a barn owl 'with phosphorescent eyes'. When the army detained her mother, she didn't think twice. She surrendered, content that she would be shot, or tried and then shot, but that Marianne would be allowed to live.

———

Michel was taken to a detention camp on the plains of Satory, south of Versailles, where she and her fellow prisoners were marched through night-time rain and mud to a ravine. They would not be shot tonight but tomorrow night – so they were told; but the next night she was spared. At the Lobau barracks on the city's rue de Rivoli, meanwhile, as many as 1,200 Communard prisoners were summarily shot on a single night. According to Michel, the swallows newly arrived from Africa that spring were 'poisoned by the flies that had been feeding in that enormous charnel house'.

In September, from prison, she wrote to her friend and fellow Communard Théophile Ferré, himself awaiting sentencing, assuring him that they would set sail for New Caledonia together, when the time came, for exile surely awaited them. She had had visions! she went on, visions of 'the great oak forest of Haute-Marne, the old tumbledown chateau where I was raised and where I heard the wolves howl in winter . . .' Again and again she returned to Vroncourt. Ferré, meanwhile, executed soon after, was never to see New Caledonia.

———

Parisians wanted to know what the infamous creature looked like. A photograph was taken and printed up as a postcard. A small rose, the red rose of socialism, pinned to her breast, is her sole adornment. You can imagine her fixing the members of the tribunal with those same large eyes, that same steady gaze; without vanity; quite at ease, if a bit cross: she does not like the photographer, Eugène Appert, celebrated portraitist, enemy of the Commune. Get on with it, man.

As a prisoner of war she was court-martialled in Versailles on 16 December 1871, charged with insurrection, fomenting civil war, carrying and using weapons, forgery and complicity (if not participation) in illegal arrests, torture, murder and, most damningly, the killing of Lecomte and Clément Thomas at rue des Rosiers.

She refused a lawyer and repudiated only what she regretted and refuted only what she knew to be untrue. She was, for example, not *short*, as the charge sheet had it; just look at her (the Ministry of War's own records from the day):

Height: 1.64 metres
Hair: brown
Eyebrows: brown
Eyes: brown
Nose: large

Mouth: average

Chin: round

Face: oval

Complexion: regular

It was alleged – the Commune's opponents being eager to associate it with international socialism – that she had both conspired with 'foreigners and rascals who had come from every corner of the globe' and fought on the frontline during the battles at Clamart, Montmartre and Issy. The second charge was true enough. 'What was the motive that pushed her down this irrevocable path of politics and revolution?' The answer was self-evident: 'Clearly, it was arrogance.'

> Louise Michel was an illegitimate child reared by charity. Instead of thanking Providence for giving her the means to live happily with her mother, she surrendered to her heated imagination and excitable character. Breaking with her benefactors, she ran to Paris for adventure.

She would not have objected to being called a 'she-wolf, eager for blood', and she had never denied she was a 'bastard' (on the contrary), but noted that she was raised not by charity or benefaction but by her mother and her grandparents. Lifting her black veil, she stared at the judges (*yeux: marron*): 'I declare that I accept responsibility for all my actions. I accept it entirely and without reservations.'

She had not participated in the murders of Lecomte and Clément Thomas, and had not expected them to be killed; unlike M. Thiers and the forces represented by the court, she added, she abhorred the killing of prisoners. But yes, she was a member of the Commune, and proud; nor did she see anything wrong with violence in the name of justice.

But – what was the point in defending herself to men whose minds were made up? 'We never wanted anything but the triumph of the great principles of Revolution.'

'You claim that you didn't approve of the generals' assassinations,' said the judge. 'On the contrary, people say that when you were told about it you cried out: "They shot them. Serves them right."'

If she had said that, she answered, it was purely with the intention of 'spurring on revolutionary zeal'.

Did she have anything to add in her defence?

'Since it seems that any heart that beats for liberty has the right only to a small lump of lead, I demand my share. If you let me live, I will not stop crying for vengeance, and I will denounce the assassins of the Board of Pardons to the vengeance of my brothers—'

The judge intervened, 'I cannot allow you to continue speaking if you continue in this tone.'

'I have finished . . . If you are not cowards, kill me.'

Learning that she was to be deported to a 'fortified place', she told the court she would prefer death. Only later did she consider that her sentence had been a kind of deliverance: 'It was better to be somewhere else, and so not see the collapse of our dreams.' To her mother she wrote words of comfort: 'Take heart and above all take care, that I may see you again. I am not going far.' The truth, as she knew, was that she was going as far as it was possible to go.

After more than eighteen months in Auberive Prison she was taken to the port at Rochefort, where Marianne came to see her off: 'I noticed for the first time that her hair was turning white,' her daughter recalled.

While Louis-Napoléon was allowed to go into comfortable self-exile in London (as King Charles X and King Louis-Philippe had before him), Michel was among more than 4,000 Communards sentenced to deportation to France's South Pacific colony of New

Caledonia: a vast traumatised army, appalled by its defeat, filled with hatred for its captors, expelled to a distant country of unimaginable foreignness.

France had been purging itself of 'undesirables' ever since the early eighteenth century, when hundreds of beggars, former prisoners and prostitutes were pressganged from the streets of Paris and transported to Louisiana, which urgently required a colonising population. But it wasn't until Louis-Napoléon's Second Empire that exile became an intrinsic element of the French penal system. By the 1870s French Guiana, which had been used as a dumping ground for seditious priests and other such dangerous elements since 1795, was deemed a failure: the ubiquity of endemic diseases meant that *exil en Guyane* was viewed as all but a sentence of death. Of the 8,000 men (and a handful of women) shipped to the colony between 1852 and 1856, half were dead within five years, a toll worse than Stalinist Siberia. The very system of penal colonialism was born of a recognition that the convict was too valuable as a source of labour to be merely executed, or allowed to die.

An earlier Napoleon, Bonaparte, had maintained that 'the best penitentiary system would be one which purged the old world through populating the new'. But a committee on deportation established in the aftermath of the Commune maintained that the objective of penal expatriation should also be to civilise its subjects, not just sanitise the metropole or settle the colonies. In the wilderness of the South Seas, wrote the head of the committee, the wretches of the Commune 'will be led quickly to realise that the laws which govern all societies are eternal and that these laws bear down on all revolts with an ineluctable and necessary authority'. Had he encountered Louise Michel, in the flesh, or even seen Appert's portrait, the utter resoluteness of its subject's gaze?

31

DINIZULU   E.E.CANSY PHO

Ghost Mountain

Dinuzulu kaCetshwayo

Dinuzulu, Cetshwayo's son, aged about twenty, at the Pietermaritz-burg police barracks in the then British colony of Natal, south-eastern Africa. It is November 1888 and he has just been induced to surrender. The photo is a mugshot, but also an ethnographic record, also a trophy. He was born in north-west Zululand, the region from which the nation emerged in the eighteenth century. As a baby he was 'Mahalena-who-comes-from-oNdini', according to the Zulu historian Magema Fuze. When his father was crowned in 1873, he commissioned the building of a huge *umuzi*, or royal homestead: oNdini, the nation's capital. He granted his young son his royal name, Dinuzulu, from either *udin'uZulu*, 'he wearies the Zulus' or, conversely, *udinwa nguZulu*, 'he is wearied *by* the Zulus'. Either way, it seems Cetshwayo had a presentiment of how the boy's life would turn out.

The new capital, in the dry thorn-bush country of the Mahlabathini Plain, was named to denote its impregnability, *oNdini* meaning rim or escarpment. It housed several thousand people, as many as 5,000 during feasts and festivals. Elliptical in shape, like most Zulu homesteads, it was ringed by a double palisade, the outer one of sharpened timbers, the inner of rushes. In its centre was a parade ground where the king inspected his men and where the royal cattle were kept.

The king's own hut and those of his wives stood in a fenced enclosure at the homestead's northern edge, while Dinuzulu and his royal sisters slept in the adjoining enclosure. To the rear was a rise from which the king could survey oNdini. Standing there, if he had dared trespass, Dinuzulu would have seen, scattered across the plain, several minor homesteads, and the royal cattle known as *inyonikayiphumuli*, 'the bird that never rests'. To the north was the Hlophekhulu Mountain, source of the spring reserved for his father's drinking water; to the south, the Mbilane Stream, from which the royal bathwater was drawn, and which, further south, fed into the fuming White Umfolozi. Beyond that river's far bank, some fifteen miles away, was eMakhosini, the Valley of the Kings, where Dinuzulu's ancestors, the founders of the Zulu kingdom, are buried. And somewhere between the river and the sacred valley was KwaNkatha, the place of execution.

The most intimate account of daily life in oNdini comes from one of Cetshwayo's teenage servants, Paulina Dlamini, who was interviewed by a missionary after converting to Christianity. Dinuzulu would be woken by the dawn song of praise to the king:

We had to rise forthwith, tidy the huts and sweep the yard. At sunrise the king emerged from his hut. By that time everything had to be tidy and orderly. As soon as he appeared, his manservants came forward; if the king wished to go on an early morning hunt, they fetched the sporting guns from the 'black house'. When he left, the whole *umuzi* appeared as if deserted, yet it was full of people; but no one was allowed to show himself.

In the afternoon, when Dinzulu's father was ready to eat, the people of oNdini would be warned to keep hidden and silent. The penalty for disobedience could be severe. Dlamini remembered the construction of the king's black house, whitewashed and glazed in the European style, where he kept his rifles and convened the royal council. The builders, from a nearby Christian mission, were to be waited upon by two of her fellow serving girls. When Cetshwayo happened to ask the men if they had eaten well, he was told no food had been arranged. The girls were confronted and, giving no explanation (perhaps they were too scared to speak), were taken to KwaNkatha. 'We did not consider their neglect of duty sufficiently severe to merit the death penalty,' said Dlamini.

Death, and the world of the dead, were close. Before the young man, like a meal laid out, was his kingdom by ancestral right, the abode of the *amadlozi*, spirits of his ancestors, who not only reside in the earth but are synonymous with it. But any safety he felt was to be short-lived, for those five years were the last settled ones he would know. When the British invaded in 1879, under the *casus belli* of Cetshwayo's refusal to disband his military regiments, oNdini was destroyed, the royal cattle were seized and more than a thousand Zulus killed. It was partly plain revenge for the shock defeat Cetshwayo's forces had dealt the British at the Battle of Isandlwana six months earlier, when an army of 20,000 Zulus had killed more than 1,300 British and colonial troops in Britain's greatest military disaster in nearly a century. ONdini burnt for four days, leaving nothing but potsherds and bones, and the discs of clay, fired hard by the flames, which had once been the floors of the royal huts.

———

Dinuzulu's friend and tutor Magema Fuze put it bluntly: 'When Dinuzulu was still a boy of about ten years, the European [that is to say British] army invaded and destroyed the nation.'

Captured by the British and confined to Cape Town, almost 900 miles from oNdini, his father Cetshwayo was obliged to watch from afar while the Zulu kingdom was partitioned once more, into thirteen chieftaincies. Banishment had been a weapon of the British in Africa since the Frontier Wars of the early nineteenth century, when captured Xhosa warriors had been exiled to Robben Island off Cape Town. Britain's priority in Zululand would continue to be the suppression of any flicker of centralised indigenous power.

Cetshwayo's greatest ally in exile was his friend John Colenso, known to Zulus as Sobantu ('father of the people'), Bishop of Natal, lifelong irritant to the British, and an outspoken critic of the invasion. By the established Church, Colenso had been despised as a dissident since as long ago as 1862, when he published a volume of biblical commentary widely regarded as heretical. The missionary, they said, had been turned away from Christian truth by the heathen subjects of his mission. His role as thorn in the British side was inherited by his daughter, Harriette. It was through the father and daughter's insistent petitioning of the government in London that Cetshwayo was finally given leave to make his case to the queen in person.

The first Zulu king to visit Britain, in 1882, he adopted European dress for the occasion – the swagger stick replacing the knobkerry, the three-piece suit replacing the *beshu*, the top hat covering the *isicoco*. The press and public in London beheld him with dazzled perplexity. 'The crowd was so great I was afraid to venture into the street,' wrote one Londoner. 'I saw him *capitally*.' Cetshwayo's presence brought home to the London public the reality of Britain's colonial engagements. If France's consolidation of its Pacific possessions, such as New Caledonia, had been partly a bid to demonstrate its clout after the 'humiliation' of Sedan, then Britain's tightening grip on south-eastern Africa was in part a competitive reaction to the *deutsche Weltpolitik* of a Germany newly unified following the Franco-Prussian War.

His outfit was understood to be in the nature of a genuflection; so too was his journey itself. After the briefest of audiences with Queen Victoria at her residence on the Isle of Wight, it was agreed that Cetshwayo would return to Zululand under the terms of a new partition, which saw the consolidation of the nation's thirteen chiefdoms into three parts: Cetshwayo's kingdom, much reduced, was sandwiched between a new British Reserve Territory to the south-west and, to the north-east, the enlarged domain of his former subordinate – and now British loyalist – Zibhebhu kaMaphitha, chief of the Mandlakazi branch of the royal family, and a famously formidable military leader. You may return to your kingdom, then, provided you accept it is yours no longer. Cetshwayo's son, many years later, would be obliged to make a similar concession.

———

In July 1883, just five months after his return, Cetshwayo's rebuilt oNdini was destroyed by Zibhebhu's troops during a surprise night-time attack. The assault followed the Battle of Msebe, in which Cetshwayo's brother Ndabuko had led an attack on Zibhebhu's homestead only to be ambushed by Zibhebhu. Ndabuko lost more than 1,000 men; Zibhebhu, ten. The failure would haunt Ndabuko. At oNdini, fifteen weeks later, along with several of his senior chiefs and advisers, three of Cetshwayo's wives were killed, and his baby son, Nyoniyentaba ('mountain bird'), stabbed to death in his mother's arms. One of Zibhebhu's British mercenaries remembered the slaughter with the wet-lipped relish of every career killer, particularly the murder of Cetshwayo's chiefs: 'Being all fat and big-bellied, they had no chance of escape; and one of them was actually run to earth and stabbed to death by one of my little mat bearers.' Dinuzulu, who was about sixteen, escaped on horseback with his uncle Ndabuko. Cetshwayo, meanwhile, having been injured, fled to the dense mist forest of Nkandla, ancient asylum of Zulu royalty. On 8 February 1884, not long after news reached him of the death of his 'father', John Colenso, he too died. The British doctor's report blamed 'fatty degeneration of the heart'.

As tradition dictated, the king's body was wrapped in a bull's hide and strapped sitting to the central post of a closed hut, to desiccate in the smoke of a fire of aromatic woods. The British resident commissioner, Melmoth Osborn, forbade his burial in the eMakhosini Valley, where the *Inkatha yezwe yakwaZulu* was kept, the sacred coil of grasses that symbolise Zulu nationhood and unity, whose previous incarnation had been destroyed by the British in 1879. To hold the ceremony there would only encourage unrest, Osborn maintained; and so after two months the king was still above ground. This was the depth of the white man's power: to dictate the body's whereabouts even in death, even as it ceased to be identifiable. While Dinuzulu remained in hiding in Nkandla, Ndabuko was finally allowed to take his brother's body by ox wagon to the Bhophe Ridge, deep in the forest, where it was buried on 10 April along with the broken-up wagon and the sacrificed oxen. Cetshwayo had become *umuntu oshonileyo*, finally, 'one who has gone down'.

Because his mother, Novimbi Msweli, was a commoner, Dinuzulu carried the taint of illegitimacy. And so when Cetshwayo died there were other contenders to the Zulu chieftaincy, including a half-brother of Dinuzulu's. His uncle, Ndabuko, and his half-uncle, Shingana, eager to validate Dinuzulu's succession, had been at Cetshwayo's deathbed. As reported by them, the old king's dying words were, 'Mpande, my father, left the country to me; I, Cetshwayo, leave the country to my son Dinuzulu.' And so Dinuzulu was proclaimed king. But Magema Fuze recorded Cetshwayo's last words differently: they were spoken not to his brother and half-brother, he maintained, but directly to his son: 'As soon as you have buried my body, mobilise the Zulu nation and attack Zibhebhu and fight against him. You will defeat him, for I will be in the midst of my army.'

———

Fastest of runners, most skilful of hunters, eyes that flash red in anger – so it was said by his subjects. According to Frances Colenso, one of John Colenso's daughters, Dinuzulu 'trod the earth as if he owned it'. Even in defeat (see that arrest photo from Eshowe), there was a kind of tender forbearance in his manner, as if he had always known his life would be one of injustice. It was simple: there were two kinds of death: timely and untimely, the life completed or the life snapped off like a green branch. 'When I die I shall not be altogether dead,' Cetshwayo had told Commissioner Osborn, 'as my son Dinuzulu will live.' Father and son alike feared only the death too awful to be given voice: the curtailment of the bloodline.

On 5 June 1884, the sun low in the sky, Dinuzulu led his men into battle against Zibhebhu. With his 10,000 warriors were a hundred armed Boers, white descendants of German and Dutch settlers, who were eager to extend the Transvaal, their territory bordering north-west Zululand. Two weeks earlier they had crowned Dinuzulu King of the Zulus. The young man had sat enthroned on an empty beer crate and in lieu of holy chrism was anointed with castor oil. (Anyone acquainted with Christian ritual would have recognised the ceremony for what it was, a mockery.) It was agreed they would give him military support, in exchange – here his youth showed, disastrously – for as much land as their leaders 'may consider necessary'.

Dinuzulu's army and the Boers pursued Zibhebhu for four days, in drought, along the sluggish brown Mkuze river. Two hills came into view, half a kilometre apart and 200 metres high: one was domed, the other craggy, their flanks thick with thorn bush. To the east, these twin peaks: Gaza and Tshaneni ('Ghost Mountain' to the British); to the north the rivers Mkuze and Phongolo. A gunshot broke the silence. The Mandlakazi were forced to pre-empt their attack. The uSuthu were driven back, only for the Mandlakazi to be driven back in turn by the Boer rifles. In an hour it was over, just the smell of cordite and of opened bodies on the wind. Hundreds of Mandlakazi were killed, including six of Zibhebhu's brothers. The survivors fled, abandoning 60,000 cattle, which were shared between Dinuzulu's warriors and the Boers to whom they owed their victory.

In exchange for their support, the Boers would eventually claim some 5,000 square miles of Zululand's most fertile farmland, including the sacred eMakhosini Valley. The kingdom's death knell had sounded, even if Dinuzulu could not allow himself to hear it. Three years later, the vanquished Zibhebhu was allowed by the colonist to return to uSuthu land. He and his men took revenge. Burning villages, raping, stealing cattle. On 23 June 1888 Dinuzulu led a counterattack on Zibhebhu's camp, a surprise rout that echoed Zibhebhu's assault on oNdini five years earlier, when Dinuzulu's baby half-brother had been knifed in his mother's arms. Dinuzulu and his men were correspondingly unsparing.

———

Such a flagrant attack on Britain's 'faithful ally' would not go unanswered. Six hundred Royal Dragoons were sent to support Zibhebhu. His uncles at his side, Dinuzulu withdrew with 2,000 men to the limestone caves of another mountain, Ceza, twenty miles north of oNdini. With Ndabuko and Shingana he watched as the British advanced, day by day, across the plains, leaving burning homesteads in their wake. He was twenty, his father four years dead, and well aware he faced imprisonment or exile, if not death.

On 7 August the British heard singing coming from Mount Ceza: the men were chanting an uSuthu war song as they torched their huts before retreating across the nearby Sikhwebezi river. Dinuzulu and Ndabuko with their bodyguard went north. Evading the British, they crossed a country in flames. For the first time, Dinuzulu was wearing across his chest the *iziqu*, the strings of willow-wood beads worn by one who has honoured himself in battle.

By night, in disguise, Dinuzulu made his way by train to Pietermaritzburg, where there lived a woman he trusted. 'I was born among Zulus,' wrote Harriette Colenso, 'and I call myself Zulu.' She was her father's daughter as Dinuzulu was his father's son. She would come to care for him like a younger brother. Born in 1847 in Norfolk, England, she had moved to Africa at the age of seven. Her father, Cetshwayo's friend John Colenso, Bishop of Natal, had died in 1883; if the Natal colonists expected Harriette to be any more accommodating than the old man, that expectation did not survive a meeting with her. Among Zulus her name was Udhlewdhlwe, 'walking stick' – she who had supported her father's every step. But her friends had other names for her: Matotoba, the slow and careful one; Mandizi, the one who flies; Inkanisi, the stubborn one. Unlike other Zululand missionaries, she accepted the practice of *ilobolo*, bride price paid in cattle, and appreciated that the Zulu nation was a unity, and not merely a collection of autonomous tribes affiliated by nothing but 'pure military despotism', as the British maintained. It would be her lifelong objective to preserve the union of Zululand under the uSuthu royal family. Following Dinuzulu's flight from Mount

Ceza, she sent a message urging him and his uncles to surrender: 'Just as your dying in a heap will cover up and make things smooth for those who have slandered you, the other road, that of putting yourself in bondage that the case may be tried, will enable us to expose the treachery by which you are hemmed in.'

––––

Three and a half months later, on 15 November, an unknown man with twenty followers appeared at Bishopstowe, the Colensos' mission station and home near Pietermaritzburg. Harriette was away in Eshowe. Her sister Agnes wondered if the man before her was indeed Dinuzulu. But who else could he be? 'The knowledge of the will and power of his enemies made my heart ache,' she remembered, 'because he still had faith in that far-off, and for the Zulus apparently unobtainable, justice of England.' Leaving Dinuzulu with her mother, she rode into Pietermaritzburg to cable Harriette.

The Court of Special Commissioners in Eshowe sat between November 1888 and the following April. Under consideration were the cases of seventeen men, foremost among them Dinuzulu and his uncles Ndabuko and Shingana, who had surrendered separately from the young king. Colenso had retained the services of the most respected lawyer in British Africa, Harry Escombe, whose fees nearly ruined her. (It was not the last time she exhausted her finances on Dinuzulu's legal defence.) Ndabuko's case opened on 15 November. The charges: disobedience, defiance, contumely, violence against Her Majesty's subjects and forces; stealing 'certain Horned Cattle'; involvement in the murder and mutilation of a tradesman named Klaas Louw. Ndabuko, who was rarely moved to anger: 'I have nothing to say to all these lies.' He insisted, furthermore, that his nephew 'should not be brought into this matter; he is still a child'.

Dinuzulu himself, meanwhile, was charged with rebellion, public violence and murder, and Shingana with murder and 'disobedience'.

On 27 February 1889 the sentences were announced: all three were found guilty, as British subjects, of high treason. Shingana was sentenced to twelve years' imprisonment; Ndabuko to fifteen. 'Dinuzulu,' announced the judge: 'after a patient hearing of your case we are justified in saying to you that we are convinced . . . that your intention was to overthrow the existing form of government in Zululand. You are sentenced by this court to imprisonment for ten years.'

But Osborn, the resident commissioner, maintaining that their continued presence in Zululand 'would be sufficient to keep alive a smouldering current of active disloyalty', recommended they be 'removed to some safe place across the sea' – somewhere far from the influence of Miss Colenso. The British Secretary of State agreed. 'In a more isolated British possession, they may, subject to good behaviour, be allowed a large degree of freedom.' On 19 January 1890 the three were led from their cells and presented to the Governor of Zululand, Sir Charles Mitchell.

Grave but polite, he addressed them as if they were headstrong children:

The Queen with Her Indunas [that is, advisers] have read over all the evidence and her wise men of the Law and Chief men have advised Her that the sentences passed are the right ones. But the Queen said, 'These men have been chiefs of their land and it would not please me, that they should work as common prisoners. Therefore I wilt send them to a country in my dominions, where they can enjoy indulgences which it is impossible to grant them in Zululand, where they would be shut up in a cell and not be able to see the grass.'

'What will become of the people remaining here?' Dinuzulu demanded. 'I mean the women, my family?'

'Do you think anybody will molest them?'

'It is a trouble to my people at home, not seeing me.'

'It is a trouble to *my* people at home, not seeing *me*.'

But as Dinuzulu observed, the governor was free to go back to England whenever he wished.

For the British in Zululand, as for the French and the Russians in their respective territories, exile was in part a practical measure, as we have seen – to decontaminate the metropole, to suppress any 'current of active disloyalty'; but it's also the case that to dictate your enemy's whereabouts on the planet, as if they were a chess piece, as if they were dust, is to flaunt a frightening and demoralising imperial supremacy.

Mitchell had been instructed to impress on the three men that their sentence constituted a 'most material mitigation' of their punishment. Seventy-five years earlier his compatriots had said something similar to another defeated enemy, Napoleon Bonaparte – 'its local position will allow of his being treated with more indulgence than could be admitted in any other spot' – before shipping him to the same remote island in the South Atlantic.

The Pale of Settlement
Lev Shternberg

Pass a magnifying glass across a studio portrait of the Shternbergs, taken in Zhitomir, Ukraine, in about 1872. Perhaps it hung in their home on Starovilskaya Street; perhaps it was printed as a *carte de visite*. Lev's twin brothers, Savelii and David, share a single chair; behind them his parents, bearded Iankel and Yenta Vol'fovna in her sheitel, with toddler Aron on Iankel's knee. At the back is Lev's older sister, Nadezhda (known as Shprintsa, and the spit of her mother), while to the group's right, removed, is Lev, 'Khaim-Leib' on his birth certificate, posed by the photographer with one forearm resting on a fretworked plinth – intended to suggest the newel of a grand staircase? Not a top-class studio – note the crude planks under the twins' feet, note the motheaten drapes – but aspiring to luxury, catering for the kind of families that can employ a maid and spend summers in the country.

Lev is eleven or twelve but looks a few years older. He has recently met his friend Moisei Krol, whom he will know all his life. A heavy serge suit, brown or grey, a dark necktie under a white collar, his dark

45

fringe scissored straight by Mama, and his lips ajar in what might be speech, or more likely a child's moue of assessment (the photographer behind his black-cloaked machine, lens cap in one hand, pocket watch ticking in the other). A serious boy, conscientious, very alert to the ease with which evil can steal into any life, and his politics already forming. 'I don't understand these Germans!' he exclaims when told about the French casualties of the Franco-Prussian War. 'Haven't they read the Bible? Haven't they heard that they must beat swords into ploughshares?'

Appalled by the suffering of others (animals, servants, the Israelites), he possessed the kind of total compassion that, for some children, is experienced as an ache so severe that they teach themselves to be cruel. Krol remembered his friend's parents fondly, especially his mother: 'I think Lev inherited his beautiful soul and rare love of people from her. His father, on the other hand,' he goes on, 'was a man of great initiative and seething energy, but a rather stern disposition.' (Iankel seems to have considered him a bad influence.) The Shternbergs spoke Yiddish first, then Russian; when he first met Krol, aged ten, Shternberg 'hardly knew a word of Russian'.

Zhitomir, which had been annexed from Poland in 1793, was a centre of Jewish culture and learning within the Pale of Settlement, the enclave of western Russia beyond which Jews were largely forbidden from living, and one of only two places where Hebrew printing presses were sanctioned (the other was Vilnius). Of a population of 40,500 in 1861, the year of Shternberg's birth, some 13,000 were Jewish. He grew up steeped in stories of his people's suffering, and not only those of the Talmud: next to the gymnasium was a mass grave of the victims of a pogrom of the previous century: it was both a memorial and a warning of what might come. His notion of 'home', therefore, was complicated. To be Jewish in Zhitomir was to learn that you were an object of official derision and suspicion, whose

community might at any time be scapegoated by the government to distract the populace at large from that government's failings. It was to learn that the State would not act to protect you. This may explain why the more radical political factions that emerged during the years of his youth included such a large proportion of Jews (a fact that, in turn, allowed the regime to paint Jews as irredeemably seditious).

Starovilskaya Street was situated a block from a tributary of the Teterov river, the Kamenka. Krol remembered 'dilapidated one-storey houses, densely populated by Jews . . . interspersed with several beautiful landowner's estates'. As Shternberg put it, 'All the residents and frequent visitors to this street knew each other, spent a lot of time together, and influenced each other. All of them were drawn, on the one hand, to revolutionary ideas, and on the other, to Jewish emotions.'

Their neighbours included prominent Jewish intellectuals, as well as two future novelists. The first, Vladimir Korolenko, eight years Shternberg's senior, later remembered a city fomenting in a 'general mood of expectation', a sense of *something's going to happen*'. It was an era of portents, 'golden decrees, peasant riots, murders'; he recalled vividly an official visit to the city by the tsar, a semi-mythical force to the young Korolenko, one who 'could do everything': 'He could come into our room, take what he liked, and nobody could say anything to him . . . he could make any man a general and cut off any man's head with his sword.' The city was also home to an infant Konrad Korzeniowski – later famous as the novelist Joseph Conrad – though he and his family were soon exiled to northern Russia due to his Polish father's opposition to Russian rule. Korolenko, who would become an inspiration for the adult Shternberg, would also experience years of political exile.

While Shternberg and Krol could visit the theatre with written permission from the school authorities, subject to a 9 p.m. curfew, the city's art gallery 'was considered a highly indecent place', and the public library was off-limits. Certain approved books were available to the boys via the gymnasium library; others by more surreptitious means. First Fenimore Cooper and Jules Verne – well, the Talmud first, strictly speaking, from the age of six – and when they outgrew derring-do: Pushkin, Lermontov, Gogol, Hugo, Dickens, Marx eventually – and had Krol read Turgenev's short story 'The Jew'?

Shternberg, who had esteemed Turgenev above almost any of the others, experienced 'The Jew' as a formative betrayal. 'Read it,' he told his friend. Krol read it: 'and I was shocked'.

'The Jew' tells the story of a Russian officer who falls in love with the daughter of one Girshel during the siege of Danzig. Girshel, a cringingly anti-Semitic caricature even by the standards of the day, is accused of spying for the French and duly hanged, in terror and misery, despite the officer's half-hearted pleas for clemency. As the noose is placed around his neck, the reader is supposed to feel pity – pity, even for this scarcely human wretch. The story's title was an echo of the curses Lev and Moisei heard daily: *Zhid, Zhid* – a term no Russian Jew would use self-referentially, and closer in its violence to 'Yid'.

'The only story by Turgenev in which a Jew is depicted,' Shternberg cried, 'and this Jew is a spy and a scoundrel!'

Zhitomir, in Krol's words, was a 'city of pensioners', thirty-five miles from the nearest train station and only recently linked to the outside world by telegraph. Even years later Shternberg, who knew true remoteness by then, would complain of its isolation. But if their home city was stifling under 'monastic and draconian rules', the surrounding countryside offered the friends liberation. They would row down the Teterev, navigating the rapids from Zhitomir to Psishchi, and spend whole days walking in the pine forest. 'On a hot day one could shelter there from the heat, and in bad weather from the rain,'

Krol recalled, remembering the 'clean, transparent air, the smell of pine, the silence that reigned in the depths of the forest . . .' During those walks, the reserved Lev of Starovilskaya Street would be 'transformed' – voluble, bursting with songs and poetry. The forest taught him the same lesson it had taught the young Louise Michel: that when the human world was threatening to destroy you, a sanctuary could be found in the non-human.

Shternberg's socialism emerged from the intellectual ferment of Starovilskaya Street in a peculiarly Jewish form, seeded in the messianism of the Hebrew Bible as much as any theory of class struggle. His belief in God might gutter, might now and again be snuffed out, but he would remain alive to the lessons of history. Fifteen years after that family photo was taken, he looked back on his childhood from Odessa Central Prison, where he spent three years, prior to his exile, for membership of a proscribed organisation: 'I was bereaved of all joys of youth,' he wrote, 'and the single impressions of these years were moral beliefs. Therefore, ideas of morality and learning grew to me as real things. All conversation of that time had one topic. Sad and hollow. Sad and fitting.' Was that really how life seemed to him as a boy? Sad? Hollow? Bereaved of joy? And what did he mean: 'fitting'? As if his misery were proper or foretold. Elsewhere in his adult writings – in Russian, rather than his self-taught English – he longs for Zhitomir, and in his letters home, later, he never expresses anything but warmth and concern towards his parents, often hiding from them the worst of his suffering. Perhaps playing down the loss, even to himself, made it easier to bear. Or perhaps those words from Odessa were merely a lapse of depression, the shadows of the prison bars briefly thrown across a past that was more light than dark.

———

The Church of the Saviour on Blood in St Petersburg, 650 miles north of Zhitomir, stands beside the Catherine Canal on the spot where Aleksander II was assassinated in 1881, shortly before Shternberg came to the city. It is a cavernous building, its interior so high that the ceiling vault appears to be veiled by some sort of meteorological haze. At one end, resembling a four-poster bed, stands the canopied ciborium dedicated to Aleksander. There the marble floor has been cut away to expose, as a kind of portal, a quadrant of the cobbled street on which he was killed. Everything is red: the marble columns, the velvet drapes, the floor. In that gorgeous, gold-lit space, the ciborium is an ugly gout, like an inflamed organ.

The killing was the culmination of no fewer than seven failed attempts the radical People's Will organisation had made on the emperor's life in the two years since the revolutionary faction was formed, in 1879. These included a bid to blow up the Winter Palace and another to bomb the imperial train. The People's Will made no secret of its ambition: a subsequent edition of its circular carried as its epigraph the words of Édouard Vaillant, one of the leaders of the Paris Commune: 'Society has only one obligation toward monarchs: to put them to death.' (Louise Michel, meanwhile, was observing events in Russia with growing excitement: 'Nihilists, my brothers, you are avenged. Liberty soars above your gallows. Russia, we salute you!')

The effect of the Commune on the *narodniki*, or Populists, had been more powerful for the violence with which it had been crushed. By the time he finished high school, Shternberg's natural compassion and his Jewish education, filtered through his reading of revolutionary thinkers like Proudhon and Marx, had been sublimated into a powerful yearning for political action. Soon the child who abhorred violence would be gone: ploughshares are as nothing against tyrants. The seeds of revolution, the Populists maintained, lay not in the cities or the universities, but among the rural peasantry. The Land and Liberty movement, precursor of the People's Will, had been founded in 1876, five years after Bloody Week, with the demand that power be decentralised and the land, all land, be distributed among the peasants. 'Our ultimate political and economic ideal is anarchy and collectivism,' read its manifesto – and that ideal was realisable only through the violent overthrow of the State.

As they approached adulthood in 'dull, bourgeois' Zhitomir, Shternberg and Krol 'began to notice that extraordinary things were happening'. Older schoolmates would vanish in the night, sending word they had 'gone to the people' – the term given to Land and Liberty's policy of embedding young revolutionaries in the country-side with the aim of encouraging revolt among the peasantry. As the pair became more committed, Krol was visited by a comrade from Kiev, a man 'of very mysterious appearance', whatever that meant, who gave him an address and instructions for the next night. Krol arrived at the address to find a table scattered with revolvers, cartridges and knives. The mysterious man and his associates explained they were planning to rob the Kiev–Zhitomir mail coach to fund the revolution, and needed a trusted local to act as a guide. Apparently shocked, Krol rushed off to Shternberg – fifteen-year-old Shternberg – who promptly went to the apartment and told the men they would have no part in violence: 'It is not the business of socialists to plunder and kill.' It seems this was accepted, and the robbery failed in any case when the would-be thieves mistimed their ambush. The incident, however farcical, makes two things conspicuous: first, the naivety of the pair, shocked that radicals might do radical things; secondly, the change that shortly came over them both, but especially Shternberg. When Land and Liberty underwent a schism in 1879, caused by a disagreement over the use of terrorism, the young men were drawn to the more extreme, more violent faction, Narodnaia

Volya: the People's Will. The decision would shape the course of the rest of their lives.

———

At 2.15 p.m. on 13 March 1881, having watched military manoeuvres at the Manege Square, Tsar Aleksander returned to the Winter Palace. Moments after the carriage, with its Cossack escort, turned onto the quay of the Catherine Canal, a young man in a fur cap stepped forward bearing a package. The ensuing explosion injured one of the Cossacks and a passing butcher's boy, but did only superficial damage to the tsar's bullet-proof carriage, leaving him with a scratch to one hand. Emerging dazed, he briefly took in his captured assailant (one report says he wagged a finger at him), inspected the crater made by the bomb, and offered a few words to the Cossack and the butcher's boy, both of whom shortly after died from their injuries. As he was about to return to his carriage, a 26-year-old former engineering student named Ignaty Grinevitzky approached him. The second explosion, stronger than the first, tore the tsar's abdomen open and shredded his legs below the knee. Aleksander uttered a few incomprehensible words. Grinevitsky didn't long outlive his target. The first bomber, nineteen-year-old Nikolay Rysakov, terrified and regretful, would subsequently give up his accomplices before he was hanged alongside them. The sleigh that took Aleksander to the Winter Palace, where he died an hour or so later, painted a red ribbon in the snow.

When Shternberg arrived in St Petersburg that winter, aged twenty, a year after Krol, to study mathematics and physics at the city's university, the People's Will was being demolished in response to the assassination – 'drained of blood', in Krol's words. Between 1879 and 1883 some 2,000 *narodovoltsy* were tried and imprisoned, with hundreds deported to Siberia. Far from heralding a new socialist utopia, the assassination prompted an increase in State surveillance and repression, while the peasantry the assassins had hoped at last to inflame into revolution instead carried out a series of anti-Semitic pogroms spurred by false rumours of Jewish involvement in the assassination. These attacks prompted the first large-scale Jewish migration from Russia to Europe and America; a subsequent wave would coincide with a second series of pogroms in 1914.

Shternberg and Krol, undaunted, joined the student wing of the remnant Narodnaia Volya, taking part in November 1882 in a stand-off between police and students demonstrating against education reforms, which culminated in their arrest. After ten days in prison, barely a year after Shternberg had arrived, they were expelled from the university.

The next year, after an interval of 'domiciliary exile' back in Zhitomir, Shternberg and Krol enrolled in the law faculty of Novorossiysk University in Odessa, where Shternberg promptly re-established the dispersed southern branch of Narodnaia Volya, while striving to unify what remained of the movement's other units. Meanwhile he took on the editorship of the organisation's proscribed bulletin, *Vestnik Narodnoi Voli*. Any of these acts alone, as he well knew, could earn him a long prison sentence or exile, and he cannot have expected to remain free indefinitely. The following year he published a pamphlet so inflammatory it caused disquiet even among his political associates. Entitled *Politicheskii Terror*, it explained in detail why Russia's unique circumstances meant that violence was the only means by which the tsars could be overthrown and socialism allowed to thrive. The peasantry was supine, the bourgeoisie indifferent; it was left to the intelligentsia to lead, and the vastness and brutality of the tsars' army meant the only realistic means of revolution was the 'violent removal of certain persons'. A 'temporary struggle' was required, albeit one whose victims would be confined to 'the very pillars of the tyranny'.

Shternberg was at pains to stress that terrorism was purely an operational tactic: as soon as its aims were achieved, 'not a single revolutionary would soil his hands with the blood of a harmless scoundrel'. Elsewhere he noted, mischievously, that Moses himself 'began his career with the terrorist act of killing an Egyptian slave-master'.

At a regional congress held in Ekaterinoslav in 1885, a divide opened up between Jewish members, who generally believed terrorism was the only means of defeating tsarism, and non-Jewish members, who maintained it could only harm their cause. The movement's most high-profile terrorist act had, after all, led only to its members being hunted down and hanged or banished, to say nothing of the death in agony of a child. Shternberg was persuaded to tone down his article on political violence before it was republished in *Vestnik Narodnoi Voli*.

Among his circle during those dangerous years was Nathan Bogoraz, who had been ejected from St Petersburg University at the same time as him and Krol and sent into domiciliary exile in his hometown of Taganrog. Like Shternberg he came from a Jewish family, but by the time he left St Petersburg had so thoroughly abandoned his faith that he had himself baptised and changed his name to 'Vladimir' – partly, he said, to facilitate his revolutionary activity, a 'Russian' name being less likely to attract attention. He and Shternberg would remain friends for life, later working together at the Museum of Anthropology and Ethnology in St Petersburg.

It was at the Ekaterinoslav congress that Shternberg announced he had succeeded, during a trip to St Petersburg, in enlisting to the southern branch two of the most influential ideologues of Populism, Albert Gausman and Lev Kogan-Bernstein. In October 1884 a leading organiser of the People's Will was arrested in St Petersburg in possession of a register of revolutionaries, leading to hundreds of further arrests. By 1886 the southern branch was almost all that remained of the People's Will. Then in April Shternberg's turn came, following the interrogation of an elderly shopkeeper whose premises had been used as a safehouse for visiting *narodovoltsy*. Shternberg's apartment was searched; he was arrested, and incarcerated in Odessa's Central Prison for three years, all but six months of which was spent in solitary confinement. Bogoraz, Gausman, Kogan-Bernstein and his old friend Krol remained at liberty for another year; but the People's Will had been effectively dismantled.

———

In Odessa Central Prison he developed a tic that would stay with him all his life, and, out of the awful silence of his cell, auditory hallucinations in the form of a repeated refrain, like a stuck newsreel: 'Gausman–and–Kogan-Bernstein–are–dead–Gausman–and–Kogan-Bernstein–are–dead–'. While the fate of his friends was a cause of anguish, Shternberg's deepest sorrow was for his mother and father at home in Zhitomir: 'Preserve the life, happiness and consolation of my parents,' he prayed, writing in his diary. 'Prolong, my God, their days, and reward them for their grief in me.'

In the political wing, a long single-storey block far from the common convicts awaiting deportation, there was little light or air, and the guards enforced an absolute, oppressive quiet. Apart from a daily fifteen-minute walk, prisoners did not leave their cell – a ferric cubicle five yards by two, with an iron bed bolted to the wall, a reeking iron *parasha* (prison toilet), and iron bars over a solitary high window. At first, the lifelong smoker was allowed neither cigarettes nor books. Towards the end of his sentence, however, once his conditions were eased, he was able to teach himself English and Italian, and, according to his diaries, wrote a nostalgic, regretful novel based in Jewish Zhitomir, though it has been lost. He took comfort in those diaries – fourteen volumes in Russian, French, Yiddish and English – recalling the serious, 'hollow' child he had been, copying down long passages from his reading: Shakespeare, Milton, Machiavelli, and – the irony can't have escaped him – *Robinson Crusoe*. One text would revolutionise his thinking. Friedrich Engels' *The Origin of the Family, Private Property and the State* is a work of proto-ethnography based on the research of the American anthropologist Lewis Henry Morgan, in which Engels, via the reading of his late friend Marx, identifies the seeds of modern capitalism in the abolition of hunter-gatherer systems of matrilineal decent. No volume would exert a greater influence on Shternberg over the years that followed.

Those auditory hallucinations proved to be a premonition, for in March 1889, just as his own prison sentence was ending, Gausman and Kogan-Bernstein were executed for participating in protests in the eastern Siberian city of Yakutsk, where they had already been exiled. 'It is difficult', Shternberg wrote, 'to reconcile the idea of a rational and noble Creator with a belief that poverty and humiliation, which are the lot of a substantial portion of the human race, are the result of his work.' While Louise Michel, who herself was in and out of prison in Paris at this time, seems to have only become more devoutly revolutionary with each phase of incarceration, some of Shternberg's zeal abandoned him in prison. But his journals are studded with the words of the prophets who remained his lodestars. 'I will gather you from all the nations and places where I have banished you,' went the Lord's words from Jeremiah's letter to the Babylonian exiles, 'and will bring you back to the place from which I carried you into exile.' In prison, on the high seas, deported to the world's edge – wherever Shternberg found himself, a home endured for him in those words.

After two years a newcomer was placed in the adjoining cell, a fellow member of the People's Will. A tap-tapping, teaspoon against iron, and then finally a voice; a voice Shternberg knew intimately. Moisei Krol would later recall that his friend looked like a 'martyr' (Shternberg wouldn't have minded this) – 'pale, exhausted, with sunken cheeks, a long beard and feverish eyes'. The descriptions we have of him are mostly from Krol's memoirs, and they are invariably bubbling with affection for the man he knew his whole life, and knew to be good. Krol retreated into the past, remembering those long summer afternoons in the pine forest of Psishchi, when they would lie side by side and gaze up to the canopy and the sky beyond. For his part, Shternberg, enlivened by his friend's presence, was still able to imagine a future: 'We will see better days, Moisei; our star is still high on the horizon.' Finally, without the inconvenience or publicity of a trial, both men were sentenced to ten years' 'administrative exile' for their participation in the Ekaterinoslav congress – Krol to north-west Siberia, Shternberg to somewhere beyond even that remoteness.

Although Siberia had been a place of banishment for Russia since the 1600s, in the late nineteenth century the number of criminals and political exiles sent to its penal-labour sites became unsustainable. By 1876 some 20,000 convicts were arriving each year. Prisoners were dying of exposure, malnutrition and disease. Escapes and crime soared, and there was insufficient labour to occupy those who remained. According to one visiting ethnographer, the region resembled a 'battlefield', such was the squalor. Sakhalin, a large, sparsely populated, coal-rich island in the far east, promised to serve the triple purpose of relieving the pressure on Siberia, supplying Russian industry with fuel, and above all consolidating the frontier with Japan. As with New Caledonia for the French, Russia's far east was also an annexe of the metropolitan penal system, an exclave where – it was anticipated – rehabilitation would be possible as well as punishment.

After three years, most of it in the blind fetor of solitary confinement, 28-year-old Lev Shternberg was thrown into the light – into the sea scent and ozone of Odessa. His journals suggest he experienced a brief surge of ecstasy, despite the months-long voyage ahead, and the knowledge that he might never see Starovilskaya Street or Zhitomir or 'Russia' again.

His parents came to see him off, just as Louise Michel's mother had come to see her off in 1873. At this moment our supposed bloodthirsty subversives are children once more. 'You will travel across the same sea the Jews crossed on foot when the Pharaoh chased them with his chariots,' his father, Iankel, told him. 'You will see Mount Sinai, from which Moses brought his tablets of the law. And just as the god of Israel brought the Jews from the house of bondage and led them to Sinai, so will He bring you back alive and allow us to rejoice upon seeing you again.'

On Seasickness

It was early May 2019 when I went looking for him, not in St Petersburg's Preobrazhenskoye Jewish Cemetery but about 4,000 miles away in far-east Russia.

From the Siberian city of Khabarovsk I took a train to the Tatar Strait port of Vanino, a journey of 300 miles and, somehow, twenty-four hours. Newly released from the snow, the dead grass had the flattened look of hair that has been under a hat all day. As we approached Vanino, the taiga for miles was black and smouldering where it had been set alight by cinders jettisoned from an earlier train's samovar.

I had hesitated about making the journey at all – had come close, more than once, to cancelling everything. My father had been ill for a while. At Christmas he had started a course of radiotherapy; in March he had first one heart attack, then another, then pneumonia and a suspected stroke. Now he was in hospital, unrecognisably frail, and delirious. In the end I persuaded myself that nowhere was far away, any more. My sisters were nearby, and even on Sakhalin Island, at the 'end of the world', as Anton Chekhov described it – *na krai sveta* – I could be back within forty-eight hours. But still the journey, as I remember it, was darkened by my anxiety about him.

At Vanino I waited at the station to be summoned to the overnight ferry to Sakhalin. I drank instant coffee from a platform stall (paper cups lined up with a spoonful of Nescafé and a spoonful of sugar, awaiting hot water), and watched the coal barges discharging, and talked to the other passengers: a teacher from Khabarovsk, a lighting specialist from Vladivostok, two Chinese platelayers, an electrician from Uzbekistan. No one knew what time the ferry would leave.

'Allahu Akbar, money-money-money, fuck you, fight you . . .'

The muttering giant was coming home from South Korea, he wouldn't say what his job was but his duffel bag was military. He sat opposite me, glowering at the electrician to whom his jumbled words were apparently addressed, and, returning from a cigarette, gave the man's parcels a kick: 'Bomb.' Grinned. '*Bomb!*'

The man looked at his parcels. People were standing up. The other man was still hissing through his teeth: 'Money-money-money, fuck you, fight you, Allahu Akbar . . .'

The ship that would take us to Kholmsk on the island's south-west coast, the *Sakhalin-8*, was a rust-striped ro-ro used mainly for freight. The *stink* – burnt diesel oil, tobacco, garlic, re-boiled sausage. (The garlic smell, it turned out, was phosphine rat poison.) The one meal served during the fourteen-hour journey was trayed up during a half-hour slot just after we departed: buckwheat kasha, latex sausage, tea. In one corner of the galley, onions were growing in a bucket.

————

If exile is a form of torture, as most reports suggest, its cruellest stage might be the journey itself, when the thread connecting the exile to their homeland is stretched to its maximum tolerance; when the prisoner becomes something else, something more pitiable and more ambiguous – and when, in most cases, the stability of land gives way to the uncertainty of water.

Having said farewell to his parents, Shternberg enjoyed a frisson at seeing a world he had only read about. It was still possible to live in the moment, to find pleasure in something as simple as movement. He was a young man, looking for symbols to match the grandeur of his plight. During the two-month voyage from Odessa aboard the crammed convict vessel the *Petersburg*, perhaps it was confirmed to him that his life was going to be exceptional, even if it was not going to be long.

After the usual Orthodox prayer ceremony on deck, the ship left Odessa; the conditions were calm, with the portholes admitting a light breeze. There were none of the 'tearing gales' or 'monstrous waves' of the body of water described by Ovid. 'One did not feel at all as if one were crossing the sea known as "Black",' Shternberg wrote. On 1 April, three days after setting sail, he wrote to his parents from the Bosporus off Constantinople. His description of 'wonderful landscapes . . . unfolding outside the window of our compartment' sounds like a cruise passenger's postcard; but then, he had reason to be relieved as well as apprehensive. 'After a long confinement, when the only horizon was the prison wall, the sea's immense expanse offered true delight.'

From the Bosporus the *Petersburg*, a steamer of the Russian Volunteer Fleet, navigated the Suez Canal to Aden before sailing on to Colombo, Singapore, Nagasaki and Vladivostok. 'Here indeed was some bitter mockery,' wrote a journalist who joined a later sailing,

to transport people nearly all around the globe, to show them a small corner of earthly paradise (magnificent, blooming Ceylon), to give them 'but a glance' of Singapore, that luxurious, divine, fantastic blooming garden a degree and a half from the equator, to allow – near the entrance to Nagasaki – just a glimpse of Japan's magical and picturesque coast (a coastline you cannot tear your eyes away from), only to deliver them, after all this, to bleak, rocky shores covered in snow.

An extraordinary voyage, some 11,000 miles, even if the destination was, on paper, the same country they had left. Shternberg's reading on board included a short story, 'Sokholinets' (meaning 'the falconer', but also a pun on 'Sakhalin'), written in 1885 by his long-ago Zhitomir neighbour, Vladimir Korolenko, who had himself been exiled to Siberia in the late 1870s for involvement in the Populist movement. His narrator (a stand-in for the author), deported to Yakutia, is disturbed one freezing night by a visitor to his hut, a former convict named Vasili, who, we learn, escaped from Sakhalin many years before. As the night goes on, Vasili recounts by firelight the story of his imprisonment and flight, beginning with his own voyage from Odessa:

Naval laws are always strict, and on board a ship with such a freight they are still more stringent. During the daytime the convicts, closely guarded, exercised in turn. The rest of the time they remained in their cabin, under deck. There were more convicts than sentries; but, to make amends for this inequality, every step and movement of the grey crowd was controlled by a firm hand, a well-disciplined crew strictly guarding against the possibility of a mutiny.

For Shternberg, aboard the *Petersburg*, Korolenko's story cannot have offered much comfort, even if his conditions, as a political exile, were for now less harsh than 'Vasili's'. Each prisoner, he told

66

his parents, received a ration of bread, tea and sugar, and meat once a day; furthermore the ordinary convicts with whom the 'politicals' shared a compartment 'treat us with great courtesy and try to do us good turns in every way . . . People in shackles are not nearly as frightening as they seem from afar. The divine spark has not died out even in the worst of them.'

When the *Petersburg* docked at Port Said, Egypt, he noticed the date on a newspaper lent to him by the ship's officer and was struck by the realisation that tomorrow was 15 Nisan – that is, 15 April: the start of Passover. Unlike many of his fellow Populists, Shternberg never rejected the Judaism of his early years. 'We ought to remember', he wrote, 'that in 600 BCE, Jewish prophets, those ethical thinkers who have not been surpassed by anyone, had for the first time revealed to the world clearly and definitely the ideas of humanity, love, equality, brotherhood, peace and God's kingdom on earth.' Gazing out at the mountains of Sinai, he finally understood the nature of his plight, its *meaning*. He was one 'who also sought freedom':

freedom not for his own people but for another people dear to him. This descendant was now destined to make a great journey, not to the Promised Land, but to the land of exile, thousands of miles away . . . And suddenly sadness disappeared from my soul and a new feeling overcame me, a feeling of pride . . . It seemed to me that a great fire had ignited in my heart, so that if millions of my dispersed brothers were with me at the moment, I would have had enough strength to use my fiery words to burn away from their hearts all impurities brought into them by centuries of oppression and slavery, and ignite a new fire in them, which would have lifted them up to the highest ideals of mankind.

———

When Louise Michel was exiled, fourteen years before Shternberg, sailing frigates like the *Virginie*, built in 1827, still dominated the French convict fleet. Economy was a priority for the French government, speed was not, provided the convicts survived. On board with Michel were twenty-five female and one hundred and twenty-five male deportees. Steerage was divided into four cages, two large and two small, with the women separated from the men in one of the small cages, aft starboard, and animals to supply the voyage penned in a fifth. They slept in hammocks slung from the bars.

She boarded with the excitement of one who had never seen the sea, or for that matter travelled further from her Haute-Marne birthplace than Paris. It was part of her strength to see beauty where others saw only ashes. 'I would never have dared to dream of such a stroke of luck . . . to me, the sea was the most beautiful of spectacles.' The *Virginie* reminded her of the toy boats her grandfather had made for her, 'beautiful little ones whose sails could be clewed up with cables of thick thread', which they had sailed on the pond near the red rosebushes in the chateau grounds.

The Suez Canal had opened four years earlier, in 1869, offering a much shorter route east, but most French captains bound for New Caledonia preferred to avoid the toll. According to another passenger, Michel's friend Henri Rochefort, several experienced mariners had refused the captaincy, considering the 46-year-old *Virginie* unseaworthy, before one Launay agreed to sail her. A wealthy newspaper owner and supporter of the Commune, Victor-Henri Rochefort, Marquis de Rochefort-Luçay, had been sentenced to 'perpetual banishment' for 'inciting civil war' and 'publishing false news', among other offences, and spent much of the voyage confined to his hammock with seasickness. Having been elected to the Government of National Defence formed after Napoleon's defeat, he had resigned in support of the Commune; but his initial hesitancy, and then his public criticism of the 'incredible casualness' of the Commune's military strategy and its suppression of the reactionary press, made him a divisive figure among Michel's comrades, and in later life he would be despised by her anarchist circle.

But aboard the *Virginie* they formed a friendship that would last until her death. He found Michel an unusual character. Almost her first act of the voyage, he said, was to give away the clothing she had been handed on boarding – two skirts, a calico dress and a bonnet. Also on board was Nathalie Lemel, whom Michel knew from Paris. A bookseller and bookbinder three years her senior, Lemel had founded a socialist food co-operative, *La Marmite*, during the Prussian siege, feeding hundreds of people daily at a time when an egg cost five francs and even wealthy Parisians were resorting to eating 'exotic meats' from the zoo at the Jardin des Plantes. During Bloody Week, she fought on the barricades at Les Batignolles and Place Pigalle. According to Michel's biographer, Edith Thomas, she attempted suicide when the Commune fell.

The prisoners were occasionally allowed to take the air. On 19 August, nine days after the *Virginie* set sail from Rochefort, another vessel came into view, a 'black ship', which reminded Michel of the *Naglfar*, the doom-ship of Norse mythology fashioned from the fingernails and toenails of the dead. For two days it followed at a distance, and Michel began to wonder if it had been sent to free them. But when Launay fired two blank cannon shots, the mysterious vessel withdrew, never to be seen again. If Michel did not discount the possibility of rescue, then nor did her captors, for Launay had been ordered to avoid Dakar in case Spanish revolutionaries attempted to free their Communard brothers and sisters.

The usual course was to cross the Atlantic with the north-east trade winds, revictualling at Santa Catarina Island, Brazil, before crossing the same ocean eastwards to enter the Indian Ocean with the Roaring

Forties. It was left to each captain to choose his parallel: the more southerly was shorter but meant a risk of icebergs, as well as endless weeks without wind, but doldrums could come out of the blue whatever road you chose. 'The voyage was as likely to take six months as three,' Captain Launay told Rochefort. Most ships set a course as close to the ice line – the *extrême des glaces flottantes* – as they dared.

'The wind blew a tempest,' Michel recalled, 'and the sun made a thousand flashes on the water. Two rivers of diamonds seemed to slide down the flanks of the ship . . .' Although she and her fellow passengers were locked between decks most of the time, she would remember the voyage as if it were an escape, a flushing into the light, even when Antarctic gales harried them as they followed the ice line east: 'All my life I had dreamed of sailing the broad oceans and now there I was, balanced between the sky and the sea.' Her comrades in Paris, she reflected, 'would be less free under the surge of triumphant reaction in France than we would be'.

In certain ways the voyage itself was as transformative as either the bloodshed that preceded it or the exile to which it led. Out of its extremity – the polar ice, the tropical heat – and the opportunity those months offered for reflection and conversation, Michel underwent a political liberation. 'I thought about the behaviour of our friends in the Commune: they were so scrupulous, so afraid of exceeding their authority, that they never threw their full energies into anything but the loss of their own lives.' During those 120 days between sky and sea, a period longer than the Commune itself had lasted, she became convinced, in debating with Lemel, that the only route to political freedom was anarchism. 'It is impossible', she realised, 'for liberty to be associated with any form of power whatsoever.' It was a belief she would maintain for the rest of her life.

Most of her diaries were lost, but despite the cold and nausea, the stench below decks, the vomiting and raging she must surely have

witnessed, Michel recalls those months with complete fondness –
apart, that is, for the albatrosses the sailors netted (Paris milliners
paid well for their feathers). Like the headless goose that had so upset
her as a child – what she called the 'dominant idea' of her life, with
its 'drunken' waddling and 'feathers spattered with blood' – the albatrosses haunted her, seeming to stand for all the suffering she had
witnessed, all the beauty she had seen crushed:

> After snaring them the sailors hung them up by their beaks until they
> died; any other method of killing them might let drops of blood spot
> the whiteness of their valuable feathers. Sadly the albatrosses would
> keep their heads up as long as possible, rounding their swans' necks,
> prolonging their pitiful agony for a minute or two. Then with one
> last grimace they opened wide their great, black-lidded eyes and died.

———

By the time of Dinuzulu's voyage seventeen years later, in 1890, the
age of sail had yielded to the age of steam. Aboard the mail ship the
SS *Anglian*, he enjoyed better conditions than Shternberg or Michel,
including his own cabin and dining quarters. Nor did he expect to be
treated as less than royalty. He was accompanied by a retinue of no
fewer than thirteen, including his personal attendant, the party's traditional doctor, and two female companions, uZihlazile and uMkasilomo. His uncles Ndabuko and Shingana each brought a wife and a
male attendant. Over the ensuing years the group's composition would
change, with some members leaving and others arriving; but its core
would remain: the triumvirate of Dinuzulu, Ndabuko and Shingana.

With the party were two Zulu interpreters and a British custodian,
Walter Saunders. 'I need hardly tell you', Governor Mitchell warned
him, 'that your chief difficulty will be with Dinuzulu, who is young,

active and enterprising and would, I think, take advantage of any opportunity offered him of escape.' Saunders wouldn't need to worry about his uncles, however, who were 'obese and indolent', albeit not so indolent that they had failed to evade and embarrass the British authorities in Zululand for the past decade. The prisoners were to be locked up at night but 'during the day allowed all reasonable freedom to take fresh air and exercise'. 'I do not expect any refractory behaviour on their part,' Mitchell went on, 'but, if such should occur, you will not hesitate to use all necessary means to ensure safe-keeping and due obedience to your lawful orders.'

The voyage from Durban to St Helena is really two: first down the hard south-east seaboard of Africa and west towards the Cape of Good Hope; then from the Cape in a straight line north-west to St Helena. The first leg, even for a seasoned mariner, can be mayhem, the kind of waters where one must stand watch constantly. No shelter, few refuges. In 1890 you were at the mercy of the waves. Where currents vie with wind or collide with counter-currents, waves of thirty feet are not rare, big enough to break a ship in two. If the *Anglian* ventured close enough to shore, Dinuzulu and his party would have seen the colonial settlements of Port Alfred and Port Elizabeth, before the ship turned south-west, clear of the foul grounds of Geyser Island and Point Danger, as the Cape loomed.

In a letter to his mother, he writes that he was 'very much alarmed at the illness of the girls' (his female companions, daughters of loyal chieftains): uMkasilomo 'vomited a great deal', while uZihlazile's 'illness commenced by her nose bleeding profusely, just as if she had been stabbed, and she had also taken a violent headache'. While both women recovered, I have often thought about uMkasilomo (whose name means something like 'wife of the famous one', though she and Dinuzulu were unmarried) and uZihlazile ('You've Disgraced Yourself', whose meaning can only be guessed at), on the ship and on St Helena, removed from their home and put to sea, the future unimaginable; the children they would bear in exile and those they would lose, the rift they would witness between their king and his uncles. 'Vomiting' we might put down to motion sickness, but uZihlazile's bleeding nose and violent headaches suggest a more profound disturbance. 'I tried medicines,' writes Dinuzulu, 'but they were of no use.'

The Cape of Good Hope was the journey's pivot, marking the end of its hardest and most perilous stage. Turning north-west, the *Anglian* maintained its bearing for some 2,000 miles. The seas are calmer, the winds drop, the weather is pleasanter. The seals that chaperoned the ship off the Cape are replaced by dolphins and flying fish. For Dinuzulu and his entourage, who had never seen the sea, let alone sailed upon it, the relief must have been overwhelming – enough, perhaps, to temporarily assuage their worries about the immediate future. When I imagine their voyage, it is not the drama of rounding the Cape that constitutes the central scene, but that period of regularisation, when the swell eases, the wind drops to a sigh, and they are granted the tranquillity to come back to themselves.

When Dinuzulu's father had been captured and exiled to Cape Town, the boy was placed by the British under the guardianship of the king's rival Chief Zibhebhu. Dinuzulu duly fled, spending much of the next four years, until his father's restoration, on the run, moving from one refuge to the next to evade the furious Zibhebhu's search parties. Those years established a pattern of near-constant mobility, as if his life were no more than an endless voyage interspersed with islands of jittery respite. While distance could not dampen his commitment to Zulu liberation, exile for Dinuzulu was an interval of unfamiliar stasis. He had been lifted out of his life.

———

During their sea voyages it is as if our exiles pass through a common space and time; or rather are freed to occupy a common realm *outside* space and time. On the deck of the *Sakhalin-8*, crossing the Tatar Strait, the sky was cloudless and the sea quite calm, and it was possible to feel that I, too, had entered that realm, and might spot on the horizon a flotilla of vessels three abreast: the *Virginie*, the *Anglian* and the *Petersburg*.

The sun's movement eastward that afternoon seemed somehow connected to ours westward. Evgeni, engineer third-class, was taking his cigarette break. I was the first native English-speaker he'd met in his thirty-one years; he'd learnt the language at what he called 'river school'.

'Are the English scared of the Russians?' he said.

'The government, yes. The people, no.'

The deck door opened and a dog, a Pomeranian, was pushed out, the door closing behind it. Constipation is a sign of good health in Pomeranians, I remembered. It looked at the door then at Evgeni and me.

Somehow Evgeni knew I was a writer. I suppose he or someone else had checked the manifest and googled the foreign name. I asked him if the *Sakhalin-8* was a good ship. He smiled and shook his head, seeing that I knew the answer. 'It is very old. From the USSR.'

To port there was a small splash – there were grey whales in these waters – then another; and I watched a plastic kettle float by . . . Another splash – dumped from the bow, what looked like a washing-machine door . . . 'Trash!' said Evgeni, as a flotilla of smaller objects bobbed past.

He showed me his phone – pictures on WhatsApp of captured Syrian armoured cars passing through his home city of Rostov on a train. Another of him gangster-posing with a Makarov pistol. He completed his army service six years ago. Did he enjoy it? He asked me to repeat the question. 'Enjoy?' he said. 'No! Boys don't like the army! Boys like *home.*'

My cabin, buried three decks down, was a cornerless bunker low in the bow, resembling the interior of a tank. Against the hull there was the intermittent swash of water, a great freezing lightlessness inches away. My thoughts returned to my father, as they would constantly over the next few weeks, in his windowless ward in Southampton General – a ward that one evening, hallucinating, he believed was the hold of a ship in which he had been imprisoned.

II

Barbarians

New Caledonia

1.

Six months earlier, I travelled to New Caledonia as a referendum on independence from France was taking place. For the first two days I didn't leave my rental apartment. The ache that had come on at the airport was so deep its source was unplaceable – was it my kidneys? My sternum? Long-haul thromboses mustering? Lying down was less painful than standing, sleeping better than being awake. All day the honk-whistle of mynah birds from the yard, all night the rustle of palms in the wind; otherwise the world behind the blinds was a void.

On the third morning, sick of confinement, I drank four petrol-station espressos with five ibuprofens and took a bus to Nouméa's central square, the Place des Cocotiers.

Next week's referendum had been ten years in the planning; the capital was jittery. I felt as if I was watching everything on CCTV. Walking up and down between the bandstand built by convict labour and the statue of the governor Jean-Baptiste Olry, three gendarmes looked ill at ease in unaccustomed stab vests. (Olry was notorious for his barbarism during the 'Kanak Insurrection', and there was a

movement to have the statue removed.) The Australian cruise passengers occupying the cafés would soon return to their ship, and next
week's dockings had all been cancelled. In a pond in front of the Café
l'Annexe a Kanak man in waders was spading silt onto the banks,
watched by the café customers. Another man, not Kanak, stood with
a tripoded TV camera propped over one shoulder, while his colleague
effused into his phone.

As long as New Caledonia's indigenous population remained a
minority, no one expected the referendum to yield anything but *non*.
It wasn't the result that concerned the authorities so much as what
it might herald. On the flight from Sydney, the man next to me, a
white Parisian born in Nouméa, returning to vote, said: 'If the polls
are right, it's too close.' Sixty–forty was the forecast. 'Eighty–twenty
would be better.'

In the supermarkets I found the alcohol aisles cordoned off; import-
ing weapons had been banned along with openly carrying ceremonial
spears; and extra cells were being prepared in Nouméa's prison. I had
come here, at the tensest time in the country's recent history, in a
spirit less of journalistic enquiry than of exhumation. Just as Britain's
referendum on leaving the European Union had unreined the past
to come crashing through the walls of the present, I hoped this cul-
minating moment would cause a rent to open to the New Caledonia
of 1873, the New Caledonia of Louise Michel. Not that my journey
was in the nature of pilgrimage, or even homage; as with Shternberg
on Sakhalin and Dinuzulu on St Helena, I just had an idea that by
setting foot where she set foot I might recover something of her life
and see how exile shaped it.

The wind was rising; a foot-long palm leaf hit the pavement. As I
sat on the grass, squinting out at the police coming towards me, and
the man dredging the pond, and the Aussies sipping their espressos, I had a kind of visitation. Call it that. A vague psychic trace of

some long-ago dispute – that is the quality of the unease by which it announced itself. I felt its memory being reeled away even as it arrived, like a self-destructing tape. And at that moment it was borne in on me, on a great surge of vertigo, that part of me was *always* dreaming, and now the membrane between dream-life and real had punctured, allowing one to flood into the other.

It's taken me three years to begin to understand what happened, but in the days afterwards – days of sweating and discomfort – I found some solace in the testimonies of the Paris Communards exiled to New Caledonia with Michel. 'Sequestration leads to dreaming, and dreaming to madness,' wrote Henri Rochefort. For his fellow *déporté* Louis Redon, the symptoms of exile were physical as well as psychological: 'My lungs are clogged up; my food doesn't digest properly; my head is foggy. At night I sweat profusely and sometimes there's a pounding in my ears which makes me nearly deaf.' For another, Achille Ballière, 'moral torments' were coupled with 'desperate physical pains'. He added: 'The thought of the distance kills us.'

———

In the archive in Nouméa, I was handed a folder containing four pencil sketches she made at sea.

The first was labelled 'En route de Palma' – La Palma, one of the Canary Islands – and showed a dark volcanic peninsula with a lighthouse rising from its mountainous tip. The other three were each labelled 'St Catherine' – Santa Catarina Island, Brazil: a jagged coastline with fortified terraces; a three-masted fishing vessel; a busy port with ships coming and going . . .

The last of these was the most touching, somehow – touching for its brevity and looseness: while the others were smudgy and darkly overworked, as if the shading had been completed in tween-decks

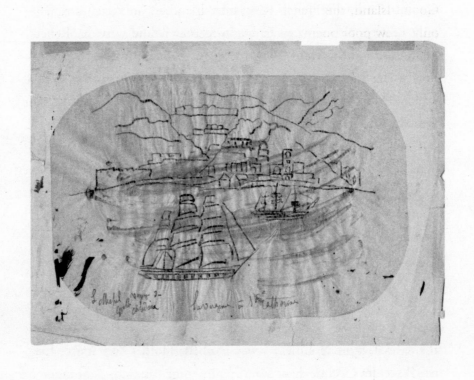

darkness, this was a quick sketch of two full-sailed sloops anchored off a harbour, done on a stained scrap of paper, made only for the moment, with no intention other than to imprint the scene on her own mind's eye, full of glitter and sea scent.

Of the rest of the voyage – the icebergs of the Southern Ocean, Gough Island, the French Kerguelen Islands – no sketches remain, only a few poor poems exchanged with her fellow convicts. Reflecting on the slow death of the albatrosses, snared and strung up to die slowly, she was moved to observe: 'Some men kill other men the same way, being very careful not to let the drops of blood soil either them or their victims.' Blood, at least, was honest.

Sixteen weeks after leaving bloody France, having sailed 17,000 miles, the *Virginie* dropped anchor off Nouméa, on the south-west coast of New Caledonia's main island. It was 10 December 1873.

———

'Grande Terre' is about 260 miles long and 40 miles wide, lying on a diagonal NW–SE axis about 900 miles east of Australia. The historic geographical fulcrum is not *Nouméa la blanche*, as Kanaks call the capital, but the *Chaîne centrale* whose foothills are visible from the Place des Cocotiers. The mountain range runs along the spine of Grande Terre, dividing the largely French '*Caldoche*' settlements of the south-west from the largely Kanak ones of the north-east. It is also a climatic barrier, with the fertile, forested coast of the windward north-east receiving twice as much rainfall, some 3,000 mm annually, as the scrubby, nickel-rich maquis of the south-west.

Eighty miles off Grande Terre's south-eastern tip is the tiny Isle of Pines; to the north-west are the three Loyalty Islands, Ouvéa, Lifou and Maré. These small islands are coral atolls, while Grande Terre and the Isle of Pines are jutting fragments of the vast submarine continent of Zealandia, of which New Zealand, 400 miles south, is also a part. Nineteen years after James Cook discovered the island in 1774, the French explorer Antoine Bruni d'Entrecasteaux landed while searching for his compatriot Jean-François de Galaup, whose ship had vanished off Vanuatu. Not until 1853, soon after taking possession of the islands of Tahiti and the Marquesas, did France claim this new archipelago, with a colonialist hauteur that colours intercommunal relations to this day. Writing to the Foreign Minister the following year, the French Minister of the Navy and Colonies explained: 'The uncivilised inhabitants of a country have over that country only a limited right to domination, a sort of right of occupation . . . A civilised power on establishing a colony in such a country acquires a decisive power over the soil, or, in other terms, she acquires the right to extinguish the primitive title . . .'

If a frontier or dominion cannot be peopled by smiling emigrants then it must be colonised by compulsion. New Caledonia was already well established as a regular penal colony by the time Michel arrived. The first convicts landed in 1865, eight years earlier, but until the coming of the Communards the colony's most notorious prisoner was Antoni Berezowski, a Polish revolutionary born in Ukraine, who in 1867 had been deported to Bourail, eighty miles north of Nouméa, for attempting to assassinate Aleksandar II while the tsar was visiting Paris (fourteen years later, The People's Will would succeed where he failed). By the time Berezowski arrived, New Caledonia had superseded France's penal colony in South America, French Guiana, as the main destination of exiled French convicts, or *bagnards*.

The Nouméa that Michel would have seen from the *Virginie* as it waited at anchor was already a well-established port city. A French missionary approaching the harbour a few years later described 'a high wooded hill, burned, corroded brown by the sun' and beneath it, 'flattened by light, the city, a cascade of zinc roofs. Here and there a coconut palm casting some shade.' Michel and her friend Nathalie Lemel were met on board by the governor, Louis Eugène Gaultier de la Richerie. As women, he assured them, they would not be housed on the exposed and waterless Ducos Peninsula with the male deportees, but in the penal settlement of Bourail, eighty miles north, where conditions were less harsh. *No*: 'If our male comrades were going to suffer more on the Ducos Peninsula,' wrote Michel, 'we wanted to be there with them.' Assuming Richerie insisted, Lemel told him, 'Louise and I, this same evening at precisely eight o'clock, will throw ourselves into the sea.' They were allowed to join their male friends in the settlement of Numbo, on the southern shore of the peninsula.

Exiles in New Caledonia occupied one of three categories: *déportés*, including political prisoners like Michel and most of the other Communards, were generally spared hard labour and even allowed to take paid work, while being confined to a particular zone. Common criminals and recidivists, known as *transportés* and *relégués* respectively, were confined to one of several penitentiaries and often forced to do hard labour. Once they had completed their sentence, transportees serving more than eight years were to remain in New Caledonia, as 'free' citizens, *libérés*, for life, meaning that many of them, watching the coast of France vanish beyond the horizon, from the stern of the *Virginie* or some other convict ship, knew they would never see the country again. This taxonomy, which was echoed in imperial Russia, revived that of Ancient Rome, where exile was methodically regulated according to the subject, the severity of their misdeed and the prevailing political winds. *Deportatio* usually meant exile to a specified place, the loss of civil rights and no hope of recall; *aqua et igni interdictus* – literally 'debarred from water and fire' – meant indefinite exile and the loss of civil rights and property; *relegatio*, meanwhile (Ovid's sentence), designated banishment to a specified locale, but with the retention of citizenship and property.

———

I have often found myself waiting for strangers in petrol-station forecourts. 'Single wave of nausea,' reads my notebook. 'Urine clear. Shooting pain in stomach. No fever. Worse with movement.'

That morning, a week after arriving in New Caledonia, I'd visited a doctor on the first floor of Nouméa's small shopping mall. He kneaded me all over and, unable to isolate the source of my discomfort, promised me there was no reason to worry and handed me a prescription for high-strength co-codamol.

Louis-José Barbançon, who arrived at the petrol station after half an hour, knew more than anyone about New Caledonia's penal history. Like many *Caldoches* (New Caledonians of French ancestry) he was descended from a convict. He had been involved with an anti-independence party during the 1980s, a party that had also campaigned for greater Kanak representation in government. He drove me to his home, five minutes away, a bungalow built by his father, a sailor, using timbers from Nouméa's old American naval base. (His father had drowned when he was three, lost in a shipwreck off Maré.)

'You can evaluate a society when you see where it places the frontier between those people it wants to keep and those it wants to banish. Read Michel Foucault. The line between the people who are mad and the people who are not mad. Every government wants to criminalise the radical.'

He led me to a library in what might once have been a pantry, its walls lined with books, including several he had written. The room was his life's centre; he had a scholarly, preoccupied air, but he was not otherworldly. He was suspicious of pilgrims and less interested in Louise Michel, another *bonne femme blanche*, than in the thousands of *bagnards* who remained unnamed let alone celebrated. 'She is not a superwoman, she is a woman! She sees things that others don't see:

okay. But you are not obliged to make her a saint. I'm sure she doesn't like that. It's the problem with icons, they have no depth, no doubts. Each time we speak about Louise Michel, all her humanity disappears.'

We were sitting side by side on a low antique chaise. From outside, where it was very still and very hot, came the squawking of the mynah birds. It was my hope that Michel's humanity would be visible here in Nouméa, where she was scarcely an icon, as it was not visible in France, where streets and schools are named in her honour and flags bearing her likeness are flown each year on the anniversary of the Commune. She was gone, but perhaps some of the places that shaped her remained.

In 1867 it was decreed that all French exiles, *déportés* and *transportés* alike, would be sent only to New Caledonia (though convicts from colonies such as Algeria continued to be sent to French Guiana, where conditions were considered too harsh for French nationals). With its subtropical climate and natural wealth, New Caledonia was considered by some to be insufficiently arduous, a sentiment shared by criminals as well as lawmakers. In the early 1870s, at the height of Communard deportations, a spate of murders of French prison guards was carried out by convicts who hoped to be sent to the 'land of eternal springtime', as one commentator called the islands. When the Jewish artillery officer Alfred Dreyfus was sentenced to deportation for treason in 1895, in a case that divided the nation, French Guiana was reopened to convicts from France, as conditions in New Caledonia were by then considered too salubrious. One French lawmaker suggested a solution: *bagnards* from both territories should be rounded up and shipped to another colonial possession altogether: the Antarctic Kerguelen Islands, some 2,000 miles south of Madagascar, where at least nobody would die of heatstroke. In New Caledonia, the majority of Communards were sent to the Isle of Pines, but the most influential spent their sentence on the Ducos Peninsula.

'The model, always, was the British penal system,' Barbançon said. 'But the British are always looking at the sea: they are sailors, islanders. The French person is different. The French are continental; the French are working the earth; are peasants.'

According to the Vicomte d'Haussonville, commenting on his country's penal system in 1875, this explained the French reluctance to settle abroad: 'A Frenchman is not less industrious,' he wrote, 'nor less able, nor less inclined to labour than an Englishman or a German. But the French allow themselves to be retained by family ties, by the attraction to their native soil.' His term for this constitutional sedentariness was *l'amour du clocher*, love of the church tower – love of the hometown.

'Take the Alsatians,' Barbançon added. 'After the Franco-Prussian War of 1870 there was the Frankfurt Treaty, which gave Alsace to Germany. Alsatians could opt to be either French or German. The question was also put to Alsatian deportees in New Caledonia, to be French or German, and 90 per cent chose to be German and return to jail in Europe.'

According to one Communard, several of his fellow *déportés* were 'struck by the worst of diseases, mental alienation'. It was accepted that such alienation – what Johannes Hofer in 1688 had named *nostalgie* and Henri Rochefort 'that strange and indefinable sensation called home-sickness' – could be terminal.

One of Louise Michel's exiled brothers-in-arms from the Commune, whom she had hoped to meet again on reaching New Caledonia, turned out to have 'died of grief at receiving no news from home. Only a few days after his death,' she adds, 'a bundle of letters arrived for him.' Another *déporté*, Achille Ballière, asked: 'What need do we have, anyway, to live this life? The weather is bad, the sky is black, our mood is dark. We think of the absent. My child, what has become of her? What has happened to my mother? Where is my father?'

How easily Hofer's 'grief for the lost charm of the native land' can be misconstrued as longing for the nation state. Michel, who abhorred the very idea of nationhood, was immune to the *nostalgie* that overcame so many of her comrades. Like the Alsatians who opted to return to a newly German Alsace, her loyalty was never national.

———

'Numbo, in the valley, was crescent-shaped, the eastern end being the top of the crescent and containing the prison, the post office, and the canteen,' Michel wrote, recalling her new domicile on the Ducos Peninsula. 'The other end, the western one, lay in a forest on low hills covered with salt-resistant plants. The middle of the crescent, running along the whole length of the bay from east to west, was where we built our huts.' On being rowed to Numbo, Michel and Lemel were greeted by the male deportees from the *Virginie* and by dozens of others they had not seen since Bloody Week more than two and a half years earlier.

She was struck by the peninsula's natural beauty:

We heard the waves beating eternally on the reefs, and above us we saw the cracked mountain peaks from which torrents of water poured noisily down to the sea during the frequent great rains. At sunset we watched the sun disappear into the sea, and in the valley the twisted white trunks of the niaoulis glowed with a silver phosphorescence.

Her friend Henri Rochefort, too, admired those sunsets 'of liquified gold, transfused with amethyst'. In his memoirs he goes on to explain that he and the other leading Communards were supposed to be held on the *island* of Ducos, a 'desert spot at least twenty leagues distant from New Caledonia, [which] would have meant a lingering death for us' – but, unable to find it on the map, the authorities had consigned them to the peninsula of the same name. Even so, Rochefort wrote, 'it was the galleys in a mitigated form, where, instead of being put to forced labour, we were kept in forced idleness'.

Michel was incapable of idleness. She treated her exile as if it were a scientific expedition. Before her departure she had been tasked by both the Société de Géographie and the Société Zoologique d'Acclimatation (dedicated to introducing non-native species to France's colonies) to undertake research; in her small plot in Numbo she built what she describes as a greenhouse, where she not only grew vegetables but also carried out a series of experiments into what she called 'jaundice' in papayas.

In reality, the mountains she mentioned were more like hills, and the sun did not 'disappear into the sea', for due west of Numbo, just a mile away across the Bay of Nouméa, was the island of Nou, which today, as Nouville, is connected to Nouméa by a man-made isthmus formed of tailings from the city's sprawling nickel works, which dominates the shoreline between Nouméa and the Ducos Peninsula. It was in the *bagne* on Nou that most of New Caledonia's criminal population, the *transportés*, were housed, as well as Communards whose crimes were considered especially grave. On windless days the Communards on the Ducos Peninsula, in their relative comfort and freedom – hardly the 'galleys', even in mitigated form – were able to have shouted conversations across the water with those of their Paris comrades who had been sentenced to hard labour. According to Rochefort, Wednesdays at 10 a.m. brought other cries:

> The warders were applying the regulation bastinado [beating the soles of the feet] to the convicts. They were attached to a form, stripped to the loins, while the 'corrector', a gigantic mulatto, belaboured them with a whip of bullocks' sinew. His energy depended on the

size of the coin the convict was able to slip into his hand before the punishment commenced.

A few months after Michel's arrival an event occurred that saw the conditions of the deportees deteriorate. Rochefort had begun plotting his escape from the moment of his arrival. At first he had planned to make his way on foot to the north of the island, from where a Kanak boat could take him to Vanuatu, about 300 miles north-east – risky, since certain Kanak clans had been 'entrusted with the duty of capturing escaped convicts'. In the end, through an intermediary in Nouméa, he arranged for an Australian coal barque to smuggle him to New South Wales. On a stormy night, he and five fellow deportees swam out to a rock off Numbo, where they were met by a rowboat that took them to the waiting ship and freedom.

'For the rest of his life he was the great escapee!' Barbançon told me. 'He did not know the suffering of Louise Michel and the other deportees, let alone the transportees. If he escaped, it was for one reason only: because he had money.'

He had paid the barque's captain 10,000 francs and was will-ing to pay ten times that. From Sydney, Rochefort sailed first to the United States, where he gave a series of triumphalist lectures, before continuing on to Ireland (as a Communard, he was stoned by a Catholic mob) then self-exile in London and Geneva. When he finally returned to Paris in 1880 he was greeted by a crowd of as many as 200,000. Michel's own escape plans, inspired by his, were thwarted by lack of finances, while Rochefort's flight heralded the further shrinking of her world. One of the authorities' responses was the removal of the governor, Richerie, and his replacement by a figure who would quickly become despised for his brutality: Louis Eugène Alleyron.

It was, wrote Michel, 'a time of desperate madness'. The deportees' overseers became crueller and more vigilant. 'One unfortunate man, who didn't have all his wits about him, was shot at, the way someone would have taken aim at a rabbit, because he came back a little late to his plot.' In May 1875, almost two years after arriving in Numbo, Michel, Lemel and four other female Communards were notified that they would be separated from the men and sent to an even more isolated location. They refused to move unless Alleyron agreed to provide private huts in their new compound rather than the shared accommodation he had proposed. 'The head guard was very annoyed with us,' Michel remembered. 'Towards evening he came on horseback so he would appear more imposing, but his horse kept breaking wind, which spoiled the effect.'

The authorities relented, since the prison in Numbo was full; the women were sent to a narrow isthmus a mile along the peninsula. Michel called it the Bay of the West. On maps, even today, it is the Baie des Dames. You could see it, the Bay of the Ladies, from the site of the penitentiary in Nouville, where the prison and the dormitories, the bakery and the administrative buildings still stand. The isthmus, meanwhile, is now occupied by the fenced compound of the Total oil terminal, with its squat white storage cylinders. I was told it was impossible to go there, let alone to the wooded hill at the tip of the peninsula, which the oil installation effectively blocked, and which Michel called *la forêt ouest*, the Forest of the West.

2.

I took a six-hour coach journey to the north-east. I was sick of Nouméa – *Nouméa la blanche* – sick of the city's nerviness and the discomfort I'd come to associate with its bistros, beaches and squares.

I was still struggling to describe to myself what had happened to me a week ago in the Place des Cocotiers, but I couldn't help feel it was somehow a product of this city. Those broad depopulated boulevards, the buses ridden solely by Kanak people, the miniature yellow road-train packed with splayed-kneed retirees from Melbourne. A sweaty, flushed-faced place, a place 'flattened by light', in the words of the missionary, it was not a plausible city, nor did it seem content.

The affable white owners of my apartment, a couple who were nearing retirement, and their teenage son invited me to dinner. We sat outside by the pool. I had been admiring the wooden sculptures: elongated ceremonial masks and ornately carved log-drums. They were not Kanak, said the husband, but from nearby Vanuatu, where he had once lived, and they were not just decorative but intended to ward off what he called 'evil spirits' – he exchanged a smile with his wife – by which he meant burglars, which meant Kanaks, who apparently feared the carvings. Later, over digestifs, he confided, 'The natives of Vanuatu, they are blacker, but prettier.' I swallowed hard, but can't say I was shocked; this way of thinking, a sort of murderous paternalistic nostalgia, would scarcely have raised an eyebrow in his social circle. 'Here, they have . . . *the flat nose*. In Vanuatu they make these beautiful carvings. Here, what do the natives make? Nothing.' And that lack of artistry, as he deemed it, that idleness, was somehow connected in his mind to Kanak people's pig-headedness over the referendum: 'They see what will happen to the economy. They know what happened when Vanuatu had independence: disaster. They do not care. We try to tell them . . .'

It was not that he wanted for education; he had lived here for years, he knew everything it was necessary for him to know. They did not seem put out when I got up to leave. Early start to Hienghène tomorrow. 'Before the referendum? Are you not afraid you will be eaten?' Another smiling glance from his wife. It was the kind of joke you could safely make in friendly company, by the flicker of citronella candles. A visiting French naturalist, writing more than 200 years ago, offered as 'incontestable proof of their ferocity' a sighting of a Kanak man chewing on a bone he judged, from a distance, to be that of an adolescent boy. The libel retained its power.

———

The 'events' of the 1980s, *les événements*, were fuelled by generations of resentment, and finally caused to explode in 1984 with the Hienghène Massacre, the shooting dead of ten unarmed Kanak men by settlers. With the threat of civil war, a referendum on independence was held in 1987, but boycotted by most Kanak people, who recognised that the extension of voting rights to all but the newest immigrants made the outcome a fait accompli. Ninety-eight per cent of voters, almost all of them white, voted against independence, and the following year on the island of Ouvéa a hostage crisis unfolded that ended in the killing of nineteen more Kanak men and four white gendarmes.

Among the dead in Hienghène were two brothers of the head of the Kanak and Socialist National Liberation Front (FLNKS), Jean-Marie Tjibaou. Later in 1988, with the co-operation of Tjibaou, the Matignon Accords were signed in Paris between the loyalists and the separatists, which gave greater autonomy to New Caledonia's government, afforded Kanaks more say in Nouméa's parliament, and provided an amnesty for those involved in the Ouvéa incident. A further treaty, the Nouméa Accord, signed in 1998, mandated that a referendum on independence take place before the end of the current year, 2018.

The coach, full of Kanak families going home to vote, rolled north across the ferrous coastal plain, past coves fringed with New Caledonia's endemic pines, trees that tilted at such angles they might have been fired into the ground from a bow. Behind us, Nouméa had vanished into the copperish cloud of sulphur dioxide from the nickel works. I felt relief. After an hour, we passed through La Foa and Bourail, heartland of the Great Revolt, before turning north and climbing into the dense forest of the *Chaîne centrale*.

Groups of men and women lying in roadside shade waved as we passed. The Kanak flag marked every driveway and, smaller counterparts, the boundaries of manioc and yam fields: three horizontal stripes of blue, red and green overlain by a yellow disc across which lies a black *flèche faîtière*, the spear-like totem that adorns the roof of traditional Kanak huts. The flag was ubiquitous as soon as we crossed the mountains, and over the next few days more than one truck rushed past me packed with young men brandishing them from back windows, as in the days after a liberation. And perhaps that's what the referendum promised: a taste of liberation, from the past, and from a future that appeared to be no more than a mirror of the past. Better to celebrate victory while it was still a possibility.

An anti-independence bill posted to hoardings, which had been erected in every community by the electoral authorities, had been torn off and the strips scattered on the grass. The pro-independence bill next to it was untouched. In the tiny, deserted settlement of Hienghène, which stood on the estuary near the sea, a hand-painted banner was slung between two closed shops, swinging in the breeze: 'Remember our brothers who sacrificed their lives for our freedom and vote YES.'

I stayed in a tribal village, Werap, on the River Hienghène, a mile from the sea. The stranger is sacred in Kanak culture, and historically the stranger, banished from the tribes of the west or washed up from a shipwreck, was not merely cared for but sometimes appointed chief. I was put up in a traditional round hut with a single mattress, a place for guests, and fed manioc and sweet-potato stew baked in the ground; but the adults and I were shy of one another. Far away, across the valley, a band was playing dub reggae. As the sun sank behind the circle of hills that cradled the village, I was joined on the patch of lawn outside my hut by four toddlers, girls, who confiscated first my pen then my notebook, one of them cheerfully blunting the pen on a rock while another tore from my notebook, one by one, the previous week's pages.

Next morning the band was playing again, if it had ever stopped. Sunbeams raked the sweet smoke of breakfast fires. As quickly as it had come on, the pain of the preceding weeks vanished – gone. Perhaps it was just the doctor's drugs working, but in my relief I couldn't help attributing it to the change of scene. I'd learnt a word in the Ajië language, spoken in the village of Haouilou to the south-west of Hienghène: *maciri*: it means 'peaceful abode'.

New Caledonia's rainforest contains around 2,000 plant species, of which more than 80 per cent are endemic. Among the tree ferns, beeches, conifers, tulip trees, kauris and palms grew papaya and bananas, dragon fruit and lemons. I asked one of the little girls what the red-flowering tree was: I was joking, surely: flame tree, flame tree! There were clearings of furrowed red soil for sweet potato and manioc and the sacred yam. A pig squealed. Peacefulness is sometimes no more than abundance. I swam in the river, smoky with silt (rain in the hills), and walked along the riverside track to Hienghène.

I knew nothing of the valley's totems or ancestor gods. I walked blindly, in a daze of touristic enchantment.

———

In one of her many letters to Victor Hugo, Michel said she hoped to be given permission to live with a Kanak clan. 'I shan't return to France without carrying out this project, because it's foolish to travel 6,000 leagues and not see anything or be of use to anybody.' That she was not allowed to do so didn't prevent her from undertaking one of the earliest Western studies of Kanak language and traditions. At a dinner held in Rochefort's honour she spoke to the first non-European she had met since leaving France. Named Daoumi, he hailed from 'Sifou' (perhaps a mistranscription of Lifou, one of the Loyalty Islands):

Daoumi had come dressed like a European in a high hat, which marred the effects of his wild man's head, and he was wearing kid gloves. With his hands thus imprisoned, Daoumi could not help . . . with the roast, nor could he help with the other preparations. That is how I was able to get him alone and have him sing a war chant to me.

She went on to write a study of Kanak legends and languages including the regional pidgin known as Bislama. She had no way of knowing the sheer diversity of languages on Grande Terre alone, but was rare in holding the 'Canaques' in anything more than contempt, at a time when that attitude was ubiquitous among Europeans in New Caledonia, from prison overseers to sandalwood traders to Communards. To some of her Paris associates, she appeared *plus canaque que les Canaques*. She never doubted that theirs was a retrograde culture, 'stone age', or that the Kanaks themselves were childlike in their 'qualities and vices'; but then, she reasoned, the Third Republic, which gunned down defenceless children in their homes, could hardly be said to govern from the summit of civilisation. 'Other races giving way before our arms is no proof of our superiority.' 'The white men promised us heaven and earth,' one Kanak informant told her, 'but they gave us nothing, nothing but sorrow.' The Kanaks had been expelled from their land by ranchers and prison officials, their taro plots had been destroyed by European cattle, their burial sites and sacred places blithely desecrated. It was as if land, to these incomers, were mere *matter*, a possession like a hoe or a boat. 'Landscape' for Kanak people, then as now, is an interface between the worlds of the living and the dead, the visible and the invisible, where place, person and myth are inseparable. 'Society' is constituted purely 'according to principles of correspondence, complementarity, equilibrium, symmetry, alterity and bilateralism'. There is no 'self'; the individual as an 'I' does not exist; even the body cannot be considered a discrete object. You are nothing but your relations with other entities.

Tensions came to a head in the insurgency of 1878–9, known as the Great Revolt. For some Communard *déportés*, as well as free colonists, the uprising represented an opportunity to reclaim a sense of identity, national identity, rendered nebulous by distance. What was *nostalgie*, but a pining for a lost part of oneself? According to one commentator, the uprising was self-evidently 'the revolt of barbarism against civilisation' – that it might be *political* in nature was inconceivable to all but a handful of the French. While many of Michel's fellow Communards willingly took up arms against what they saw as a common barbarian enemy, a few, like Michel, instinctively sympathised with the rebelling Kanaks. She, after all, had always thought of herself as a 'savage'. 'The whites shot down the rebels as we were mowed down . . . on the plains of Satory.'

The uprising, led by Ataï, a chief from the Komalé region, can be seen as the culmination of a series of smaller colonial wars dating back to 1856, but it was triggered by the expansion of the penitentiary in La Foa, fifty miles north of Nouméa, and particularly the destruction of Kanak crops by roaming French cattle. Advised by the French governor that he should build fences if he wished to protect his crops, Ataï is said to have replied: 'I will build fences when my taro start eating your cattle.'

On 25 and 26 June 1878, nearly five years after Louise Michel arrived in New Caledonia, 125 settlers were killed in surprise attacks in the Ouraïl-Bouloupari district. The Europeans were astonished by the suddenness of the violence, which seemed to come out of nowhere, and by its 'savagery'. They, too, had considered the natives 'children' – again and again, foreshadowing every colonial atrocity – incapable of co-ordinated resistance. The violence of the French response, therefore, was energised by moral offence as well as territorial interest. It would have been ineffective, however, in the dense country around La Foa, without the guidance of the Canala clan, which as a rival of Ataï's Komalé had allied itself to France, guiding the white troops in suppressing the resistance on its own terms. 'Fire and destruction have been applied to the native villages,' wrote one local missionary. 'It was the Canaque system of warfare.' The 'children', meanwhile, had shown themselves to be 'ferocious beasts'.

Attack and counterattack followed, with the Kanaks under Ataï withdrawing to their heavily barricaded villages. On 1 September 1878 an expedition set out from the La Foa military post to attack Ataï's encampment, with a hundred French and more than twice as many Canala men. It would mark the beginning of the end of the Great Revolt, even if it was not to be the total conquest the French anticipated. Ataï was killed by an axe blow, Michel was told, and fell 'like a tree that has been chopped down', before his head was removed and handed to the authorities in Nouméa, whence it was shipped to France.

Michel says little about what practical assistance, if any, she gave the rebels from the remote Ducos Peninsula, only admitting that she advised them on methods for severing the telegraph wires vital to the French counterinsurgency; and that she gave her red scarf, torn in half, to two visiting insurgents before they went to face her countrymen – 'the red scarf of the Commune that I had hidden from every search'. Solidarity was the one religion available to her as an anarchist. On St Helena and Sakhalin, too, unwilling exiles and unwilling hosts would discover a sympathy that confounded colonial power.

At the Paris Anthropology Society, meanwhile, Ataï's head arrived 'in a perfect state of preservation', still ponytailed with its top few vertebrae. 'It is very expressive; the forehead especially is very handsome, very high and very broad. The hair is completely woolly, the skin quite black.' His hand, which was also acquired, was 'large and powerful . . . very well formed, except that one of the fingers is retracted as a result of an old wound. The palmar folds are similar to ours.'

———

At Hienghène, the beach behind the razor-wired gendarmerie compound was a dumping ground for the sea, heaped with rotting palm leaves, the air so thick with midges that you walked spitting. Under a tree a large bearded man was sitting on a lawn chair, a little girl perched between his legs. He was slowly brushing her hair while she watched cartoons on a tablet. The sand was braided with snake tracks and he warned me about the small tricolours: if he bites you here – he pinched the web of skin between his forefinger and thumb; here – between the nostrils; or here – the inner whorl of the ear – 'then in two hours you will be dead'. He went on brushing the girl's hair.

On the promontory above the bay a wedding party had gathered for photos, each member dressed in a shirt or dress of lime green. I walked south along a quiet coastal track, accompanied by a succession of near-identical white dogs, which seemed to follow at my heel in a kind of pre-agreed relay, each one staying with me for half a mile before passing me over to another as I left its territory. Locusts rose from the verge with the sound of papers being shuffled. There were black swallows, black crows, a black pony stepping back and forth in the centre of the road. When the dog barked in its face the pony stared at it, unflinching.

The road was divided from the sea by a narrow strip of forest, the density of which was occasionally broken by a fishermen's path forming a tunnel to the beach, so that you ducked from the shaded road into the close darkness of the forest, with fishing nets slung from branches like discarded wedding dresses, only to emerge into the dazzle of the beach, with its white sand, sea-glitter, gulls and distant unpopulated islands. Every few hundred metres one of the palm trees overhanging the beach would be machete-carved with a mark designating the individual or clan whose name was assigned to the stretch by ancestral right. In the shallows around clumps of mangrove the dog went after the tiny zebra fish with jubilant, fruitless pounces.

And like this, with my dog (which was really several), I threaded south, walking along the beach for a while before taking a path through the forest to the road, and then, after a few minutes' walking, crossing back to the beach, and so on between these two incoherent worlds. I could have walked like this forever; the world's beauty, the island's, was inexhaustible. You cannot live on a small island and be unaware of the wider planet; to this extent an islander, an Oceanian especially, is less isolated than a continental. The sea is not a barrier but a highway, as Louise Michel had appreciated; the shore the start and end of every journey. One effect of colonisation was to cut off this highway, quite literally to *insulate* Kanak society from the wider community of Oceania.

——

Under a Kanak flag I met Charles, who was sitting in his shack boiling coffee. He was in his early fifties, undernourished, grey beard. I sat down in the broken lawn chair he gestured to while he took a knife to a grapefruit as big as a football, handing me half. 'Eat.' It was all pith and juice; I ate like a toddler. 'Then we'll drink coffee.'

The air was full of swallows and at once salty and sweet (the sea and the forest), and that salt-sweetness seemed to be the swallows' element.

The coffee boiled and he handed me a plastic cup. I'd been warned the referendum was a subject it was unwise to broach with Kanak strangers; but it was men in Nouméa who had given me that warning, and Charles wanted to talk. I knew nothing about him but he spoke as if it were too late for him – as if his life were a plant sown in poisoned soil. 'Independence is getting back our identity,' he said: 'It was stolen from my sisters many years ago. If the vote is yes, then we regain our identity. The other nations can stay. But the French government must end. The real name of my country is not *New Caledonia*. That name was given by Cook, because he believed the big island looked like Scotland. Its real name is Kanaky: the place of the Kanaks.'

————

At Wan'yaat, half a mile along the track from Werap, were two shot-up trucks. The vehicles were wreathed in bolts of bright cloth and strewn with plastic flowers and Kanak flags. The party had been returning from a meeting in Hienghène in 1984 when they came to a palm tree dropped across the track. As they attempted to reverse, they were attacked with dynamite and gunfire by a group from two local settler families. Among the ten who died (six at the time, the remainder in the days afterwards) were two brothers of Jean-Marie Tjibaou, the Kanak leader, who was foremost among the intended targets. He was away in Nouméa, but Tjibaou had always expected to be assassinated, to go to *le grand trou noir*, as he called it, the big black hole. Afterwards he never travelled anywhere with his family or without his bodyguards. 'The hardest thing to do may not be to die,' he wrote; 'the hardest thing is to stay alive and feel like a stranger

102

in your own land.' However different their lives and their battles, Tjibaou shared with Michel a quality of idealism across the hundred years separating them. His story, too, was a story of exile. To feel like a stranger in your own land.

As had already happened on the other side of the island, where Kanaks were ultimately confined to barbed-wire reserves, French settlers successively pushed Tjibaou's ancestors from their lands on Hienghène's fertile valley floor to the relatively barren mountains. The rich loams of the lowlands were not for them. Alongside the guillotine, which was shipped over from France, deportation became the colonists' chief tool in suppressing Kanak resistance. During the Great Revolt, hundreds of Kanaks were deported from Grande Terre to both the Isle of Pines and, much further away, France's colonies in Tahiti and Indochina. (In turn, rebellious subjects from French Indochina were deported to New Caledonia.) The banished included Jean-Marie Tjibaou's ancestors, leaders of one of the clans that ruled the Hienghène Valley. He himself was born in Tiendanite, upriver from Werap, in 1936, the son of a tribal chief. During the Northern Rebellion of 1917, his grandmother had been shot dead while fleeing an attack on the village of Ouélis by the French military and its Kanak auxiliaries. She had been carrying his father, who was four. 'He rolled down in the ferns and his big sister picked him up,' Tjibaou wrote later.

Catholic missionary activity in the Hienghène Valley went back to 1897; but not until 1965 did the first Kanak from the north-east of Grande Terre enter the priesthood, the son of the chief of Tiendanite, no less: Tjibaou. His training took him away from his home valley and its totems to the white seminaries of Canala and the Isle of Pines. When he returned to Tiendanite after ten years, having spoken nothing but French during that time, he opened his mouth to greet his brothers – and found he no longer knew Pije, the language of his childhood in Tiendanite, his means of naming the world. It was a transformative moment. Exile can be linguistic as well as geographic: the loss of his native tongue alarmed him, for it was a metaphor for his people's dispossession. But he understood that the weapons he needed to resist that dispossession were to be found not in 'Kanaky' but in France.

In 1968, the young priest won a scholarship to study theology, and found himself in Paris during the most intense period of civil unrest the country had seen since the Commune. Tiring of religion, he started studying ethnology, writing a thesis on 'the problems of Kanak cultural identity'. While his years as a seminarian might have distanced him from village life, his studies in Paris – resting place of Ataï's skull, at once his world's antipode and the epicentre of the earthquake that shook Kanak culture to its foundations – showed him a way back to the 'local, inhabited earth'.

Returning to a country where Kanaks felt their alienation more than ever, he left the priesthood and committed himself to politics, even as he recognised that independence could not be realised, under the French system, while Kanaks remained an electoral minority. Addressing a conference in Geneva in 1981, by which time he had become mayor of Hienghène and a spokesman for Kanak rights, he highlighted the importance of ancestral land to his people: 'Genealogies are rooted in the earth. Genealogies have no meaning if they are not inscribed in space, in a specific place . . . Otherwise, one has no history. One is a citizen of the world and of nowhere.'

The quest for Kanak autonomy was neither a matter of nostalgia – a return to the old ways was a 'myth' – nor of yearning for Western values: white men had been to the moon and were still unsatisfied, still 'searching', as he put it. But political radicalism in the European mould would itself be an expression of subjugation. There could be no 'Nouméa Commune'.

In 1984 the FLNKS was formed out of a number of smaller independentist groups with the objective of creating a Kanak socialist republic. For the first time the Kanak flag was raised. Green for the land, blue for the sea, red for the people's blood. When the perpetrators of the Hienghène Massacre, killers of Tjibaou's brothers, were exonerated, further violence became inevitable. One of the ringleaders of the *embuscade* was later executed by a Kanak sniper.

'Nonviolence, yes,' as Tjibou said, 'but with the gun at our feet.'

––––

The morning before I was due to return to Nouméa, walking in the forest between Werap and the Hienghène river, I came to a clearing the size of a football pitch, and for the first time saw the source of the music that had been echoing around the valley these past three days.

The sun, already hot, was steaming the night's moisture from the banana-tree leaves, and as the heat increased and the shadows rose from the valley, the bird noises (not quite calls or songs) from the surrounding forest, the parakeets, bulbuls and thicket birds, became louder and more discordant, discordant as a bell tower in an earthquake. In one corner of the clearing, tethered without shade, stood a deer with one antler snapped off above the base. It stood absolutely still – the stillest thing in the whole valley, it seemed – in the centre of a disc of grass nibbled to the soil. In the opposite corner, under two giant banyan trees, was a shack and about twenty young people, dancing in the absolute shade characteristic of banyans, to music from a single large speaker set on the ground under one tree.

I was greeted by the men (it was mostly men dancing, the women sitting on a terrace in front of the shack), who had the crumpled appearance of those who have been up all night, the bright eyes and glistening skin of dwindling euphoria. Their dancing was more like a rhythmic swaying, the music an accompaniment rather than a stimulus. They were from Werap and Tjibaou's home Tiendanite and the valley's other villages, still celebrating yesterday's wedding, though the bride and groom were not there. They were almost too weary to talk, but I was embraced and my hand was shaken and into it was placed an almost-empty bottle of whisky. They knew where I was staying, of course, and how long I had been there, no visitor going unobserved and news spreading quickly within and between villages. And perhaps it was because of this – the debasing fame of the tourist or policeman, the toll to be paid, which meant that an idea of me preceded me like the sound of a helicopter – that one of the older men barrelled over to me and insisted I dance, only for his mood to sour – something in my face he didn't like, something standoffish about my manner. 'If he doesn't dance, I'll fucking kill him! *Je vais le guillotiner!*' He wasn't about to kill me, but a week before the referendum, his words didn't feel casual. A few miles up the coast was the memorial to twelve rebel Kanaks who had been guillotined by the French in 1868. I was a *kamadra, un blanc* – who cared if I was French? – and I didn't belong here. The land forgot nothing.

His friends pulled him away, lovingly, arms wrapped around his chest, and I left, as the one-antlered deer looked on and the man who wanted to dance laughed and tugged at the front of his T-shirt, showing me what was printed on it: KANAKY – the name Jean-Marie Tjibaou and the FLNKS had given their dream republic.

3.

Sequestration leads to dreaming, and dreaming to madness. Rochefort's words. Back in Nouméa I moved to an apartment in the city's Latin Quarter. The air conditioning was broken so I spent a lot of time lying in the palm-tree shade on the beaches south of the city. I found myself thinking about the mysterious black ship that had briefly trailed the *Virginie*, a vessel that seemed to promise Michel the same liberation she had sought in execution. It had reminded her of the *Naglfar*, the Norse ghost-ship made from the toenails of the dead. Exile itself has often been seen as a sort of death, as for Ovid on his 'barbarous coast' 1,900 years earlier: 'When I lost my country . . . was when I died, an earlier, grimmer death.'

At a café on the marina I met another poet who seemed distracted by the horizon, Nicolas Kurtovitch. We had been introduced by his older brother, Ismet, the city's archivist, who had showed me Michel's drawings from the *Virginie*. Where Ismet had the tentative inwardness of one who'd spent a lifetime in windowless library stacks, Nicolas was tall and tousled, a broad-chested hill-strider, and a bit louche.

'People here are too *égocentrique*,' he said. 'For me it's not possible, because my name is not a French name, it's from Sarajevo. People always know you are from somewhere else. So you see, I am always looking away. You have the horizon; but then there is something behind the horizon.'

His father, the son of a Bosnian imam, fled Nazi Sarajevo in 1945, first for Paris, then Australia, where he met Kurtovitch's mother, the daughter of an old *Caldoche* family. The couple married and lived in Nouméa for a few months, before moving to Paris in 1952. It was not a happy alliance. 'My father was too hard, not a good husband.' In 1961 his mother 'escaped', as he put it, back to Nouméa, with her three children. Kurtovitch was seven. 'One evening, my father came home and – nobody! Nobody. We were on the plane.

'I've always felt I am a refugee. I don't feel I have a true home anywhere, not even here. A long time ago I wrote a poem about a journey in the desert. It reads: "Who will talk about the exiles who have no country to be exiled from?" Take Victor Hugo: he was exiled from somewhere, at least. Where is my country? When I go to France, I live in a hotel, like every stranger.'

107

His father never returned to Sarajevo, said Kurtovitch, but nor did he become a French citizen; he remained *apatride*, stateless. His son had inherited that condition, its spirit at least.

'I used to be militant, an activist,' he said. 'We called it independence, but in our mind it was decolonisation.' It was hard to understand what the difference might be in practice. But if Kurtovitch had once favoured independence, indeed campaigned for it, he had changed his mind. Assuming the result on Sunday rejected independence, as was all but certain, the Nouméa Accord allowed for a second referendum to take place in two years' time, and another in four.

'But in two years' time we will win again,' said Kurtovitch (it turned out he was right). That was the point: 'In four years' time also. The only way for this country to reach independence is if lots of people who now vote no, vote yes. But why? We have our own budget, our own employment law. France has no say. Only in justice, money, army and university. And all the people working in hospital, they are paid directly by France. Each year France sends us one and a half billion euros. If we have independence, this is finished. So we need to stay with France for economic reasons. But not only that. France is the guarantee of the republic. They had coup d'états in Fiji, in the Solomon Islands. We do not live alone. We Europeans, we have to deal with Kanak people; and Kanak people have to deal with white people. We cannot behave as if each other does not exist.'

It was hard to think of him as a refugee; he was not his Muslim father, fleeing war. True, he *was* a kind of *étranger*, a foreigner, in Nouméa; but then perhaps that was merely the condition of being a *Caldoche* – to feel yourself, at some quiet level, an outsider. The history of French New Caledonia was a history of displacement, universal displacement. There could be no reversal, no true independence for anyone; all that was on offer was 'reconciliation', which really just meant that the Kanak people, who did not own the land but *were* the land, must reconcile themselves to perpetual pain, which meant the *Caldoches* must do the same.

Victor Hugo spent nearly twenty years in exile after fleeing Louis-Napoléon's France, only returning after the emperor's defeat at Sedan. Over his dining-room door in Guernsey, where he settled, had hung a sign: *Exilium vita est.* Life is exile; exile is life. 'Exile is not a material, but a moral matter,' he wrote. 'It does not matter where on earth you are.'

———

Across Nouméa Bay, with its superyachts and French naval destroyer, you could make out what Louise Michel called the Forest of the West, rising to a summit at the tip of the Ducos Peninsula. For her it was a numinous place, a reincarnation of the wilderness of her childhood Vroncourt. For me it took on the qualities of an Edenic citadel, as unreachable as a rainbow's end. The hill – almost an island, so narrow is the isthmus of the Baie des Dames, where Michel was confined – is one of Grande Terre's few preserves of dry tropical forest, a rare plant community that has otherwise been wiped out in the vicinity of Nouméa. My longing for the place – to set foot there, to live there forever? – I realise now was connected to the inaccessibility that protected it; connected, as well, to the ache that had returned no sooner than I set foot back in Nouméa.

Her hut had stood on a terrace to the west of the bay, at the edge of the forest, on a slope overlooking the isthmus and the huts of the other women. What she calls the Forest of the West – 'Koumourou' on modern maps – measures about 1,300 metres by 800 metres and extends into the Pacific like the half-submerged head of a lizard. One of the pleasures of Michel's descriptions of her walks in the forest is her unconcern with naming. She doesn't know what most of the plants and animals are called and she has no way of finding out, save what she can glean from her few Kanak contacts; but the glee she takes in itemising her finds isn't spoiled by her ignorance. What matters is the abundance, the wilderness that provides a retreat without threatening her life or psyche. She had become hardened to solitude (or softened to it) as a child in Vroncourt, where she had learnt that she needed no companion but nature. Her discovery of the Forest of the West was a return to nature, but more than that, a return to childhood. Surrounded by water on three sides, in the dense unpeopled forest she was safe again, as she had been in the Haute-Marne. ('At Vroncourt,' the child Louisette had written long ago, 'you're separated from the rest of the world.')

As she walked and climbed she would pick and eat the forest's fruits – figs, mulberries, yellow plums, blackcurrants, tomatoes – fruits that differed from those she knew from the markets of Paris or Vroncourt: the figs smelt like ashes, the mulberries had a powdery white coating, inside the plums was an enormous spherical pit, the blackcurrants gave barely any juice. Again and again in her memoirs she mentions the forest's lianas, with 'their branches floating in the air or thrown in mad arabesques', and New Caledonia's endemic niaoulis, *Melaleuca quinquenervia*, a white-barked tree of the myrtle family.

Trees, especially oaks, were always important in her life's symbology, from Vroncourt to Paris to New Caledonia. Perhaps it was their rootedness, their steadfastness, that drew her to them. In Vroncourt an ancient oak had traditionally been the place where oaths were exchanged; at the height of the siege of Paris she had experienced a vision, or was it a memory, of a giant oak with 'an axe embedded in its heart'; during Bloody Week, while she was carrying out reconnaissance in Montmartre Cemetery, 'shells tore the air, marking time like a clock'; her comrades urged her to take cover, but she was ever fatalistic. 'Always the shells arrived too early or too late for me. One shell falling across the trees covered me with flowered branches.' When a comrade was killed she removed her red scarf – symbol of the Commune – and laid it on his grave. 'A comrade picked it up and knotted it in the branches of a willow.'

The Forest of the West, two years later, is a kind of fairy-tale realm, seething with supernatural excess; and yet, Michel insists, nothing that can harm her. 'Even the water serpents pose no threat to man,' she says, telling us she kept one in a pond, as a pet, until she worried that it would crush her elderly cat. 'Certainly it followed her movements with its little reptile eyes filled with an expression that held very little sympathy.'

Alongside her anthropological studies and her investigations into papaya jaundice, she sought to demonstrate the viability in New Caledonia of silkworm cultivation. For years she corresponded with 'scholars' in Paris, who sent her batch after batch of silkworm eggs, only for them to arrive dead after the months-long voyage. Had her plans come to anything, they might in any case have been scuppered by the swarms of locusts that descended on the peninsula twice a year. 'Leaves, vegetables, tender grass, old bushes – everything except the trunk of the trees was eaten.' What might look to any other deportee like a portent of the world's end was sheer delight for her. 'Nothing', she writes, 'was as beautiful as the grey and turbulent snow of the locusts. Their uniform colour filled the whole sky, and the insects filtered the sun's rays . . . From the sky, grey flakes fell in a strangely blurred chiaroscuro.'

She is, I think, being healed of the horror of the barricades, is being allowed, briefly, to forget what has happened to her cause and to her friends. The smoke, the noise, the gaping wounds, the sludge of blood and powdered lime. During those intervals of solitude, among the niaoulis, the sandalwood and the nameless fruits of her

Forest of the West, it is as if she allowed herself to forget she was a political being.

———

'Love, love, love,' said Koma. 'This is what my father-in-law taught me. Open your heart to the world.'

She was eighty, with a crown of grey frizz and an air of serene forbearance that slipped into imperiousness when she tired of dull questions. She was the daughter-in-law of a pastor and the widow of a pastor – the pastor who had overseen the inter-tribal reconciliation process following the death of Jean-Marie Tjibaou. When she spoke about love she meant something specific, connected to the land; something forceful, with the power to annihilate.

I'd taken the short flight to the atoll of Ouvéa, sixty miles north of Grande Terre. The Loyalty Islands have always been distinct from Grande Terre, and not only geologically. Rising only a few metres above sea level, they were not even noticed by Cook or d'Entrecasteaux. About thirty miles from tip to tip, the most westerly, Ouvéa, is a broken limestone crescent measuring about four miles across at its widest, and connected by a bridge to the tiny island of Mouli to its south. A strip of white dunes extends along the islands' western coast, looking onto a shallow lagoon, flanked by a row of taro plots and most of Ouvéa's homes.

The Loyalty Islands had never been part of New Caledonia's penal archipelago, but the influence of missionaries remained potent and visible: the north of the atoll was mainly Protestant and the south mainly Catholic. Every few miles was another church, some of them primped and white, some of them roofless, their plaster spalling. The island's history of trade with Anglophone visitors from Britain and Australia – sandalwood, pearls, *bêche-de-mer* (sea cucumber) – meant that its people were more kindly disposed to English Protestant missionaries, when they arrived in the 1850s, than to their French-Catholic counterparts. When trade with the English dried up, however, French Marists from the main island exploited the vacuum and persuaded most of Ouvéa's population to adopt Catholicism.

These tribal divisions of faith had entrenched political loyalties: the north did not share with the south a coherent memory of what had happened in the 1980s, let alone the 1880s. Tjibaou was a Catholic; most of those killed at Gossana, the site of the 1988 hostage crisis, were Protestants or at least from traditionally Protestant clans. Ouvéa was different from Grande Terre in another way: while it had been annexed by France as far back as 1864, and was subject to French law, it had never been settled as the main island had been (the land was virtually barren, there was no nickel and no source of fresh water), and today the white population was so small as to be invisible, apart from the police enjoying a leisurely salad at a beachside diner, who were perhaps more vigilant than they appeared to be.

Koma had been there with her husband when Tjibaou was shot. Among the artefacts that provide a context for that event is a photo of Tjibaou, taken at the signing of the Matignon Accords in Paris in 1988, shaking hands with the leader of the New Caledonian republican party, Jacques Lafleur, the man who had approved the acquittal of the Hienghène murderers.

Today she runs a restaurant from her garden, ablaze with frangipani and bougainvillea, and it was there that we were sitting, in the shade of a palm-leaf shelter. She occasionally turned away to devote herself to a filter-less Gitane, intervals during which, it became clear, she was unwilling to speak.

'I want to say something that will disturb you,' she said finally, stubbing out her cigarette. 'Are you prepared?'

'Disturb me.'

'I disagreed with the handshake,' she said.

'A compromise too far.'

'It was not from the heart. It was politics. It was – *business.*'

And because the sentiment was not heartfelt, because Tjibaou in his heart distrusted Lafleur, true reconciliation could not be possible. It was this display of dishonesty, she felt, that made Tjibaou's death inevitable, more than the betrayal the handshake represented in the minds of his assassin and other independentists.

After the killings in Hienghène and the French government's hardening resistance to dialogue, the FLNKS had adopted a strategy of active confrontation. The events leading up to the Ouvéa Crisis, as it came to be known, are cloudy and disputed, many of the organisers having since died, but it seems that the FLNKS's constituent parties – including Tjibaou and his deputy Yiewéné Yiewéné – had agreed that its activists would occupy the main gendarmerie station on each of the three Loyalty Islands. Why only the station on Ouvéa was ultimately attacked is unclear.

On the morning of 22 April 1988, two days before the French elections, four Kanak men entered the police compound in the settlement of Fayaoué in south-west Ouvéa. In the scuffle, a lieutenant shot and injured one of the Kanaks, who in turn knifed him to death. When two other gendarmes went for their rifles they were killed. The Kanaks' reinforcements – some twenty Ouvéans – arrived to find three police dead and the rest under armed guard. What had been planned as a peaceful action was already a catastrophe.

The man who led the attack, Alphonse Dianou, had, like Tjibaou, trained as a Catholic priest (but not as a militant in Libya, contrary to the French government's later assertion). He and his men corralled the twenty-seven surviving gendarmes into several trucks and drove north to a hidden cave near the village of Gossana (being limestone, the atoll is honeycombed with cavities, many of whose entrances are known only to local villagers).

Meanwhile 300 French soldiers and armed police were sent to Ouvéa, including a special forces 'shock unit' flown in from France. With the French election two days away, and having just paid a huge ransom for the release of three French hostages in Lebanon, the president, Jacques Chirac, wished to give an impression of unassailable strength. The captain of the French special forces, Phillipe Legorjus, was seized while attempting to negotiate with the hostage-takers, along with five soldiers, another gendarme and a local magistrate. On 5 May, two weeks after the attack on the police station, the cave was finally raided by forces deploying a helicopter and a flame-thrower. Nineteen Kanaks and two French soldiers were killed. Despite the reported ferocity of the gun battle, there were no bullet marks on the surrounding trees or cave walls. All twenty-three hostages were freed uninjured, while autopsies suggested that as many as twelve of the hostage-takers had been shot at point-blank range. In the sheer cold fury of the French response it was hard not to recognise an echo of the suppression of the Great Revolt of 1878–9, not to mention the massacre of those other 'savages', the Communards, in 1871.

The chief hostage-taker, Dianou, having been shot in the leg after surrendering and given no medical treatment, bled to death. (This was corroborated both by Kanak witnesses and the disgraced Captain Legorjus, who was later forced to resign.) In a rare switching of the historical poles of deportation, thirty-two surviving Kanaks involved or implicated in the hostage-taking were flown to France, tried and imprisoned.

———

On the surface of the road as it passed through Fayaoué, where the gendarmerie had been raided, the words *Je ne voterai pas* had been chalked across a speed hump. Who could blame the islands' indigenous people for boycotting a referendum they deemed fixed? A few metres away was a low stone dais strewn with photographs and plastic flowers, marking the spot where the seventeen dead were buried in a mass grave.

Jean-Marie Tjibaou, who had kept his counsel during the crisis, finally arrived on Ouvéa a year later for the ceremony to mark the end of the traditional grieving period. It was well known that the people of Gossana still resented his inaction. They were owed reparations. Tjibaou was nervous, and eager to complete the evening's mourning ceremony as quickly as possible. 'The blood of those who are gone is still with us,' he said, addressing the mourners. 'And we rush forward because this blood of the dead and the living calls out to us. It is our blood; it is the blood that demands liberty for our people.'

As the ceremony was drawing to a close, the names of each of the dead having been spoken, the attendees lined up to shake Tjibaou's hand. Djubelly Wéa stepped forward. A fellow independentist, he was mourning his elderly father, who had died after being beaten by French forces during the siege. He was opposed to the FLNKS's moves towards reconciliation with the Nouméa government, as exemplified by that other handshake in Paris a few months earlier. Taking a machine pistol from his bag, he shot Tjibaou – he was wearing a bullet-proof vest – point-blank in the face. Wéa then killed Yiewéné Yiewéné, before he himself, despite having dropped his gun, was shot dead by one of Tjibaou's bodyguards. To the seventeen names inscribed on the monument were added two more.

———

It was All Saints' Day and the roadside forest was full of machete-wielding children gathering wildflowers. In the many small cemeteries, with their driftwood crosses, the grass was being scythed and the kids' flowers crammed into jars of water. At mass, St Mary's church in Mouli was empty apart from six old women, and children dashing in and out like birds. The walls were white, the pilasters and the corbels bright blue, the skirting and the window embrasures bright red. The holy-water stoup by the door was a scallop shell. The flowers having been arranged around the altar, the women settled in to wait.

Palm fronds were swagged like bunting under the windows and across the beseeching arms of Christ and around the Virgin's neck. A breeze from the sea climbed the hill and, funnelled by the pines that lined the lane, entered the church, flicking through the palm fronds like a reader seeking a particular passage. The women, themselves garlanded in yellow flowers, were growing restless.

For another forty minutes we sat in silence, waiting for the service to start, listening to the roof beams creaking in the wind. Sometimes one of the women would shout at the darting children with tremendous anger, subduing them for a few minutes. The pastor arrived in jeans and a floral shirt, lighting a single candle on the altar before slipping into the vestry. Four young men entered, hefting two speakers, which they positioned on chairs either side of the altar. A long wooden bench was placed at the top of the aisle. A few families drifted in.

The pastor reappeared in vestments, and a muffled commotion behind us caused people to turn in their seats. Up the tree-lined hill, fifty metres away, a row of men was sauntering towards us, ten abreast, and behind them, turning rank by rank onto the road to the church, more people, women and children, and amidst them finally, a flatbed truck, and it was the truck that was setting the pace, even for those preceding it, a pace that was slower than the natural walking pace of an adult.

When the truck reached the church after five minutes there were eighty or ninety people around it, and they streamed in until the pews were full, and finally the truck was unloaded by four pallbearers, who carried the coffin at waist height and laid it on the bench that had been placed in the aisle. Nobody intimated that my presence, as the only white person, as a complete stranger, might be less than welcome; but I was embarrassed, and once the hymns began – the icy sweet harmonising of South Sea Christianity – I backed out and returned to Fayaoué.

——

There was to be no independence. Nor did even the pro-independence leaders truly believe that a second or third referendum would yield a different result. The Kanak ideal would continue to meet with forces that would deny it; the result would always be more or less violent; even if the crime rate was low, this country was fundamentally a violent place, as it was during Michel's time, as it had been since 1853.

When the news came, the day after I returned to Nouméa, there was no relief, and the atmosphere of wariness did not lift. In St Louis, a Kanak village that had become effectively a poor suburb of Nouméa, the through-road was barricaded by burning cars; the police, when they arrived in their armoured buses, were bombarded with rocks. You could see the smoke from the city's beaches, which remained busy. The closeness of the result meant that the independentists were able to frame it as a partial victory, the first step towards independence. Nobody believed it. In Kaméré and Tindu, the main settlements on the Ducos Peninsula, passing cars had been pelted with stones. But those extra cells in the prison stayed empty.

——

A local man who had agreed to go with me to the Ducos Peninsula, to Koumourou, Michel's Forest of the West, emailed me to cancel. His name was Bernard Suprin, he was New Caledonia's foremost botanist, and his interest was the peninsula's rare dry tropical forest. The only road to Koumourou passed through Kaméré and Tindu and he was worried about 'the climate'. Then he said he would take me if I signed a document insuring his vehicle against damage. I refused, but I couldn't blame him: things might seem calm, and I could usually smell danger when it was close, but what could I really know about the 'climate'? No taxi would risk the journey, either. It had taken me three weeks to find someone who knew Koumourou and how to circumvent the oil terminal, and I was leaving in three days' time. I badgered him until crossly he said: 'Then I take the risk.' He didn't believe the TV reports that claimed the peninsula was calm. 'They can only tell us the good news.' We would have to leave early, before the stone-throwers of Kaméré rose.

Dry forest is the world's rarest kind of tropical forest and was once the dominant habitat of south-western Grande Terre; but since colonisation all but 10,000 hectares has been destroyed. The remaining fragments contain 379 native plant species, of which 59 are unique to dry tropical forest. Following the Second World War, when Koumouro was home to a herd of feral goats, almost all of its vegetation was destroyed. Aerial photos taken by the US army, which briefly had a base on the peninsula, show the hill stripped almost bare. Since then, the goats have been culled and the relative isolation of the place has allowed the forest to return. Koumourou is now densely covered, apart from a few beachside shacks – 'squats', M. Suprin called them – owned by Kanak fishermen.

His Land Rover was noisy in Kaméré's silent streets. Lying in bed you could have heard every gear change minutes before we passed. We saw no one. On the hillside sloping to the sea a slender white tower rose from dense forest: the derelict church of the old leper colony, Suprin said – off-limits, and home today to Nouméa's addicts and homeless. On the shore below was a medical-waste incinerator and the hulk of a grounded trawler. The peninsula remained a dumping ground.

Numbo, where Louise Michel and the other Communards had been confined after their arrival, was dominated by small marine industry. The Communard cemetery had been preserved and the grass around the headstones closely cut. Shaded by palm trees was the wharf where the Ducos exiles had been offloaded. There, by the water, France's first Pacific guillotine had been reassembled back in 1873. Across the Bay of Nouméa was Nou, today's Nouville, from which the Numbo Communards had been able to hear – unable not to – the shrieks caused by the *bastinado*.

From the next headland we looked down onto the isthmus: the Bay of the Ladies, now a place of men, occupied by the Total oil terminal, with its white tanks and pipe-threaded jetty. And rising beyond the isthmus, the lush round hill, Koumourou – Forest of the West.

———

Michel and the other female Communards had been sent to the bay on 21 May 1875. Soon after, a cyclone struck. True to form, she who had been invigorated by the cannonades of Paris was thrilled. 'I am a savage, and the poetry of the tempest took over my heart.'

It came during the night, preceded by a day of silence and stillness, during which her goats and cats were uneasy. As night fell, clouds of red and black gathered out at sea, compasses began to spin wildly, and from Nouméa an alarm cannon boomed. Perhaps she remembered her friend Henri Rochefort, who had escaped two years earlier. Through the wind and rain and darkness she rushed across the headland to Numbo and the hut of an old Communard, Perusset, a former naval captain. She describes the encounter in her memoirs:

'Who's there in this weather? Idiot.'

Breathlessly: 'The boat that guards the harbour isn't rowing any more. It won't be in the harbour the rest of the night. On a raft we could float off with the cyclone and be carried to the next landfall. Sydney, probably.'

Perusset looked at her, soaked through and red-faced. Finally he said: 'We have nothing to make a raft with.'

'There are some old barrels. We could fasten them together.'

Old barrels.

'How would we know where we'd land?'

'We must take our chances.'

He refused, knowing – as she surely did – that even if they could cobble together a seaworthy craft before morning, they would be torn to pieces against the island's encircling reef. Ludicrous to perish here, out of vain imprudence, having survived the bombardment of Paris.

Slamming the door, Michel marched back over the headland to the Bay of the West, and as the cyclone died, hour by hour, her plan came to seem like a momentary madness. The following morning dawned still and bright. The shore of the isthmus was a wreck of storm debris: dead plants, shells, 'the wreckage of old shipwrecks'; and in her description of a 'half-dead octopus [opening] its human eye' and an unidentified 'pink gelatinous substance', it is hard not to see the aftermath of war.

The guard boat resumed its patrol.

The Forest of the West remained a sanctuary, a place where it seems no one else ventured. She had made it hers, but even at the time it was far from pristine. For years, the Ducos exiles had ransacked it for wood. 'Nevertheless,' she recalled, 'at the farthest point, around a rocky cape imitating a fort, the wild vegetation has taken refuge in savage silence.'

———

Bypassing the oil terminal, it turned out, was as easy as walking along the beach between the barbed wire and the sea. There was a constant hydrocarbon odour that was not dispelled by the wind, and while fish flourished in the bay they were ignored by the fishermen because of their taint of oil.

On the other side of the fence, between the low-lying isthmus and the double hill of Koumourou, was the terrace where Michel's hut had stood. The shrubbery had been cut back and the turf was strimmed short to minimise the risk of fire. Beyond the perimeter fence the dry forest was an impenetrable wall of thorny acacia. There was nothing for it but to edge around the waterline as the tide rose.

M. Suprin, aged seventy, was always ten metres ahead, his bare legs latticed with a lifetime's thorn-scars, splashing between clumps of mangrove. Always, as we went: the tender sea to our left and the white trunks of niaoulis to our right, rising from white sand or white limestone cliffs. Every hundred metres or so were shaded coves where the beach was made of shattered white coral, beaches rarely visited by humans, even with a city of 100,000 people a mile away. At a longer beach was a boat hauled onto shore and a fisherman's shack shaded by a niaouli, and nearby, outraged, three dogs barking on their tethers. There was smoke in the air, but when we called no one came. A stranger was unlikely to be offering anything good, and we did not call again. I felt a traveller's unease, a traveller's shame, which is the shame of the trespasser. We came to other shacks, corrugated-iron lean-tos, with a similar air of recent abandonment, a feeling that we were being watched by unseen eyes, not that we should be fearful but that we were a cause of fear. There was a meticulously weeded manioc patch and, hanging from one of the shacks' supporting posts, a red, blue and green flag. On the far side of the peninsula – Michel's 'rocky cape imitating a fort' – an opening in the forest allowed us to leave the sea.

Around its mouth grew a thick curtain of vines starred with tiny white flowers, and dancing in their dozens were white butterflies – the same white butterflies, caper whites, that Michel had described. Into the hillside, helical trails had been cut – by the US army during the war, M. Suprin reckoned – so that we rose through the woods in increments towards the hill's summit.

'The forest was beautiful,' Michel wrote. 'Lianas cover it with creepers twice a year, their branches floating in the air or thrown in mad arabesques.' She went on to describe what might be the forest's heart:

Deep in a gorge between little knolls impregnated with the bitter odour of the sea, there is an immense tree very like a European olive tree, and its branches stretch out horizontally, like a larch. No insect ever lands on its bitter-tasting black leaves, and no matter what the time of day or season, there is a grotto-like coolness in its shadow, refreshing to thought as well as body.

La forêt sèche, the dry forest, was a thicket of lianas, niaoulis and banyans, dominated by prickly acacia. The undergrowth was dry and leafless, but the ground was strung with fine green vines, lianas, at tripwire height, so that with every other step you had to stop to unsnare an ankle. So dense was the canopy that the sky was hardly visible and it was hard to gauge how far up or around the hill we had come – and yet it wasn't gloomy, as jungle can be, but quite bright, as if a light of its own presided beneath the canopy. There was no plant M. Suprin did not know. The forest was not the innocent Eden Michel had imagined. False mango: a poison favoured by prison suicides. Fire vine: brush against it and your skin will burn for weeks. White mangrove: rub its latex in your eyes and you will never see again.

Finally, when we were both exhausted, and I wondered if we were not simply walking round and round the hill like twine being returned to its reel, the trees opened onto a crown of exposed limestone. 'At the top of the high knolls in the Western Forest,' wrote Michel, overdramatising as usual, 'enormous rocks have collapsed like the ruins of a fortress.'

Through the trees, the sea was visible as glimpses of a blue deeper than the sky; but we were awarded nothing so satisfying as a 'view'. Nearby, below the hill's brow, grew a giant old banyan under whose canopy we rested, sitting side by side on its bronze-coloured roots, eating slices of coconut from a plastic tub, tender as sushi. You could make out the hum of the oil terminal. We were not far from anywhere, but this, I supposed, was as close as I could hope to get to Michel.

———

On 16 October 1879 she was told her exile had been commuted; but she refused to accept special treatment while her fellow Communards languished in Ducos, Nou, Bourail and the Isle of Pines. 'With them all, or not at all,' she said (it was her motto), renouncing her supporters' pleas for her pardon: 'Please consider as null and void all steps which, though taken in my name, outrage my honour.'

Earlier that year she had been allowed to leave the Ducos Peninsula to work as a schoolteacher in Nouméa, teaching the daughters of *déportés* and, on Sundays, Kanaks, who crowded into her home to learn reading, drawing, mathematics and music, which she taught on an out-of-tune piano. When her work was mocked by newspapers back in Paris, a former member of Nouméa's board of education came to her defence: 'She discharged her duties with unfailing devotion,' he told her slanderers, inspiring nothing but 'respect and admiration even from her political enemies.'

Not until an amnesty for all *déportés* was declared on 11 July 1880, eight months later, did she agree to leave. With the money she had earned as a teacher, and not without some reluctance, she bought a ticket home, promising her Kanak friends she would return. Not that she held out much hope of a better life for either herself or her fellow amnestied Communards back in France; but her ambivalence was tempered by her concern for her mother, perhaps the only thing she truly missed about her homeland, whom she had just had word of: 'Weariness had overcome her, and she was fearful she wouldn't live to see me again.' And so she boarded the steamer to Sydney, as her Kanak students called out sadly, 'You'll never come back!', for they knew that only a mad person returns to prison when their sentence is over.

———

I ended my own time in Nouméa where it began, at the Place des Cocotiers. The Café l'Annexe was shuttered and the statue of Jean-Baptiste Olry seemed forlorn on its plinth. (It has since been announced that it will be replaced by one depicting the famous handshake between Jean-Marie Tjibaou and Jacques Lafleur.) I remembered that strange mental disturbance – was it only three weeks ago? – as a sort of gasping flailing, a protracted instance of the feeling you sometimes get on the edge of sleep, of having unexpectedly stepped off a kerb.

Back home, a psychiatrist friend, unwilling to offer anything so concrete as a diagnosis, mentioned that physical or mental stress sometimes gives rise to episodes of disassociation or even mild psychosis. I found myself returning to Ovid, who compared his fate to that of the warlord Mettus, who, in Virgil's *Aeneid*, is bound to two chariots and torn limb from limb as punishment for betraying Rome. Exile was a cleaving in two, for Ovid, a literal *dislocation*. It was, he wrote, 'as though I'd lost a limb; a part of me / seemed wrenched from my body'.

The Communards-in-exile felt that dismemberment viscerally. They were not just castaways, after all, but survivors of a brutal civil war; they had witnessed – participated in – extremes of cruelty and violence and injustice. Friends had died awfully before their eyes; their life's greatest desire had been exposed as blind idealism. It is impossible to disentangle the effects of exile from those of traumatisation. *Nostalgie*, as they experienced it, was perhaps then the body straining to forget, at the same time as the mind strained to hold the self together. Meanwhile reality threatened to rend that self into unrecognisable pieces.

The thought of the distance kills us. But 'the distance', in Achille Ballière's formulation, was not an interval between two places so much as an unbounded void – what Jean-Marie Tjibaou called *le grand trou noir*: the big black hole. Louise Michel's solution was this: to live as if you are not French or Kanak, not Russian or Zulu or English, but as if the whole world, the universe, is your native city. The price of this stance, as Tjibaou recognised, is perpetual homelessness.

The Man in the Moone

St Helena

1.

It was Maundy Thursday when I landed on St Helena. All day the men fished from the wharfs and the cliffs and out at sea. The coastguard plied the shores until everyone was home. At the Wicked Wahoo bar in Rupert's Bay they gave away what they had caught: wahoo, dorado, bull's-eye, soldierfish, five-fingers: bony, fatty fish deep-fried in a giant pan. It was a family event; there were toddlers playing a game that involved flinging a towel in the air and catching it on your head. I was the only non-Saint Helenian.

All week Johnny Cash had been echoing down the valleys, and here, too, Cash was being played: 'I Walk the Line'. The band was a man named Seabird on keyboards and a singer named Squares, who read the lyrics off his phone. Like many islanders he had worked for a spell in England: during an interval he told me about the hologram manufacturer in Basingstoke whose workshop for some reason hovered on a cushion of air; and about the time a suitcase was found at the railway station, packed with body parts. 'A taxi driver had helped lift it into his trunk!' said Squares. That was England. I asked him about his nickname: this amused him: 'They say it's because I have a square head.' He tapped the corner of his head.

We were sharing a picnic table with an eighteen-year-old called Nathan. All night people refilled his plate and brought him cartons of juice while he sat beaming. He was there with his grandma, who seemed to be his carer, and when Squares returned to the stage we all three sang along, Nathan looking across at me to make sure I was joining in. He was a part-time DJ at Saint FM, his grandma told me, and when I listened to his country-music show on Easter Sunday he was playing 'I Walk the Line'.

———

Dinuzulu kaCetshwayo and his party, when they arrived in 1890, were treated far more respectfully by their 'hosts' than they had been by the colonial powers 2,500 miles away in Natal. After eighteen days at sea, the *Anglian* docked off Jamestown on 25 February, a carronade fired from deck to announce the ship's arrival to the excited capital. According to a British soldier stationed on the island at around this time, it might not have been necessary, for 'the sharp eyes of the street boys in Jamestown can even detect the signal man on the look-out when he bends on the signal, so that the cry of "Steamer-r-r!" is often re-echoed in the town before the flag is at the mast head.'

How did St Helena appear to them, to Dinuzulu and his female companions uZihlazile and uMkasilomo, to his uncles Ndabuko and Shingana, as they looked out from deck before the tenders were allowed to take them to shore next morning? Ten years earlier, in 1879, a British visitor observed, 'Near to the coast the rough lava is quite bare, and presents the most forbidding aspect to the stranger as he approaches from the sea.' As for the capital, 'Did you ever see such a town,' asks another description from the period, 'so neat and prim, and painted so smart, with white and yellow walls, and green verandas, placed in such a deep and dismal rock-hung valley-rent?' UZihlazile and uMkasilomo, exhausted and dehydrated, must have been eager to set foot on land, no matter what awaited them.

———

I was staying in the hills at the head of James Valley, in a district called the Briars. When he was not singing, Squares was employed to inspect and maintain the giant steel nets pinioned top to bottom across the valley walls, like Christo wrappings, to protect the town from rockfalls. (In April 1890, shortly after Dinuzulu's arrival, a rockfall in Jamestown killed nine people.) After it had rained early one evening, sitting on my terrace, I heard what I took to be distant fireworks, realising just as the noise stopped that there'd been a rockfall. People had come out of their homes and were standing looking out to the far side of the valley; but it seemed no harm had been done.

The bungalow's small garden adjoined the grounds of one of the two residences of Napoleon, who was confined on the island from 1815 until his death in 1821. He had been miserable here as he had not been on the Tuscan island of Elba, where he had been exiled by Britain a year earlier. Confined he may have been, but during that previous exile he had retained his title and was conferred all the powers of a potentate. There was always the hope of restoration. But in 1815, soon after escaping from Elba, he was defeated at Waterloo and deported to this British colony 4,500 miles from Paris, where escape was all but impossible.

Until 2016 the only way on or off, for most people, was aboard the fortnightly RMS *St Helena* to Ascension or Cape Town, which has since been decommissioned. The airport had been spoken about for decades. When the airport lights were switched on the whole island came out to watch. Only when the Boeing 737, which the airport had been built for, touched down did the turbulence issue become apparent. After all the delays, after the opening party and the celebratory press releases, a new term entered the islanders' vocabulary: wind shear. You used it in conversation and watched a weariness settle on the listener's face. The airline withdrew, and the island returned to its seclusion, reachable only by sea.

A feasibility study before work started on the airport had mentioned concerns about turbulence. Even Charles Darwin, visiting in the *Beagle* in 1836, described the island's 'impetuous winds'. The only advance testing had been with a small propeller aircraft rather than the twin-jet 737 stipulated in the government's business case. Not until 2017 was an operator found that was willing to land on the runway at all. Using an aircraft much smaller than the 737, it flew from Johannesburg once a week, carrying just seventy-five passengers. £300 million, the airport had cost. The developers of a luxury 'eco-lodge' hotel pulled out. The new four-star Mantis hotel in Jamestown was all but empty week after week, a couple of waiters standing in the doorway, looking hopefully at every passing stranger.

———

Papillon – Papillon! – was dragging her arse along the ground as the French honorary consul and I walked towards Jamestown. Worms. She was his dog, a svelte black retriever with a salt-and-pepper chest, and her name was a little joke, *Papillon* being the title of Henri Charrière's memoirs of his imprisonment in French Guiana in the 1930s.

The consul lived nearby, and we often saw each other when he was walking Papillon. His name was Michel Dancoisne-Martineau but the St Helenians called him simply 'the Frenchman'.

'Post-colonialism', he was saying, 'is much more poisonous than real colonialism.'

He managed the Napoleonic properties on the island: Longwood, where Napoleon spent most of his exile; Briars Pavilion; and Napoleon's tomb. He was fifty-three and had been on the island since he was eighteen, having inherited the job from his father. But he wasn't parochial – he might have been a rich Parisian holidaymaker, and cultivated a sort of suave, priestly aloofness. His memoirs, *Je suis le gardien du tombeau vide* ('I am the keeper of the empty tomb'), had been a bestseller in France, he said. The empty tomb was that of Napoleon, whose remains were repatriated in 1840 following a campaign orchestrated by Adolphe Thiers (president at the time, he would later become Louise Michel's blood enemy).

I'd spent a morning at Longwood House, now a museum, soon after I arrived on the island. I was the only visitor. The house retained a mahogany darkness, a block of solid shadow in brightly planted grounds. The rooms were cold and redolent with beeswax. His billiards table, his astronomical globe, his copper bathtub deep as a sarcophagus, his black-canopied deathbed. The English contributors to the comments book were protective of their victory. Richard from Bath conceded that the displays were interesting but wondered 'why was he treated so well?' John and Joan from St Osyth – the handwriting indubitably John's – found the exhibits 'delightful' but added: 'Do remove that dreadful EU flag. The Tricolour is enough.' This was after the Brexit referendum.

'Believe me,' said Dancoisne-Martineau, 'the flag will stay. Longwood House is part of France and we are proud Europeans.'

But St Helena itself is British. The island, roughly teardrop-shaped, measures no more than ten miles across, and lies 1,200 miles west of Angola and 1,800 miles east of Brazil, too remote for there ever to have been a truly indigenous population. On one wall of Anne's

Place, the bar overlooking the public gardens in Jamestown, was a sea chart of the South Atlantic. Brazil was on the left and Africa on the right, but where tiny St Helena should have been, roughly midway between the two, there was nothing – nothing but a coarse white smudge, the island effaced from the paper's surface by a thousand sweaty fingertips – 'There we are!'

The number of people living on the island, around 4,000, has not changed much since Dinuzulu arrived in 1890. It was discovered by the Portuguese in 1502, probably on 21 May, the Catholic feast day of St Helena, then claimed by the Dutch, though neither country settled it. Who would want to spend their days here, floating in outer space? Finally, in 1659, recognising its value as a resupplying post for ships returning from India, the British East India company established a colony on the island. It's remained under British control ever since and is administered today as a dependent territory.

'This is British hypocrisy,' said the consul. '"Dependency" is just a hypocrite's way of saying "colony". Call a cat a cat.' He was enjoying his indiscretion.

We followed the dog along a private footpath that overlooked the waterfall at the head of James Valley. Mynah birds squabbled in the dwarf ebonies; the white specks of terns wheeled in the vapour wafting off the waterfall.

'There are worse places to go into exile,' said the consul, and I supposed he meant it to be unclear whether he was referring to Napoleon or himself. He had heard of Dinuzulu, but he was dismissive. The African's exile was nothing compared to Napoleon's, who was restricted to a few guarded hectares around Longwood House, while Dinuzulu was free to roam wherever he wished. 'We call it "exile",' he said of the emperor's confinement, 'but it was actually imprisonment.'

He himself was, he went on, just a 'spectator'. He was nostalgic for the old days when he first arrived as a young man, when the island endured as an outpost of a colonial lifestyle that had become impossible else-where, impossible and absurd. 'I was eighteen, I fitted in straight away. It was very relaxed, there was no judgement.' He had socialised with the British then? 'Yes, but I would form an . . . attachment, a fondness, and then the person would leave. It was very painful for me, so now, no. It's a very comfortable seat, to be the one who is just watching.'

We finished our walk and sat on the terrace of my bungalow. On the lawn a rabbit nibbled a green mango knocked from its tree by the mynah birds.

He rubbed Papillon's flank. 'You cannot compare the expatriates back then with the expatriates today,' he said. 'They had a colonial mentality. They didn't know how to live otherwise, those British captains and their wives, from Burma, from Africa.' I imagined the island as a kind of empire-themed retirement home. 'They were unfit to go back to the UK. But they behaved towards the locals much bet-ter than today's expatriates. Today it is about money and position.'

In 1982 St Helenians were temporarily stripped of their British citizenship due to a blanket ruling designed to prevent mass migra-tion to Britain from Hong Kong, which was about to be returned to China. But even then there had been no anger, said the consul, only bewilderment, and a pain that endured.

'They are proud citizens of Britain,' he said. 'Britain, which treats them like shit.'

———

When, back in 1889, it was suggested that Dinuzulu be shipped to the island, the Colonial Office in London was sceptical: 'We have negatived proposals in other cases to send any petty offending savage to the island . . . for sentimental and international reasons. If we did so, we should never hear the last of it either here or in France.'

But St Helena's history as a place of exile long preceded the Emper-
or Napoleon, beginning soon after the island's discovery by the Portuguese. Having converted to Islam as a soldier in Goa, Fernáo Lopes
sided with the Muslim resistance there against his fellow Portuguese,
was captured by his countrymen, tortured and disfigured – nose and
ears hacked off, scalp rasped to the bone with a clamshell – and on the
way back to Portugal in 1515 marooned on St Helena. He became
something of a secular saint among Portuguese sailors stopping at the
island to replenish their supplies, and in 1525 was allowed to visit
his homeland. In Rome he was absolved of apostasy by the Pope.
Come home, they said. *Stay. Your exile is repealed.* But Lopes missed
the volcanic mountains and the fairy terns and the sound of the sea,
and the cockerel that was his friend. He returned to St Helena, to his
solitude, dying in 1545, content enough, we can assume.

One of the earliest descriptions of the island in print appears in 1638
in a book attributed to Domingo Gonsales, which suggests that even
by then the island was famed for its remoteness. He had been set down
on its shores, having fallen sick en route from the East Indies to his
native Spain, and found it to be a miniature Eden, its hills thick with
'fig trees, vines, pear trees, palmitos, cocos, olives, plumms', and bless-
ed with an abundance of fauna – 'cattle, and fowle, as goates, swine,
sheepe, and horses, patridges', as well as 'wild fowle beyond all credit'.

Among the fowle was a 'certain kind of swan', which he calls *gansa*
(from the Spanish 'goose', presumably):

> I took some 30 to 40 of young ones of them and bred them up by
> hand, partly for my recreation, partly as having in my head some
> rudiments of that device, which afterwards I put into practice. I
> began to craft in my head how I might do to joyne a number of
> them together in bearing of some great burden: which if I could
> bring to passe, I might enable a man to fly.

134

To fly, it turns out, to the moon. Gonsales's account constitutes the opening pages of *The Man in the Moone*, which in fact appears to have been written by Francis Godwin, Bishop of Hereford, who didn't visit St Helena any more than he visited outer space.

———

If Napoleon's exile was a sort of death in life – 'he no longer had any preoccupation with the future, did not reflect on the past or care for the present', according to the Comte de Las Cases – Dinuzulu's was a period of transformation. It was no capitulation, certainly, and unlike his uncles, he was, like Louise Michel, largely immune to wistfulness. But where Michel had been dazzled by the tropical novelty of New Caledonia seventeen years earlier, Dinuzulu comes across as a worldly figure on St Helena, despite his youth: pleased by the unfamiliar, and above all confident in his entitlements, assured that he is no less the king of his people here than he is in Zululand.

'Dinuzulu', the *St Helena Guardian* said, 'evidently came ashore prepared to ride to Rosemary Hall, as he wore gaiters and carried in his hand a riding whip.' The article continued: 'He and his party are evidently unaccustomed to travel by boat, or so far as we could judge, by carriage either; the women almost crawled out of the boat on landing, and the three carriages which conveyed the party to the country proceeded at slow pace.'

Rosemary Hall, one of three homes successively occupied by Dinuzulu and his party, has long been demolished, but stood three miles west of Jamestown. 'A very large and very nice house,' is how he described it in a letter to his mother. 'It is cool and away from the mass of people.' The eleven Zulus slept upstairs in rooms divided by sex and seniority, and 'we have a bathroom and also a kitchen'. However accurate the translation and transcription of

his sentiments, it's clear Dinuzulu wished it to be known he was comfortable.

In April the *Illustrated London News* caught up with developments on the island, publishing a drawing of the group disembarking at Jamestown, surrounded by a crowd. Most of the island, it seemed, turned out to see them, much as thousands had turned out to see his father during his trip to London eight years earlier. There are women in white dresses and men in white pith helmets and boaters. Dinuzulu is wearing white jodhpurs and cravat, and regards the people he is to live among with curiosity, but no apparent anxiety.

'Although an exile, he still maintains his dignity,' reported the *St Helena Guardian*, and this sentiment seems to have held, in the eyes of most of the islanders, throughout Dinuzulu's stay. He maintained his 'dignity', maintained his European attire, understanding that it was a shield, perhaps a weapon.

After the Suez Canal opened in 1869 St Helena became largely obsolete as a revictualling station, plunging the island into a decline from which it has never fully recovered. 'Nothing can be more deplorable than the state of the island at the present,' wrote a resident in 1875. Jamestown had an 'everyday look of dejection . . . The shops themselves have a dusty, neglected and uninviting look, as though the wares exposed in their windows had been there since the days of Noah.' Hundreds of islanders emigrated to South Africa in search of work as servants and miners at this time, with 493 – about one-eighth of the island's population – leaving between January 1893 and June 1894 alone. The Zulu historian Magema Fuze, when he joined Dinuzulu on the island as his tutor in 1896, noted that the 'arrival of a steamship is the occasion for great celebrations among the "ladies" of St Helena. Adorned in their finest clothes, they get into small boats which transport them to the ship, which they board, to ask for money.'

A 1905 book confirms that in the early 1890s St Helena was at such a 'very low ebb' that even those wishing to leave could sometimes not afford the steamer fare. Perhaps then the islanders welcomed the *Anglian* as a quiet seaside village welcomes a coachload of foreign tourists – money, but also something *novel*. Even a century earlier, ten years before Napoleon made the island synonymous with exile, a visitor writing a *Description of the Island of St Helena* found that 'few of the inhabitants . . . seem to live satisfied with their present condition or without a longing desire to quit it; and a wish of "going home", by which is meant going to England, is fondly and familiarly expressed, as well by the native inhabitants as by the recent settlers. They appear to consider their situation as a state of exile.'

2.

Soon after meeting Michel Dancoisne-Martineau and his 'little doggy', as he called Papillon, I was invited to a lunch party near my bungalow, at Briars Pavilion, which was briefly Napoleon's home when he first arrived. It was hosted by the British deputy governor, who now lived there, and attended by about thirty young British expats. A power-metal cover version of Lloyd Webber's 'The Phantom of the Opera' was being blasted from the pavilion's veranda when I approached, and as the guitar solo reached its climax the mynah birds fled shrieking from the trees.

In the kitchen one of the guests showed me her new tattoo, still raw: on her wrist a compass rose with an outline of the island at its centre. It was a sort of pledge. The pavilion had the air of a museum: the Napoleonic etchings, the period furnishings and arsenic-green wainscoting. The dining-room table was crowded with food the guests had brought – salads and dips and crudités; a baked ham; arancini, goujons, terrines and pastries. Among us were the hospital's

English pharmacist, an English soil scientist, an English meteorologist, an English government lawyer, an English policeman on secondment and his wife, as well as various teachers and the deputy governor, who was herself English. Most of the island's expertise was imported, and most of it transient.

The science teacher from Prince Andrew's, the island's secondary school, a bearded, sunburned fellow in his twenties, stood with me on the veranda and pointed in turn at each of the two dozen young people lounging on the emperor's lawn: 'She's leaving,' he said, 'he's leaving; they're leaving in a month; he's leaving in May; she's someone's mum – they leave on Saturday; two months; three months; October; June . . .'

Everyone was leaving soon, the expats were always leaving soon. That was what 'expat' meant: it was a temporary condition. They came for a year or two, earned good money, then went home to Britain. It was partly for this reason that relations between them and the islanders went only so deep. On the government website was an ad for a maths teacher, a role for which only an outsider would be qualified. The salary offered was £35,000, on an island where the average was about £7,000.

He himself planned to stay for another two years – his hours were good and he was well paid. Then he'd teach privately in China or the Middle East, until he'd saved enough for a deposit on a house in the UK. 'I make no apologies,' he said, and went on cataloguing the exodus: 'Leaving, leaving, leaving. In a year none of them will be here.' On the lawn, the recumbent guests glanced up briefly when introduced, but weren't inclined to remove their sunglasses or offer room in the shade.

Emma, who was working as a primary-school teacher, seemed separated from the others; then I understood: she was with Henry Thorpe. She was wearing a shoulderless powder-blue dress, and the women on the lawn did look up when she and Thorpe stepped from the veranda. Thorpe was untypical of the 'Saints' I met, in both affluence and education. Still a young man, he was tall, old-fashioned, quietly spoken, very courteous, gently proprietorial. The family owned much of the island and several old businesses, including the grocers in Jamestown. Proprietorial without being lordly; imagine a senior naval officer benevolent in the security of his rank.

Emma was working on a novel, she said, inspired by the two years she had spent on St Helena. 'An island that shouldn't be here, filled with people who shouldn't be here.' She had first visited with her mother, and was conscious of herself as a European transplant, transplanted in time as well as space: her gaucheness and her elegance; that dress; her thoughtful word choices. She mentioned her idea of the 'shadow island', invisible but coexisting alongside the island of expat revels and tourist-board itineraries ('Swim with whale sharks!' 'Meet Jonathan, the 190-year-old tortoise!'), and exemplified in my mind by the contents of a particular outhouse on a Jamestown backstreet. As my days on the island passed, the idea of the shadow island, as substantial but as hidden as its volcanic preponderance under the sea, became more and more vivid.

Soon Emma would be gone to start her studies in creative writing in Paris. Henry had lived in England and was educated there; but he was a businessman and there was no question that his home was St Helena, where his family had lived for generations. I left early, and from my terrace a hundred metres away I listened to the party continuing as darkness fell. After an hour or so the remaining cars left, and there was only the sound of the lawn-sprinkler, a sound that continued night and day.

———

Dinuzulu's friend and tutor Magema Fuze was a Christian convert and former student of John Colenso. Having lived and worked at Colenso's mission station in Bishopstowe, he was also close to Harriette. Six years after the royal party's departure, he was summoned to St Helena by Dinuzulu. In his *The Black People and Whence They Came* (one of the first Zulu-language books, originally published as *Abantu Abamnyama Lapa Bavela Ngakona*, in 1922), Fuze remembers the dinners hosted by the young king, where 'there would be dancing in European fashion, the two royal uncles sitting as onlookers'. It was precisely this kind of licence, and worse still the reciprocation of Dinuzulu's hospitality by the island's governor, that incensed the authorities back in Natal. *Why was he treated so well?* But colonial Eshowe was a long way away, and when in 1897 the *Natal Witness* claimed that the Zulus had 'of late made themselves extremely obnoxious', the *St Helena Guardian* was quick to respond. 'We believe we are expressing the unanimous opinion of the Inhabitants of St Helena in giving the most unqualified denial to the accusation,' went the editorial. 'In fact, such relations as exist between the residents of the Island and the Zulu Chiefs are, and always have been, of the most friendly character.'

Fuze remembers particularly three young St Helenian girls, who led the dancing, 'Miss Cummings and Miss Cressy and her sister, who were brown in colour, their fathers having been captured as children while bathing in the Congo.' Later he mentions four men, whose names he gives as Cummings, Williams, George and Mbilimbili ('I have forgotten the name by which the Europeans called him'), who had, he said, been 'rescued from the white men who had seized them by the ships of the Queen, and taken to the island of St Helena by her orders'. He goes on, 'Now they are old men with homes of their own, except Mbilimbili, who has no home and who still has a slight knowledge of our language, but the other three no longer know it except for a few words.'

Today the students at Prince Andrew's saw Napoleon's *tombeau vide* in its tranquil, hibiscus-festooned valley, tended by the consul's gardeners as if it contained the True Cross; then they saw a small, dirty-walled building in Jamestown, hidden down an alleyway behind the prison, its door hung with wreaths and bead necklaces, containing, according to the laminated notice, 'the bones of 325 Africans'.

———

In *The Black People and Whence They Came*, Fuze describes 'the ships of the Portuguese and other evil white men, going about hunting for black children bathing in rivers',

> to collect them and sell them to other white people to be turned into slaves in order to acquire money. This evil practice was eventually brought to an end by the gracious English princess, Queen Victoria, who sent out great warships to patrol the sea, which on finding ships containing black children, apprehended them and deprived them of these children, who were sent to certain places established by her, and they were not sold.

The 325 whose bones lie in Jamestown were among more than 24,000 'liberated Africans' (a legal term) brought to St Helena following the passing of the 1839 Act for the Suppression of the Slave Trade. Because the so-called Middle Passage, the route taken by slave ships from Africa to the New World, passed close to St Helena, it was the obvious place to establish a 'processing depot' – this was located first at Lemon Valley, west of Jamestown; and then, as the navy's seizures increased, at the broader Rupert's Valley, to the east. In other words, the royal party when they arrived just forty years later were far from being the first expatriated Africans to have appeared on St

Helena in living memory. Memories, stories, of those earlier arrivals cannot have been suppressed, when a number of survivors were still alive on the island. The evidence was there in the ground, too. Without warning or consultation, a concentration camp – the term would be coined sixty years later by the British during the Boer War – sprang up on the people's doorstep.

In December 1840, 215 enslaved people were brought ashore from the Portuguese vessel *Julia*. The following year the numbers burgeoned:

256 from the *Marcianna*.

305 from the *Euro*.

316 from the *Minerva*.

420 from the *Louiza*.

Dozens of cultures, traditions, religions and languages and dialects. Invariably they would be sick and many were found dead before the ships reached St Helena. John Charles Mellis, who wrote a book about the island, visited a 'full-freighted slave ship' when it docked at Jamestown in 1861, less than thirty years before Dinuzulu's arrival. The vessel, he wrote,

> scarcely a hundred tonnes burthen at most, contains perhaps little short of a thousand souls, which have been closely packed, for many weeks, together in the hottest and most polluted of atmospheres . . . the whole deck, as I picked my way from end to end, in order to avoid treading upon them, was thickly strewn with the dead, dying and starved bodies . . . Many died as they passed from the ship to the boat, and, indeed, the work of unloading had to be proceeded with so quickly that there was no time to separate the dead from the living.

Between 7,000 and 8,000 'liberated Africans' died on St Helena. The graves of the 325 awaiting reburial in the shed in Jamestown were among thousands uncovered in Rupert's Valley, a few hundred yards inland from the Wicked Wahoo, during the construction of a supply road to the new airport.

St Helenians have always known about the bones. They were occasionally uncovered by dogs or ploughs. But the extent of the burials only became clear when archaeologists began excavating the site in 2007. Rupert's Valley turned out to be a site of international importance. Nowhere else do the remains of first-generation African slaves exist in such numbers. Most of them were under eighteen when they died, the average age being around twelve. Some were mothers with children. There were signs of malnutrition, naturally, as well as scurvy. Two of the children had been shot – onboard or afterwards? Among the remains were copper bracelets, clay pipes, buttons and remnants of goat-fibre textiles. In several graves were found hundreds of tiny brightly coloured beads, the remains of beadwork mattresses. The road was built and the gravesite sealed under tarmac. A decision over the fate of the bones in the shed in Jamestown had been postponed indefinitely – where should they be interred, what should be the nature of any memorial? It had proven impossible to reach any agreement, and so there they remained.

Liberation for the 'liberated Africans' was not liberty. Most of the 24,221 brought to St Helena ended up in the Caribbean as indentured labourers. More than 500 settled on the island, however – among them the fathers of the three dancing girls Magema Fuze had mentioned – of whom the last died as recently as 1928. Most of those dumped on St Helena had been abducted from Central Africa – Congo and Angola – but some were shipped from Mozambique, and it is possible that these included Zulu subjects of Dinuzulu's grandfather, Mpande.

Dinuzulu's plight was as nothing compared to that of the mass of forcibly displaced people throughout history: the refugees, the captive and enslaved. He was a king, after all. Until the early twentieth century, most political exiles enjoyed a privileged status, however acute their sense of loss. The mass displacements of the Second World War, however awful the reality, lent the word 'exile' a sort of glamour, a veneer of heroic estrangement that has stuck to this day. That mouldering windowless outbuilding in Jamestown, with its laminated A4 notice, was a reminder that for every celebrated political exile or émigré novelist, countless millions of people, never to be named, have been swallowed by slave ships, penal colonies, gulags, death camps and the sheer lightless void of dispossession.

———

Two hours' walk from Jamestown is St Paul's Cathedral, where Dinuzulu and his uncles worshipped, and a very different burial site. In the yard I found a small double grave with a single low headstone and two empty glass jars containing the dry stalks of flowers. The graves belong to a girl named uNomfino, who died of pneumonia, aged four months, in 1891, a year after the Zulu party arrived on the island; and uMohlazana, a boy, who died in 1894, aged three, from enteritis. In small letters at the bottom of the headstone were the words 'Children of Dinuzulu' and then: 'Thy Will Be Done'.

UNomfino was uMkasilomo's child and uMohlazana was uZihlazile's. Between them the women would give birth to five more children during their time on St Helena, including uMkasilomo's son Solomon, who would inherit the kingship of Zululand. Magema Fuze lists the royal offspring living on St Helena, in addition to Solomon, as: 'Nyawana . . . Mphaphu (Victoria), Mshiyeni (Arthur) who was then very young, and Bhekelendoda.'

There were other children of Dinuzulu's, too, born to island women. On 14 October 1895 Emma Henry, who delivered goods to the household, gave birth to a son, George Edward, whose own son

– known as Johnny Chief – is still remembered on the island today. Dinuzulu's few other descendants were mostly reluctant to acknowledge the connection, but even before I arrived I'd heard about one of them, a royal granddaughter, now in her eighties. She called herself Princess Dinuzulu.

Most of her life, I was told, had been spent in Britain, where she had been a nurse and a jazz singer. She had returned to St Helena in retirement. Apparently Princess Dinuzulu wore traditional Zulu regalia and adorned her home with tribal artefacts, though she had never visited her famous ancestor's homeland. 'Regal' was the word people used. She was very frail and it was thought she was living at the elderly-care home in Half Tree Hollow. But when I called she was no longer there, and the receptionist couldn't say what had become of her.

———

After Dinuzulu's sentencing, the resident commissioner in Natal, Melmoth Osborn, had insisted that 'the very fact' of the chief's continued presence in either Zululand or Natal 'would be sufficient to keep alive a smouldering current of active disloyalty', and that they would 'undoubtedly find means to communicate to the partisans and to carry on intrigue'. The party's letters home from St Helena therefore were translated by the British and carefully monitored for any hint of sedition. Dinuzulu was soon writing to his people to demand supplies: eating utensils, a new gourd to replace one broken during the voyage, medicinal plants, fibres for weaving prepuce sheaves, tobacco, snuff, cash and cannabis (the mule drivers who had taken them from Eshowe to the port at Durban having stolen his stash). 'My uncles and the girls [uMkasilomo and uZihlazile] wish to be remembered to everybody. Nyosane [his male attendant] and Paul [his traditional doctor] ask you to send them some snuff. Nyosane wants you to remember him to his wives, see that they don't run away and get other husbands while he is alive and well.'

St Helena is bigger than they were led to believe – 'From one side of the island to the other is as far [as] from the White Mfolozi to Habanani.' He is lonely, and he expresses his loneliness as resentment. 'You are at your homes drinking beer and happy,' he complains, 'and I am thrown away, and yet you don't give me any news . . . Have Nenegwa's people built a kraal for my cattle? are all my horses alive? and are my dogs well?' Elsewhere he arranges for thirty cattle to be sold, adding: 'Au-au-au – our time on St Helena is very long!' (His concern for his cattle was of a part with his concern for his people and his kingdom; his cattle's well-being was Zululand's well-being.)

At the end of May, three months after their arrival, Dinuzulu and his uncles joined a parade celebrating the queen's birthday and afterwards attended a reception held by the governor. In November they visited a bazaar in the botanical gardens in Jamestown, 'expressing great pleasure and amazement at the display of fireworks'. When, in January 1892, the colonial surgeon, Dr Welby, gave a garden party, the Zulus were among the guests, and two years later Dinuzulu was recruited in a tug-of-war contest against a team from the British army garrisoned on the island.

Nor were they mere novelties. In March 1891 Antony Daniels, Dinuzulu's secretary, married Ellen Ann Augustus of Half Tree Hollow, in St Paul's Church. (Daniels, who had been appointed against Harriette Colenso's wishes, would betray Dinuzulu in dramatic fashion.) Three years later Paul Mthimkhulu, the Zulus' doctor, married Caroline Brown, she a widow, he a widower. 'We wish Dr Paul and his bride every happiness,' said the *St Helena Guardian*. Other marriages would follow, and births, as we've seen. A few months later, it was Dinuzulu's turn to host the festivities for the queen's birthday, with toasts drunk to her and the governor. 'It is a great pleasure to note the genteel manners of the Prince,' wrote the *Guardian*.

Dinuzulu's most frequent correspondent was Harriette Colenso, his confidante and ally from Eshowe days. Having urged him to surrender in 1889, to 'put himself in bondage', she now devoted her life to campaigning for his release. 'No one has helped me,' he complained to her. He was restless, and like Michel, felt the asceticism of island life keenly. 'I greatly desire to learn. Indeed I am like one who has long been athirst receiving no water, until he feels he must swallow a whole river. But then, too, I am like the fly wrapped round in the spider's web, though its heart is yet alive.'

Descriptions of Dinuzulu on the island often remark with a smirk upon his dapper English dress, his *gentlemanly* conduct, the soirées, his piano-playing ('I play the "Mariner's Jog",' he told Colenso, 'and the "Hornpipe", and "Für Elise".') Within a year of their arrival, the group's new custodian had written to the governor that his charge took 'pride in being well-dressed, at all times, even distinguishing the difference between gaudy-coloured apparel – so attractive to the eyes of savages – and the sombre but more becoming hues of the garments of civilised races'.

Dinuzulu's uncles were less accommodating of their condition, especially Ndabuko. He had been sentenced to fifteen years – fifteen years in this dank, impoverished outpost! He would be nearly sixty when he saw Zululand again, if he lived that long. According to an account written by an islander some years later, both 'uncles were much more unsociable [than Dinuzulu], and had set their faces steadily against any innovation . . . they would not use chairs, tables, nor beds, neither would they wear European dress, except on occasion when they walked abroad and were compelled to do so'. (It was a condition of their liberty on the island that they refrain from wearing traditional Zulu attire in public, though I doubt Dinuzulu threw off his Jermyn Street suit on closing the front door.)

In photos – most of them taken for PR purposes by Colenso's arrangement – Ndabuko is the serious one. There is always a weariness in the way he holds his mouth, the weariness of a despair that pre-dates his exile. The slaughter into which he had led his troops at Msebe, following Dinuzulu's father Cetshwayo's return from exile, weighed on him all his life. His eyes have a mannequin fixity that might be the vestige of some long-ago moment of terror, but more likely is simply the glaze of surrender.

There are touching reports of Ndabuko, whose name translates as 'I remember', poring over a copy of Angas's *Kaffir's Illustrated*, a large folio of colour lithographs, subtitled 'Sketches of Landscape Scenery in the Zulu Country, Natal and the Cape Colony', published in London in 1849. The retired colonials who were its intended audience were not alone in being susceptible to nostalgia.

In 1891, a year after their arrival, Ndabuko and Shingana wrote to Colenso with a supplication. They were, she was to understand, 'like beasts' in their appearance. It was not the islanders whose opinion concerned them, but their own party. 'We are too shamefaced to be seen moving among our fellow men.' They were writing to ask her to 'plead for us, that a person from Zululand be sent to dress our hair'.

The *isicoco*, or head ring, was a distinguishing adornment of Zulu men, originating in pre-colonial times, worn by the king and his chieftains and by ordinary men once they had married. A circlet of grasses was woven into the hair with cattle sinew, coated in a special gum, oiled, and buffed to a gloss. In photos of the party it can be seen that the *isicoco* is a perfect ring, like something rolled from clay, firmly woven to the hair at the crown, and as smooth as if it has been glazed. Magema Fuze explains that its significance was not only symbolic, however (and we should bear in mind the uncles were neither young nor unaware of their importance): 'A man grows up even as you are watching him, with beautiful black hair, but after he has attained fifty years of age, you will notice that his head shows signs of disarray. Long before the appearance of grey hairs you will notice that there is a bare patch at the back of the head without a single hair on it.'

Fuze goes on, 'I do not think that a little bald-headed grey-haired old man is an object of beauty; in fact he is known by all as a little old bald-head.' It is for the same reason, he adds, that white men wear hats: 'If they did not do so, they would look even worse and more unbecoming.'

But Colenso understood there was no narcissism in the uncles' plea; it was simply that they did not wish to emulate the young prince with his 'sombre hues', his bowler hat. The *isicoco* was a 'mark of distinction', they explained. 'We shrink from leaving the house for any purpose.' But on this occasion, she was unable to help.

I picture Ndabuko in the drawing room of gloomy Rosemary Hall, his *isicoco* a reeking, matted mess of hair, grass, sinew and grease, the boy his nephew turning more 'English' by the day, the smoky old house creaking around him like a ship. He lifts the weighty pages: women making beer; hippos languishing in a river; a solitary lion padding along a deserted beach . . . The artist's gaze is not his gaze: the people, and even the animals, are caricatures; but he recognises the light.

In February 1893 the Zulus finally left Rosemary Hall, which they found damp, for Maldivia House in Jamestown. The governor received a report on the condition of the vacated residence – arch, amused: 'The Zulus quite declined to recognise that the chimney was a convenient or suitable channel for smoke and made a fire in the centre of the room.' It was, on the contrary, a question of propriety – of literally squaring the circle of their dislocation. In a traditional Zulu circular hut, the hearth, the *iziko*, is at the centre. The European fireplace, conversely, is no place for a fire, for it occupies the position of the *umsamo*, the platform that stands against the wall of every

151

hut, opposite the entrance, which is at once a shrine to and an abode of the ancestors. On the *umsamo* you place offerings – meat, corn, tobacco; but to use it as a hearth would be to do the unthinkable: to make a sacrifice of fire.

I'd been shown the new square house, Maldivia, at the end of a switchback: a tall wooden residence with a broad, covered veranda, situated by a stream on several bosky acres. Drier and more central than Rosemary Hall, but like the rest of the town, in its 'deep and dismal rock-hung valley-rent', shadowy even at midday, and always the valley walls looming over you, with their threat of falling boulders.

———

Something happened that seemed meaningful, something I think of as a defining event of those weeks on St Helena, but whose significance I find it hard to describe. History sometimes expresses itself in metaphors too complex for clear-cut interpretation.

On the plane from Johannesburg I had noticed a grey-bearded man in his fifties wearing short cut-off jeans and a sheer black singlet. I saw him repeatedly over Holy Week: he was hard to miss, marching about Jamestown with his tanned legs, radiating such easy joie de vivre that I assumed he must be a resident glad to be home after a long absence.

This, it turned out, was the 'moth man' people had told me about, and although he didn't live here, he knew the island quite well. His name was Dr Timm Karisch. He was a German lepidopterist, and he had been seconded to St Helena's National Trust from the Museum of Natural History in Dessau. I must come and see his light-trap, he insisted, when I met him one evening at Anne's Place.

The lepidoptera of St Helena, he explained, haven't been studied much, but are of great interest because of the large proportion of endemic species among them. The smaller ones, particularly the genus *Opogona*, a kind of fungus moth, are barely known at all. He and an entomologist friend, a lacewing specialist, first came here one Christmas, in 1995, on something of a whim, a two-week voyage from Wales (in those days the RMS *St Helena* sailed from Cardiff). On Boxing Day night, having been given Christmas dinner by a local family, they set up their first light-trap in the island's cloud forest.

On the evening we agreed to meet, he was waiting at the door of the National Trust office on Jamestown's main street. At his feet were two butterfly nets and a cardboard box containing two white sheets, four wooden poles, a giant lightbulb in its cabled socket, a portable generator and a can of petrol, and a plastic bag full of specimen tubes and killing jars.

We packed his kit into the National Trust's Land Rover and drove out of Jamestown towards Thompson's Wood, one of the last natural redoubts of the endemic St Helena gumwood.

The sun setting over the sea had the translucency of a satsuma segment squeezed of its pulp. As we climbed towards Thompson's Wood, we penetrated a bank of fog that seemed to precipitate darkness before the sun had quite gone out of the sky. The coastal cliffs below were a smudged charcoal black against the still bright sea. I had experienced it nowhere else – it wasn't dusk so much as the co-existence of night and day.

It was dark by the time we reached Thompson's Wood. By torchlight we waded through dew-soaked grass to the edge of the wood. Karisch built a frame of the poles and over it pegged the two sheets, one on top of the other, then attached the bulb in its socket. When the generator twenty metres away hummed into life, the bulb heated from pale green to pale pink to red to white. The moths of Thompson's Wood were roused.

In the light it was possible to see where we were: the corner of a sloping field scattered with giant volcanic boulders, at the edge of an ancient forest dominated by the low, crooked forms of gumwood trees growing where they had grown for millennia. It was the association between them and the island's endemic moths, especially those of the tiny *Opogona* genus, that interested Karisch.

'If you know where you are looking you can find very special things.'

The outer sheet was soon a flickering veil of hundreds of common gold-green grass moths; among them crawled an ichneumon wasp, dragging the stiletto of her ovipositor. Here was *Helanoscoparia transversalis*, pale yellow with a white band across its wings; here was the spangled blue-and-white *scintillulalis* of the same genus.

And among the quivering profusion, vigorous as a beehive broken to the sun, were the tiny folded-winged *Opogona*, each no more than a millimetre long. He recited their names, *Opogona sachari, Opogona divisa, Opogona vilis*, and in our island of light it was like hearing the liturgy of some persecuted sect.

'It's very special, this subject,' he said. 'Because they are so tiny. Because they are uncommon. I try to identify them, but nobody will really care, of course. If it is an elephant, you can interest more people.'

Into the specimen tubes he coaxed the *Opogona*. In the glass jars – they'd once contained pickled herring – he placed the larger moths. At the bottom of each was a wad of cotton wool impregnated with ethyl acetate.

'They are sleeping now. The long sleep!'

'What draws them to the light?'

'They are not attracted to the light but *irritated* by it.'

By 10 p.m. we had started to cough. The moths found their way into your clothes, beneath the lenses of your glasses. They perched on your earlobes and fluttered between your lips. And rising from the light was a haze of dust – moth dust, the microscopic scales from their wings, filling the air, filling our lungs.

There was a moment when it was too much and I retreated into the darkness, looking back at Karisch at his work. The moths contained within the column of light above him and the trap were as numerous as embers rising from a fire. A Joseph Wright painting: the spellbound scientist in his sphere of luminance, oblivious to the infinite dark around him. On the sheet at his knees was a small pile of specimen tubes, each containing its imprisoned *Opogona*. When I rejoined him he passed one to me – in the light I could make out a moth no larger than a grain of barley, with a feathery grey back flecked with black, a wedge-shaped head and long proboscises. With a nonchalance that didn't seem affected, he said: 'Here we have a moth never before seen in the world.' It would turn out he was right.

When the generator was turned off, silence and darkness flooded into the field with the force of a tidal wave. We were provoked to look up. The moths had been freed from the light. All the stars of the southern hemisphere were subtly in motion.

———

Among the museum's absorbing clutter was a hand-carved wooden beer vessel inscribed around its base 'Mrs Welby from Dinuzulu' (the surgeon's wife, perhaps). Alongside it was a painting by another of the island's prisoners. It showed, viewed from the land, between two masses of pink rock, the sea, and beneath it an expanse of yellow. In the sky was a long cloud of a stagnant yellow-green. On the horizon, beyond two rocks, was a three-masted barque.

It appeared to be sailing away. And though it was small, the ship, not the sea or the coastline, was the painting's subject. It was the work of Willem Merk, a Dutch captain whose yacht, the *Frontier*, had been apprehended by St Helena's police while anchored off Jamestown in 1991, following a tip-off from Interpol. On board was a large amount of cannabis. Merk – a career drug-smuggler, it turned out – was arrested, tried, and sentenced to fifteen years in Jamestown's small prison, while the *Frontier* was stripped and scuttled. He had told the story of his last days on the island to various journalists back in Holland.

While a prison officer was admiring one of his paintings – perhaps even the one now displayed in the museum – he was able to make an impression of the officer's key in a bar of soap. From this impression he somehow sawed a replica out of a piece of scrap metal. On the night of 4 April 1994, four years into his sentence, he placed a set of stuffed clothes under his blankets and pressed play on a Dictaphone on which he had recorded himself snoring. He unlocked his cell door with his replica key, and after several days spent hiding in the hills outside Jamestown, swam to a raft, which had been built and anchored offshore by a friendly unnamed St Helenian. Aboard this vessel made of foam and pallets, Merk said, he arrived, three weeks later, in Brazil, 1,800 miles away, having navigated by the stars. He christened the vessel *Napoleon's Revenge*.

HMP Jamestown, where he was held, squatted between St James's Church and the police chief's office. You entered through a steel-barred wooden wicket. Such an incongruous sight was the Victorian prison, in the centre of Jamestown, that day-trippers from visiting cruise liners sometimes rang the bell requesting a look around, assuming it must be a museum. They were put straight.

Leslie, the manager, disliked the terms 'warders' and 'inmates'.

'We're officers and prisoners; remember that, please.'

She was blank-faced and terse when she'd come to meet me at reception. It was irregular for visitors unconnected to prisoners to be given access. The prisoners weren't zoo animals. Her mood had not been helped by an article that had just appeared in the *Sentinel*, one of the island's two newspapers: 'Prison Lacks Procedures to Help Young Offenders Back to Work/School'.

'Not us,' she said flatly, meaning the charge wasn't hers to answer.

'The state of the existing prison,' the story read, 'and updates needed for the new prison, have been getting in-depth attention recently as the Equality and Human Rights Commission begins its inquiry into the "Condition of detention at Her Majesty's Prison, Jamestown" and as councillors finalise a new prison site.'

'I'm not very happy,' she said. But she eased into a disarming talkativeness once we sat down. Her office was painted in institutional lavender. Partially visible under the lavender were a hundred tobacco-stained layers of distemper and wallpaper. She was English but, like the French consul, she didn't seem to socialise with the other expats, and wasn't asked to their parties. She'd been recruited two years ago, having previously been governor of a prison in Kent, to manage the relocation of HMP Jamestown to Half Tree Hollow, the densely populated headland overlooking the town. Her contract ended in a few weeks.

Only once was she distracted, when an elderly male prisoner became visible in the doorway and she silently shooed him away as if he were an extra who had wandered into shot. She was protective of her wards. There was little distinction in the prison between the prisoners' area and the rooms restricted to officers. The small, blue-carpeted hall we'd passed through on the way to her office was both the staff meeting room and the prisoners' common area.

Even in the office there was an atmosphere of shipboard claustrophobia. The place had none of the bright, echoic quality of modern prisons. You were conscious of the great thickness of the walls, the warm, motionless air. I'd imagined cells infiltrated by the free world – the sounds of gulls and children, the smell of the sea – but actually the town felt distant. We might have been under ground, except for the window of Leslie's office, which, she noted, looked out onto the empty £200-per-night 'heritage suites' of the new Mantis hotel.

You might be on an island but your world could still be made smaller. The nature of corporal punishment, of course, is to impose tighter and tighter limits on the body's mobility: a tether ratcheting you in. Thus, as Dancoisne-Martineau had maintained, Napoleon's exile was harder than Dinuzulu's, because he was confined to Longwood, while Dinuzulu had the freedom of the island. Similarly, when Louise Michel was allowed to travel beyond the Ducos Peninsula, towards the end of her time in New Caledonia, she felt it as a liberation. None of them, of course, was any closer to home.

The lack of outdoor space within HMP Jamestown meant that offenders spent a lot of time working elsewhere on the island. In Longwood, near Napoleon's house, I'd met a party of three men in orange prison T-shirts, weeding the churchyard under the supervision of two prison officers. Everyone said hi. It was a warm day and there was an air of co-operative industry; the smell of cut grass. More like community volunteers than a chain gang.

'It's much harder for my staff,' said Leslie. As native St Helenians, they were likely to be acquainted with their wards; they might well be blood relatives. If in a British prison an officer happens to know one of the prisoners, the prisoner will be relocated. Here that wasn't possible.

There were several recidivist domestic abusers – 'He hits her and does his turn; she hits him and does hers' – but most of the prisoners were sex offenders, including several paedophiles. Among them was a lifer and a British former police officer convicted of possessing child pornography and raping a minor. Group counselling for paedophiles, routine in British prisons, didn't happen here because it was perfectly possible that your victim would be this man's sister, or your nephew was raped by the man to your right, with whom you also went to Scouts or whose father is your daughter's boss. On an island of 4,000 people there was no secure psychiatric unit and no secure geriatric-care unit. Human-rights legislation prohibited the transfer of prisoners overseas because visiting rights would be impossible to uphold. How often would your mum bring you magazines or tobacco in HMP Wormwood Scrubs, London, return flight £1,600?

The inquiry that had just been launched would survey 'the physical infrastructure of the building, the size and conditions of the cells, sanitation, temperature control and ventilation, access to food and water, clothing, washing facilities, access to medical treatment, recreational facilities and opportunities for exercise, access to complaints-handling mechanisms and protection from violence'.

In other words the provisions of the modern State were to be available, and every regulation enforced, and world-class expertise magicked up, on an island 1,200 miles from continental landfall, whose population was equal to that of a small British town.

'Every prisoner, wherever I've worked, complained about the same things,' said Leslie. 'Mainly the food. I wish I could send some of this lot to a British prison, just for a week.'

A plan to relocate the prison to a site on the road between Longwood and the new airport had been shelved because it was felt it would give an unfavourable impression of the island to newly arrived tourists (most of whom were only here because of the island's famous prisoner). The earlier plan for Half Tree Hollow, the plan Leslie had been recruited to oversee, was abandoned because of objections from the community. For now the prison would stay where it was.

Hers was the loneliness of the specialist, the loneliness of some of those I'd met at the deputy governor's party. Even the chief of police didn't understand the prison service or how a prison operated. HMP Jamestown wasn't fit for purpose – the cells were dark and hot, the toilets were on full view. Her budget was small and fixed, her staff insufficiently trained: to send them overseas was expensive; to bring instructors to the island was expensive. You felt that every ideal would be frustrated by an arcane bureaucracy beset by filibustering, infighting or lack of expertise – think of the bones of the 'liberated

Africans' awaiting burial next door: innovations were delayed, postponed, cancelled, mothballed or just consigned to the category of wanly remembered dream.

Home time: she picked up her handbag. Stopping at the gate to lean through the reception hatch, she patted the bald head of her colleague, who was writing something in a logbook. He looked up with a tight smirk.

'Nice walk on Friday?' she asked him. I wondered who he'd been with. There was a pause.

'How did you—?'

'I've got eyes, you plonker.'

Captain Merk's yarn was bull, incidentally: true, the Dutchman escaped, but he had inside help. Nor had he sailed to Brazil alone on a jerry-rigged raft. No, a former cellmate, released before Merk and well paid for his assistance, was waiting offshore aboard a yacht provisioned and fuelled for their flight to Brazil. There had been no *Napoleon's Revenge*, no solitary weeks navigating by the stars.

———

As Dinuzulu and his entourage were sailing to the impoverished island in February 1890, Harriette Colenso and her mother and sister were on their way to England. They remained there for the next three and a half years, campaigning for their friends' release. 'My object in coming to England', she told a journalist, 'is to present the cause of the Zulus as I understand it . . . Those now being punished as traitors and rebels', she went on, 'are the very people who have done most to keep order in the country.'

She was treated with wary reverence by the Colonial Office. What to make of her, a daughter of an English bishop, who appeared to believe she was African? She seemed, somehow, immune to their condescension. For her part, she found them dull, cruel and negligent. And England stifling. It was not her home and she had no fondness for it. Unused to English formal dress, she arrived at a meeting with a Liberal politician in a gown bearing – according to one curtain-twitching commentator – 'half a yard of London mud on the tail'.

In the spring of 1890 she gave a speech at the National Liberal Club, where several statesmen of influence were present. As a result, in August, the 'Zulu question' was debated in Parliament. A sparsely attended, late-night session. Colenso listened from the Ladies' Gallery as the Undersecretary of State – Baron de Worms – assured his colleagues that 'the condition of [Zululand] is satisfactory'. The debate did not trouble the newspapers.

Colenso spent the rest of the year lecturing to Liberal associations and churches across the country. The political climate was unreceptive to a figure, a woman, who was so assertive in her opposition to Britain's increasingly aggressive imperial policy – a policy whose embodiment in Africa, the prime minister of the Cape Colony, Cecil Rhodes, had proclaimed in May that year that he 'preferred land to niggers'.

A second parliamentary debate, in July 1891, eighteen months after Colenso's arrival in London, was more heated. Again the baron spoke. For many years, he declared, Colenso had 'played a part in Zululand which has not been conducive to the welfare of the natives or the peace of the country'. As for Dinuzulu and his uncles, who after all had surrendered to the British army, 'They are rebels in the true sense of the word.'

There would be no reprieve. Colenso could only listen in stifled silence as the Liberal MP Osborne Morgan mounted a defence, after a fashion: 'We all know that in a country like South Africa human life is far less sacred than in a country like England.' But, he went on, while Miss Colenso might have indulged in 'feminine exaggeration', she herself was 'honest and generous in spirit'.

In British Zululand, meanwhile, a boundary commission had begun to divide Dinuzulu's kingdom into dozens of petty chiefdoms in preparation for its incorporation into the neighbouring colony of Natal. The troublemaker was not to be allowed to go back while he still had a kingdom to reign over. The following year, Baron de Worms denied rumours that Dinuzulu's enemy Zibhebhu was to be allowed to return to Zululand. Should there be any disorder in the colony, 'it will be in great measure due to the action of persons like Miss Colenso'.

In 1893 she published a 32-page pamphlet, *The Present Position Among the Zulus and Some Suggestions for the Future*. Dinuzulu and his uncles, she insisted, should be repatriated, and Dinuzulu himself appointed as 'head induna' of the annexed Zululand, thus recognising both his kingship and the authority of Zululand's other chiefs. It was a suggestion she would regret. In September that year, three and a half years after she and Dinuzulu left Africa, Colenso returned to Bishopstowe with her mother Sarah and her sister Agnes. It may be that Sarah knew she was ill, for two months later, she died. The night before, Colenso told Dinuzulu, her mother dreamed of her late husband, 'Sobantu', as he was known by the Zulus; but not only of him: also of Dinuzulu's own father, Cetshwayo. 'Our mother has now laid afresh upon us the command to have courage to persist in our work.'

In England she'd had her photo taken. In black taffeta she gazes rigidly at the camera with a rookish head-tilt. She seems *tired*. Her gaze isn't for England but for her people. She wishes them to understand what the English viewer would not. See what I am holding. The *tshokobezi*, the whipped cow's tail that symbolises the royalist cause; and, slung from its wooden handle, a string of *iziqu*, the beads of honour worn by those who have proved themselves in battle. But she had yet to win any victory.

———

It was a rift with his uncles in 1895, five years after their arrival, that caused Dinuzulu and his consorts uZihlazile and uMkasilomo, with their children, to abandon Maldivia, the communal house in Jamestown, for a smaller one an hour's walk away high on Francis Plain at the head of James Valley. What did they argue about? Was it simply the pressure of their continued confinement, and the hopelessness of their case, coming to a head around the young king's embrace of European ways – the bowler hat, the organ-playing, the liaisons with white women? Far from the eMakhosini Valley, had his authority begun to wane?

Today Francis Plain is the site of Prince Andrew School. The steep zigzagging track taken by Dinuzulu is overgrown, but still used by children who miss the morning bus. Wave after wave of silver-gold moths rose from the dew-laden grass as I climbed. The recent rain had caused rockfalls here and there.

Dinuzulu's house, with its girdling veranda and balcony, is used as the school staff room, and three teachers were sitting on the balcony drinking tea when I approached. Yes, come in, come up! Somewhere a kettle was boiling and a microwave pinged; but the house was largely unchanged in the past 130 years – the same dark oiled floorboards, the same heavy doors and blacked fireplaces – but surrounded by light, as Maldivia is not, and with thin curtains flapping in the sea breeze. I joined the teachers enjoying the view from the balcony: over the cricket pitch to the headlands that wall in Jamestown – and then the gigantic clouds mirrored in the Atlantic. Rarely, on St Helena, were you afforded such a powerful sense of your extraordinary isolation. You are one among just 4,000 humans, on a pinnacle of volcanic rock 1,200 miles from continental landfall. Look north, as we were, and there is nothing but water until you reached the Arctic, 5,500 miles away.

Coming to Francis Plain, one of the few level expanses on the entire island, must have felt like clambering out of a pit. Finally a seat befitting your status. Zulu custom dictated that the women and children and their midwife lived apart from Dinuzulu, as they had at Maldivia and Rosemary Hall, though that cannot have been easy in a house so small. How did he occupy himself? Well, learning the piano and the 'American organ'; improving his English and his written isiZulu; entertaining guests and ordering suits from London; and writing letter after letter, to Colenso and to his people in Zululand (those suits weren't free): 'everyone who remembers my father will contribute a small amount'.

Looking out at the scene Dinuzulu had known – the edge of the land and then the unchanging sea, every exile's fixation – I was aware that I was here for the same reason I had gone to New Caledonia; out of a conviction I couldn't suppress, that the trace of any presence somehow endures. But to believe in haunting is not to believe in ghosts. Coming here was in the nature of visiting a place you know to have been dear to a deceased loved one. They are retrievable to us there as they are not elsewhere.

3.

On 24 January 1895 St Helena's British governor informed Dinuzulu, Ndabuko and Shingana that they and their party should prepare to leave. Colenso's efforts in London had been successful, up to a point; as she had proposed, Dinuzulu would be chief of the uSuthu and salaried *induna* to the Zululand government. But his kingdom was gone. They would board the *Umkuzi*, to Natal, in under two weeks' time.

An auction of their effects was advertised: furniture, a mirror, carpets, flowerpots, bedsteads, ducks, Dinuzulu's piano and 'that well-known gelding Black Prince'.

St Helena's *Guardian* would be sorry, on balance, to see them leave:

It is now just five years since the Zulus arrived here, and during
that time they have been gradually weaned from their uncivilised
and savage life . . . This can be said especially of the young Prince,
who has become very refined, his gentlemanly manners and bearing
promising well for the speedy reclamation from barbarism of the
tribe over which he may hold sway.

They would be missed: 'Over a thousand pounds a year have been
expended upon the establishment, a loss the Colony is bound to feel
in the present aspect of affairs.'

Three days before their departure a gunboat, HMS *Swallow*,
anchored off Jamestown. The Zulus' release had been countermand-
ed. When the *Umkuzi* did arrive it was carrying official documents
confirming the order. They would be staying.

Harriette Colenso arrived to console her friends, whom she had
not seen since their imprisonment in Eshowe in 1890. What had
happened? The original order having been sent, it seemed the Colonial Office had received a demand from self-governing Natal that
Dinuzulu not be allowed to return until the incorporation of Zululand into Natal. 'Loss and suffering may dispose natives to disorder
owing to despair,' read a telegram from the governor's office.

Colenso spent more than a month on the island, mostly with Dinuzulu. Together they dined with the governor and rode (on the Black
Prince?) to Diana's Peak, the highest point on St Helena's central ridge,
and to Napoleon's Longwood House, at the time a termite-infested
ruin. I imagine them like siblings reunited, a kind of homecoming
for them both. Colenso arranged a magic-lantern display at the
Garrison Theatre in Jamestown, featuring a 'series of photographs of
Zululand'. She also attended mass with Ndabuko. His 'nostalgia' had

not abated, and the magic-lantern show, following hard on the news that they would be staying after all, may not have helped. 'I thought I knew before how lonely he was!' she wrote to Agnes.

Perhaps it was the memory of Cetshwayo's visit to London and the Isle of Wight in 1882 that prompted Dinuzulu and his uncles to plead that they be given leave to visit England. If they could not go home, they should at least be allowed to go to the land of their tormentors, to make their case. 'We are beset with a feverish cold,' Dinuzulu wrote to Colenso after her departure. Mubi Nondenisa, a friend of Colenso's whom she had sent to the island to aid Dinuzulu's education, reiterated his plea: 'There is feverishness among the children and their parents also; it clings, and got worse when there was a tremendous three days' rain, and fall of rocks.' Colenso agreed that a sojourn in England would be salutary, if not for the party's health then to help lift their spirits after the outrageous blow they had received: 'Their visit to England need cost little trouble, and comparatively little money,' she wrote in a published pamphlet addressed to the Colonial Office. In London they could visit the museums and the zoo, and Westminster Abbey, she suggested; in the countryside, 'the English cows and corn might occupy them'. But no, the British government was not in the business of laying on pleasure trips for native agitators. On St Helena they would remain.

———

I'd abandoned the idea of meeting his granddaughter, when, a few days before I was due to fly back to Johannesburg, I received an email. I was to visit 'Princess Dinuzulu' in Longwood.

I walked the four miles from my bungalow. The verges were strewn with the reds of wild currant, lantana and fuchsia. Fodies, watchful scarlet finches, moved songlessly through the scrub, dashes of red as

167

surprising as those in a Constable landscape. The trees, like the flowers and the fodies, were invasive: eucalyptus, pine, cedar. The island's few remaining endemic plants existed in scattered fastnesses like Thompson's Wood – the gumwood, the cabbage tree; the island's own species of ebony, lobelia, whitewood, tree fern, jellico, plantain and rosemary.

The princess no longer wore her regalia. In a ground-floor apartment she lay curled on her bed in pyjamas. The window was open and the curtains flapped in the breeze coming off Longwood Plain. Between the curtains you could see the 600-metre-high volcanic remnant known as the Barn. Two hundred metres down the lane was Napoleon's despised Longwood House.

Two nurses helped her to sit up and moved her to a wheelchair and fitted her hearing aid. She was eighty-two and she had 'good days and bad days', one of them told me. When they left she let out a small cry. We sat and listened to the mynah birds outside her window.

She sat not slumped but tilted. She lifted her eyes to me but didn't speak. In her gaze was a certain alertness; she knew why I was there, but when I said hello and she offered her small, strong hand, she only murmured a low affirmation.

'I came about the king,' I said.

She mouthed his name and smiled. I was longing to know about her life, but I knew she wouldn't speak. I regretted disturbing her.

Much later, from a pamphlet published by an island historian, I learnt that 'Princess Dinuzulu' was a kind of stage name. She'd been born Maglan Francis, in 1936, to a father who soon went to war, and a mother (Dinuzulu's daughter) who, having contracted leprosy, was quarantined in some abjured corner of the island. Thus 'Maggie' was brought up largely by her grandmother, Julia (she who had been Dinuzulu's lover). The girl was mocked by schoolmates, who knew the story that she did not – the story of her 'royal' lineage: 'Look at the princess now!' Aged fourteen she was sent to Scotland as a maid

168

to Lord and Lady Glenarthur, before training as a nurse. It was as a nurse and midwife – eventually as a part-time jazz singer – that 'Princess Dinuzulu' spent the rest of her working life. Her mother's favourite hymn, she remembered, was 'When Lamps Are Lighted in the Town', with its final verse:

> God hath watched o'er the fishermen
> Far on the deep dark sea,
> And brought them safely home again,
> Where they are glad to be.

Outside, as I walked the short distance to Longwood House, the mynah birds were still crowing.

———

'I call it a *lieu de mémoire*, not a museum,' the consul had told me. A site of memory. This explained Longwood House's sparsity of explanatory labels. 'I don't pretend to restore the humidity, the smell, the rotting, the rats, the sickness. It's a monument to the memory of the man.'

The house's centrepiece is the recreation of the black-canopied bed where, on 5 May 1821, Napoleon took his last breath. He was racked by vomiting, at once horrified by the light and drawn to it. 'Hello, sun!' he would cry. 'Hello, sun, my friend!' '*Il s'est éteint comme s'éteint la lumière d'une lampe,*' his valet wrote of his final days: his light has gone out like the light of a lamp.

I thought of the visit Dinuzulu made here with Colenso in 1895, having learnt that he would not be returning to Zululand; knowing that his kingdom was being picked apart. Perhaps he was to share Napoleon's fate and die on 'this evil rock' (the deposed emperor's words), far from his forebears' graves.

169

It was not until December 1897, more than two and a half years after the original order, that the party was allowed to return to Zululand. Joseph Chamberlain, the British Colonial Secretary, instructed St Helena's governor to be frank with his charge, just as Saunders had been when he had banished him in 1889: 'He must clearly understand that he does not return to Zululand as Paramount Chief.' Dinuzulu would be chief *only* of the uSuthu, confined to land assigned to the uSuthu by the British Boundary Commission. 'He will govern amongst them and will rule them by the same laws and form of Government as other chiefs of tribes in Zululand, and he will himself, like those chiefs, be under the laws of the Government of Zululand.'

The royal party that had numbered eleven when it arrived in 1890 was much bigger by the time it left – records vary from twenty-four to more than thirty – and included various tutors and translators, a midwife, eight children born on the island, and the new, St Helena-born wives of the Zulu attendants. There had always been St Helenians who, as the historian put it, 'consider their situation as a state of exile', and in those impoverished times there must have been those who envied them.

Among Dinuzulu's island companions was a certain Mary Johnstone. Learning that she planned to go with Dinuzulu when the ship left in two days' time, Colenso, who had returned to ensure the trip went smoothly, wrote an uncharacteristically hurried and direct letter. Granted, she said, the girl was 'useful' to Dinuzulu on St Helena, but, she warns: 'I do not see that you can help him in Zululand as you do now, because you know that it is not an English custom for a gentleman to be waited on and served by a young woman as you serve Dinuzulu.' A young white woman, she meant. 'If you did that in Zululand it would injure you and injure Dinuzulu also with English people.' She would be a stranger in Zululand; how much of a stranger, an island creature such as Johnstone could not begin to comprehend. 'It is my business,' Colenso felt it necessary to explain, 'because I am an older woman than you, because I am an English-woman, and a Missionary. It is my business because I believe that if you go now, unexpected, you will go to great misery, and perhaps you will get killed. Dinuzulu does not see this, he thinks perhaps that it is kind to take you – and unkind to leave you.'

She signs off by saying she expects an answer that evening. *If* Ms Johnstone persists in her plans, she, Colenso, will not hesitate to repeat her warning to the girl's mother. Maybe she saw in the young woman a threat to her own alliance with Dinuzulu, an alliance that, for both of them, was an expression of filial piety. After everything Sobantu and Cetshwayo had sacrificed, after the life-energy she and Dinuzulu had expended, she would not now allow the future of Zululand to be jeopardised by some pert island innocent. But she must also have known that, in a polygamist society, the girl would no longer be able to consider herself any sort of favourite, and that she would suffer.

And so Mary Johnstone stayed on the island, and we can't know if she was among those who lined the dock at Jamestown, five days before Christmas, watching as the party was rowed out tender by tender to the waiting SS *Umbilo*; and then as the ship plied its way to the horizon and the last plumes from its smokestack were lost on the wind.

The island was changed; so was Dinuzulu – subtler, more sceptical, surer of his entitlements, prouder. But it is easy to mistake going home for going back in time, and the Zululand he was returning to was not the country he had left. Re-entering open sea, for Michel and Shternberg, too, was like submitting to a chloroformed handker-chief. To what would they awaken? None of them could know.

171

The Island of the Black River

Sakhalin

1.

In Moscow, a year after my visit to St Helena, the intersections around Red Square were blocked by orange municipal dumper trucks; bullet-vested police were guarding the approaches and by 9 a.m. bands of bearded young proto-Cossacks were standing in circles roaring battle songs into the sky.

It was Victory Day, celebrating the surrender of Nazi Germany, and later President Putin would be addressing the troops. By design or accident, an international a cappella festival was also taking place. The outdoor stages were set up in the same squares as makeshift screens playing looped war footage, so that the singers' earnest harmonising – a beatbox version of 'Superstition', for instance – vied for your attention with, say, the Red Army Choir doing 'Arise the Great Country', reaching an equilibrium of volume that became intolerable until the a cappella people broke into the chorus.

On Pushkin Square three hundred members of the Moscow Communist Interbrigade were carrying flags bearing the hammer and sickle and Lenin's face. Among them was a green flag with another stencilled likeness – Che? No, Gaddafi. '*Net kapitalizmu! Net fashizmu!*' a man was chanting into a loudhailer. Over the heads of the crowd it was possible to glimpse, beyond the barricades, a ballistic missile as big as a grain silo creeping down Tverskaya towards Red Square.

Meanwhile, a mile away, Putin was mid-speech: 'Our nation is well aware of what war is. It brought grief and immeasurable suffering to every family. We have not forgotten anything. We remember everything . . .' But the past wasn't for everyone. In the bars of Kitai Gorod half the women seemed to be wearing the same brand of denim trench coat, printed across the back with 'Good things come to those who hustle'.

In the Pushkin State Museum of Fine Arts I lingered over Lucas Cranach the Elder's *The Fall of Man*: Adam and Eve as pale and delicate as rhizomes, about to be kicked out of the Garden of Eden. No longer innocent, perhaps, but unable to imagine what their new life will be like.

Over the next three weeks, as I dogged Shternberg's ghost across Russia, I realised that my preoccupation with exile wasn't about mourning a lost Eden, so much as simply wanting to think more clearly about loss. The ninth of May being also the feast day of St Nicholas, patron saint of travellers, I lit a candle in the Cathedral of the Assumption – for the journey ahead, but also for my father, in hospital, 1,600 miles away.

———

In the spring of 1890 Anton Chekhov made the 4,000-mile journey to Sakhalin from his home in Moscow, a journey of eleven weeks by road, river and sea. He spent two months on the island, mainly in the capital, Alexandrovsk, interviewing convicts and former convicts, administrators and prison overseers. The resulting description of squalor, sexual abuse, incompetence and systemic cruelty became a cause célèbre when it was serialised, then published as a book, *Sakhalin Island*, three years later.

The overland route he chose to take, with all its journalistic colour, was largely a thing of the past. But until the sea passage from Odessa had been established in 1879, thousands walked across the continent in miserable 'marching convoys', trudging for thousands of miles across steppe and taiga as monotonous as any ocean, a journey that might take not merely two months, as the sea journey did, but up to two years. Indeed, the journey itself, with its extremes of cold and heat, and its chaotic lawlessness, was often the hardest and most dangerous element of any Siberian exile's sentence. To travel to Sakhalin by ship, as Lev Shternberg did, was to travel in relative ease, whatever the particular hardships of life aboard the *Petersburg*.

'I regret that I am not a sentimental person,' Chekhov told his publisher and mentor Aleksey Suvorin before he left; 'otherwise I would say that we should make pilgrimages to places like Sakhalin as Turks go to Mecca.' At about the same time, Shternberg was beginning to see that the island might, however ghastly, become the centre of his own life's work.

———

At 4 a.m. I watched from the deck of the *Sakhalin-8* as we approached the lights of Kholmsk, on the island's south-western shore. Sakhalin is not, despite its reputation, a St Helena in its remoteness. At more than 30,000 square miles, it is Russia's largest island, almost as big as Austria. It sits in the Sea of Okhotsk opposite the Amur River delta, its southernmost tip just twenty-eight miles north of Japan, which has historically contested the island's sovereignty. But by the time Chekhov, and before him Shternberg, arrived, it was a byword for bleakness and isolation, 'the final destination of the un-shot [and] the unhanged', according to one commentator; a 'land of moral darkness and abject misery', according to another.

A steamed-up *marshrutka* – one of Russia's ubiquitous shared mini-bus taxis – took me to the capital, Yuzhno-Sakhalinsk, two hours east. Sakhalin is often described, in the few tourist guides where it is mentioned, as *sturgeon-shaped*, just as New Caledonia's Grande Terre is often called *baguette-shaped*; and Sakhalin does resemble a fish – a long, slender, bony fish, with two parallel peninsulas in the south forming a forked tail, and another, a dorsal fin, extending eastward into the Sea of Okhotsk. Between Lazarev on the mainland and Pogibi on the island's north-western shore, the Tatar Strait narrows such that until 1855 even the neighbouring Japanese believed Sakhalin was a peninsula, despite the insistence of the island's indigenous people that it was surrounded by water. Sakhalin's largest indigenous group, the Nivkhi, believed that the god of thunder lived beneath the sea between Pogibi and Laza-rev, and so it came as no surprise to them when a tunnel ordered by Stalin in 1950 – a symbol of Russian unity as well as a military asset – collapsed during construction, drowning hundreds of forced labour-ers. (Putin has commissioned designs for a bridge at the same spot, inspired by the one he had built between Crimea and Russia.)

The southern half of the island is dominated by two parallel mountain chains, the eastern Sakhalin range and the western Sakha-lin range, between which extend the floodplains of the island's two rivers – rivers that somehow seem too great, on a map and in reality, for the landmass they drain: the Tym, which meanders north-east, and the Poronai, south. The north of the island is flatter, wetter, barer, colder and windier, mostly bog, tundra and open taiga, its coastline a scalloped lattice of lagoons. Off the north-eastern shore lie the enor-mous oil-and-gas fields of the Sea of Okhotsk shelf. Yuzhno, as the capital is known, lies just north of the fish-tail's cleft.

I was staying in a business hotel surrounded by oil-firm offices. The city had grown affluent on the industry, and the restaurants were full of young Americans on short-term contracts, noisy with the buzz of easy money. I met a Sakhalin-Korean translator named Alisa. A brilliant yellow dress and a dented black Fiat. A giant weltering sadness she tolerated as one might tolerate a vicious dog adopted in puppyhood. It was not only Russians who had been prisoners on the island. Of a population of just under half a million, some 55,000 are of Korean descent, mostly living in Yuzhno. During the Second World War, when southern Sakhalin (known as 'Karafuto Prefecture') was under Japanese rule, around 150,000 Koreans were removed from their homeland and brought here to bolster the Japanese labour force serving the island's mining and timber industries. The conditions were little better than they had been for the Russian convicts doing the same work fifty years earlier. When Russia invaded in 1945 and recaptured southern Sakhalin, most Japanese and Koreans fled; but around 43,000 Koreans were prevented from leaving (some say Stalin himself ordered they be detained to supplement the island's gulag workforce). When the borders were sealed they were trapped.

Alisa was born in Yuzhno to second-generation Sakhalin-Koreans. She earned a living as a translator for the oil-and-gas industry, but most of her time was devoted to her three-year-old daughter. All her life, she told me over dinner, she had struggled to manage the energy in the world, to distinguish positive energy from negative energy, and to master the energy she herself possessed. Energy? It was hard to explain. As an architecture student in Moscow she had suffered an episode of something like demonic possession. It traumatised her. She had no doubt that God and the devil exist. She had inherited from her mother a profound belief in the pre-eminence of fate. She would make or cancel plans without warning, according to her assessment of the associated 'energy' – a lucrative contract in Korea, for instance, cancelled the day before her flight. 'They were angry, of course, but I had my reasons.' She'd spoken to many psychologists, and to others who possessed this 'energy' – she mentioned an elderly man in Kazakhstan whom she once visited for guidance when she was ill. I asked what his occupation was, his specialism: 'No "job"! Just a very unusual person. You'd understand if you met him.'

With her daughter, Mia, we went to see her mother in the hills above the expat enclave of the island's main oil consortium, Sakhalin Energy, known as 'Strawberry Hills', with its un-Russian lawns and employee-only restaurant and health club, the first health club in Sakhalin, Alisa said. Her parents' house was an old shiplap two-storey with a garden planted with flowers and blossoming cherries and rows of actual strawberries. On the balcony there was a cool breeze and a view of the Yuzhno plain and the city, with its gold cathedral dome, sparkling far below.

Sandra, her mother, was famous in Yuzhno-Sakhalin, recognised on the street, a TV presenter and critic, and secretary to the oblast's former governor (he'd been killed in a helicopter crash, and if you believed it was an accident, well, okay). We sat and drank green tea. Sandra's parents and uncle, she said, had been among those Koreans who had come to the island voluntarily in the early 1940s. 'Then the borders were closed, and they were completely cut off from their homeland, their parents, their families. They couldn't even write letters.' It was her uncle, a teacher, who took exile hardest. 'A teacher had a very high status in Korean society. But because he spoke no Russian he couldn't teach in Sakhalin. He had a girlfriend in Korea, but he couldn't write to her. The only way out was alcohol.'

It was not until after Gorbachev came to power in 1985 that the borders were reopened, and Koreans born before August 1945 told they were free to return to South Korea. 'But only if they left their children and grandchildren here in Sakhalin,' said Sandra. 'My father decided to go home. We had to shut off so many tears. I knew he wasn't going to Korea to live – his life was here. He was going there to die, and he was going to die alone.'

The stairwell was hung with paintings given to her by Sakhalin artists, grateful for her early patronage: a full-length portrait of Alisa, which captured something Alisa disliked; a vase of flowers in a summer garden; the island's fatigued, sackcloth landscapes: taiga, steppe, sea . . . Alisa showed me the room where she and Mia had stayed after her divorce. A beautiful room lined with golden timber and full of golden light, dominated by a rubber plant so overgrown that to move from one side of the room to the other meant edging past its giant brown leaves.

'When I left home as a girl to study in Korea,' she said, 'my mother bought this plant and told me "It will be *you* while you are away."' When she returned to the room with her daughter ten years later, the plant was ailing, pressing against the walls and ceiling. 'I showed the leaves to my mother,' said Alisa. 'For the first time, she understood why I have always wanted to leave Sakhalin.'

———

Alexandrovsk-Sakhalinsky, Shternberg's 'Alexandrovsk', lies on the sturgeon's belly, halfway up the west coast, where the mountain south meets the boggy north. By 1888 the island was the largest penal settlement in Siberia. Any man sentenced to more than two years and eight months, for any crime, could be sent here, as could any woman under forty serving more than two years. As in New Caledonia, with its *déportés*, *transportés* and *libérés*, and Ancient Rome, with its *deportatio*, *relegatio* and *aqua et igni interdictus*, exile in Russia had its own taxonomy. As well as common criminals or 'convict-exiles', known as *ssyl'nokatorzhnye*, on Sakhalin there were three further categories.

'Settled exiles', like the *libérés* of New Caledonia, had completed their sentence but were obliged to remain on the island. After six to ten years they became 'peasants-in-exile', free to leave provided they did not return to European Russia. There were also those who had come to the island voluntarily. 'The clever are brought here,' went an island saying; 'the idiots come on their own.' Among the 'free' were the wives of convicts, some of whom were enticed by letters from their husbands, describing a land of warmth, fertility and opportunity. 'The climate here is marvellous!' went one, glossing over those occasions when the temperature dropped below −20°C.

Russian has a useful word, *rasputitsa*, 'time without roads', meaning spring, when the snows melt, and autumn, when the rain comes. In Sakhalin it's safest to travel any distance by air or rail. On the outskirts of Yuzhno, the train passed through sidings dense with fresh young bamboo. The birch taiga was coming into green: in the dark of the forests, the young leaves were bright as the spots of light from a glitterball. Lying in my bunk, with the onset of night, I pondered the story Alisa had told me while we waited for my train, a coda to her mother's.

As a young teenager, she had gone to South Korea on a piano scholarship. A TV crew had come to interview her, and the presenter learnt that her grandfather, whom she had not seen since she was a baby, had come to Korea from Sakhalin many years before. Seeing an opportunity for a tearful reunion, they tracked him down in his nursing home and arranged for Alisa to visit him. She was told by her teacher that she must comply, that it would look bad if she were to refuse, after the TV people had gone to the trouble of finding him. And so in a provincial town she did not know, the cameras filmed her meeting an old man she did not know. 'When they stopped filming, he begged me to take him back to Sakhalin to die. But I knew my parents couldn't afford to look after him.' It was an experience familiar to the Sakhalin exiles of an earlier era, as well as to Louise Michel and Dinuzulu kaCetshwayo: to finally be allowed to go home, only to discover it was home no longer.

2.

My train pulled into Tymovsk, fifty miles east of Alexandrovsk, just after dawn on 13 May.

I was met by Aleksander, a driver sent by the director of the Chekhov Museum, Mr Miromanov. The road from Tymovsk to Alexandrovsk rolled through taiga swamped with snowmelt. Water flowed everywhere. It was as if the island had just been winched out of the sea. Around the borders of the forest bogs were the blooms of what Aleksander called lopukh, which turned out to be Asian skunk cabbage. He let out a flurry of grunts and squeals – it took me a moment to realise he meant the plant was used as pig fodder. Its white spathes, resembling arums, were flame-like or jug-like or like hands in benediction, rising out of the anaerobic black in groupings that seemed to correspond to the clustering patterns of anxious human crowds.

We stopped for a smoke at a churned-up field where, said Aleksander, thousands of victims of Stalin's purges had been shot and buried. A rusted iron cross swung from a birch tree. From the hills the road followed the streams towards the Tatar Strait, through tiers of white housing blocks.

———

Natalia was a retired English teacher who had lived in Alexandrovsk all her life. She was worried I'd have a poor opinion of her town, of her country; that I would find the hotel, the canteen, the roads disagreeable. We walked to Alexandrovsk's defunct harbour, with its thickets of knotweed and angelica and its grounded and half-sunk trawlers. When Chekhov's ship the *Baikal* anchored offshore on the evening of 10 July 1890, the hills surrounding the town were aflame. 'Through the darkness and smoke spreading over the sea,' he wrote, 'I could not see the landing stage or buildings and could make out only the dim lights of the post, two of which were red . . . it looked as if the whole of Sakhalin was ablaze.' He did not need to add that it was 'as if we were in hell'.

Lev Shternberg's initial impression of the island, fourteen months earlier, was more positive: he was met, on that warm May day, by the 'courteous' district head, who explained that as a 'political' he would be granted an allowance, spared hard labour and permitted to take paid office work. Indeed, he was able eventually to send money to his parents back in Zhitomir. However, he wrote to his old friend Moisei Krol: 'My own privileged position does not make it easier to watch the suffering of people deprived of all their rights.' Nor was it only his fellow exiles whose ill-treatment he noted. Soon after arriving he saw an old Nivkh man being harangued by the children of the bathhouse owner – 'Look at the old shaman! He'll tell your fortune, sir, he will!' In his diary Shternberg noted that the man was likely to be 'his tribe's semi-god, feared by everyone. He probably comes from an ancient clan . . . Maybe, even now, when he returns to his tent, he feels once again that he is a wise and self-assured divine figure . . . Someday,' he concluded, 'I will study them.'

For his part, Chekhov claimed that the 'mild-tempered Sakhalin mongrels' barked only at the island's indigenous people. Even for a writer so probing as Chekhov, the Nivkhi were little more than an incomprehensible shadow at the edge of his field of vision. 'The Gilyaks never wash,' he writes, 'so that even ethnographers find it difficult to put a name to the real colour of their faces.' He conceded, however, that they were neither warlike, quarrelsome nor violent, and that lying was repugnant to them.

The largest indigenous group on the island, the Nivkhi are one of the five indigenous peoples of eastern Siberia known by ethnographers as 'Paleoasiatics', whose language has no known connection with other linguistic groups. Nivkh, famously, has twenty-six different ways of counting from one to ten according to the physical and social characteristics of the thing being counted. Traditionally they were semi-nomadic fishers, with an animist belief system based around four 'spirit masters': the sky, the hills, water and fire. Today most of Sakhalin's approximately 2,500 Nivkh people live on the other side of the island, in and around the oil towns of the northeast, having been ejected from their traditional settlements first under the influx of Russian immigrants of the late nineteenth century then under several phases of Soviet collectivisation.

The harbour where both strangers, the writer and the revolutionary, came ashore was vanishing into mud and sand. 'Nothing is sadder than a boat on land,' said Natalia, looking through a gap in the hoardings that fenced off the old harbour. Pining for the past was a form of self-comfort. It was also a way of explaining the present to strangers. Things haven't always been this way. When she was a child the town had 20,000 people and nine schools; today the population is half that and there are three schools. At least in Shternberg's day the place had a purpose. Now, said Natalia, the young people fled to Yuzhho, Moscow or Vladivostok the moment they left school.

On the outskirts of the town, as in the villages I would see over the coming days, occupied houses were often surrounded by dozens of rotting dwellings shrouded in weeds, home only to feral dogs and the occasional bear. Natalia remembered the sunny days of Young Pioneers camps in the hills; the days when the port was thriving and she and her schoolfriends would return from summer afternoons on the beach glittering with black dust from the coal barges.

Now the coal industry was defunct and most of the logging firms had moved to Japan. Alexandrovsk, like much of the island, saw little of the wealth being siphoned from the oil-and-gas fields of the north-east (Sakhalin Energy reported revenue of over $6 billion in 2018, but most of the tax was skimmed off by Moscow). There were no longer enough fish in the Tatar Strait to sustain the town's fishing industry, and the water had risen to submerge Natalia's childhood beach at high and low tide alike. Global warming was causing sea levels to rise across the Pacific, but this wasn't a present to which she wanted to reconcile herself; it was not her country.

As I was taking a photo of the rusted plaque to Chekhov's arrival, I felt a surge of pain in my calf so deep and startling that I was caught, like Buridan's ass, between shrieking and puking. Natalia screamed. It felt like I'd been harpooned. The dog – one of Chekhov's 'mild-tempered Sakhalin mongrels' – had been barking from its lookout of rubble with the squint-eyed ripping motion of serious dogs, and I'd turned away. It did its job so well that all memory of its appearance has gone – big or small; what breed or colour. There was too much blood to examine the wound. I took off my sock and tied it ineffectually round my calf and, shoe slopping with blood, flagged down a car.

Pushing the needle into my back an hour later (for rabies, I understood; for tetanus, it turned out), the nurse in the town's clinic said: 'Now you have something to write about, don't you?' The doctor's nostrils flared as he suppressed a smirk. I went back to the town's solitary hotel, the Three Brothers, shook the blood from my shoe into the toilet, swallowed some antibiotics and went to bed. For the rest of my time on Sakhalin I showered with a plastic carrier bag taped around my leg. Next morning, when I was told that a minor earthquake had struck in the night, it didn't come as a surprise, and not only because Sakhalin lies in a region of seismic unrest.

———

When I met Miromanov, the museum director, the following morning, he asked after the dog's health. Had it been given a jab? Natalia, who introduced us, knew him from forty years ago, when they were trainee teachers at Young Pioneers camp. She spoke about him as if he were famous – which he was, in a limited sense. She didn't think he would remember her. 'He did something very special. It was really remarkable. He would say, "Tell me any word, and I will make a poem." And he did just that: you gave him a word and immediately, he would recite a perfect rhyming verse; I don't mean doggerel.'

If Miromanov, who had once been the town's mayor, was not directly employed by the federal security service, I had been told he was probably an informant. Not that informants were rare. On the ferry there had been a thin, grey-faced man in an oversized black suit, who I think had been tasked with watching me; later – less surreptitiously – there were the two young men who sat in on my meeting at a museum in Nogliki, unintroduced and fingering their phones as I spoke; then there was the time Alisa, in my hotel room in Yuzhno, looked up at the light fittings and the smoke alarm and waved at them and said, not quite joking: 'Hi, guys!'

Miromanov was shaven-headed and grey-bearded, with the complexion of a fisherman. He was impatient with anyone who was not a young woman. He'd been born in Alexandrovsk, like Natalia, and for a while had been mayor. Before that he had travelled the world. When I asked in what capacity, he changed the subject with such deftness that I only realised he had done so hours later. He was popular, and the way others addressed him, with a cautious smile, suggested he still wielded the power of a person known to be influential. I asked him many questions and not once did he ponder his answer for more than a second, even when it was a snapped 'I do not know!' You wouldn't take him for a museum director or, for that matter, darling of the town's am-dram soc.

The museum, in a single-storey wooden house built on the spot where Chekhov stayed, had been founded in 1896 by Shternberg and others as a museum of history and anthropology, and run by Miromanov's father before him. He showed me in with the manner of someone presenting the family business to an investor. The rooms were immaculate, the letters and artefacts (Chekhov's desk; Chekhov's samovar; Chekhov's pre-printed census forms) displayed with none of the pathos – blown lightbulbs, sticky-taped labelling, lurking cats – of some Russian regional museums. A cleaner followed us from room to room, wiping the vitrines, like the women employed to clean lip smears from the icons in Orthodox churches.

When Shternberg and Chekhov were here, Miromanov said, Sakhalin had four subsets of *ssyl'nokatorzhnye*, or convict-exiles. Most slept in the town's prison, were not shackled but worked each day in the coal mines at Dué, on the coast a few miles south ('a dreadful, hideous place', according to Chekhov). A second group was shackled, and laboured for four hours per day. The third and most wretched, the *tachechniki*, or 'barrow-pushers', were chained for life to wooden wheelbarrows. The *tachechniki* did not work, the barrow serving only as ball and chain. There were photos of these men standing with their barrows, wearing the almost-rapturous expression of those who have discovered that pain is not finite. Finally there was a small number of 'administrative' political exiles, no more than fifty in 1890, including Polish revolutionaries and Russian Populists like Shternberg.

In 1890, when the authorities in Alexandrovsk learnt about the arrival of the famous author, clutching his wretched notebook, they saw to it that one political exile, a tiresome agitator for prisoners' rights, would not be around to testify. Shternberg had been in Alexandrovsk for more than a year, and had become sickened by the ill-treatment of the convicts he lived among, especially the overseers' often arbitrary meting out of punishment beatings. One of the most memorable scenes in *Sakhalin Island* describes the birch-lashing of a failed escapee, a counterpart to Henri Rochefort's description of the beatings undergone by convicts in New Caledonia. The victim was a child-killer named Prokhorov.

Prokhorov's hair is stuck to his brow, his neck is swollen; after five or ten blows his body, still covered by weals from previous lashings, has already turned crimson and dark blue; the skin on it splits from every blow.

'Yer Excellency!' we hear through the screeching and weeping. 'Yer Excellency! Be merciful, yer Excellency!'

Chekhov notes a 'kind of curious stretching-out of the neck, the sound of retching'. He leaves, unable to watch any more. Writing a few years later, another visitor, Charles Hawes, describes the *plet*, a whip with lead-tipped thongs. Hawes tells the story of one victim who, sentenced to a hundred strokes, promised to pay the executioner with a bottle of vodka if he refrained from applying the leaded tips. But with five strokes remaining, the prisoner reneged: 'You can't hurt me now; you needn't think you'll get your vodka!' The executioner silently adjusted his stroke. Three more blows and the man was dead. 'It was only necessary to draw back the plet, as the stroke was spent,' explains Hawes, 'for the ends to injure the liver and send a clot of blood to the heart.'

That same year, after Lev Shternberg had repeatedly decried the treatment of his fellow exiles, he was persuaded by the authorities to sign an agreement promising to cease his appeals, on pain of being banished to the 'most isolated corner of Sakhalin'. He persisted; he was sent, as promised, to a tiny settlement fifty miles north: a place called Viakhtu, the site of what he called his 'ethnographic baptism'.

Shternberg's *The Social Organisation of the Gilyak*, published in 1905, is a rather staid work, often impenetrable to me, but its pages are enlivened by jailbird drollness: 'I became interested in this study', Shternberg opens, 'when late one winter I found myself involuntarily on the solitary shore of the Tatar Strait, about one hundred kilometres from Aleksandrovsk.' (His Russian readers would have understood both where he was and why.) 'Here on the broad pasture of the mouth of the Viakhtu River,' he goes on, 'the representatives of such tribes as the deer-breeding Tungus and the dog-breeding Gilyak organised an annual rendezvous . . . Occasionally they spent several days with us, and in exchange for tea and bread they let me into some of the secrets of their primitive life . . .'

He had first read Friedrich Engels's *Origin of the Family, Private Property and the State*, published in 1884, in prison in Odessa. In Viakhtu he returned to it and to Lewis Henry Morgan's seminal 1877 book, *Ancient Society*, to which Engels's book was a response. It was a meeting with Charles Darwin that shaped Morgan's own belief in the successive stages of human social evolution: from 'savagery', where 'group marriage' and promiscuity were norms; to 'barbarism', with its loose husband-and-wife pairings; to the monogamous, present-day phase of 'civilisation'. 'As it is undeniable that portions of the human family have existed in a state of savagery, other portions in a state of barbarism, and still others in a state of civilization,' Morgan wrote, 'it seems equally so that these three distinct conditions are connected with each other in a natural as well as necessary sequence of progress.' This three-stage system of social evolution – savagery; barbarism; civilisation – would become central to Shternberg's own ethnography.

It was the Gilyaks – Nivkhi is the preferred modern self-naming – who would occupy Shternberg's studies. 'Despite my complete ignorance of their language, I was struck from the very beginning by the terminology used by the Gilyak when addressing relatives of various categories.' He noted that 'children addressed by the common name of *imk*, mother, not only their own mother but also all her sisters, and the wives of their father's brothers. Similarly, with some variation, they addressed their father and all his brothers as *tuvng*.' It was these clan relations, and the language used to describe them, that would become Shternberg's preoccupation in Viakhtu. It's hard to say how far, if at all, he considered his study of 'social organisation' an extension of the activism that landed him on Sakhalin; what is not in doubt is the use to which others would put this research in furtherance of their own political ends.

Having deeply mythologised that small place, I kept returning to Viakhtu in my mind's eye, worrying at its grainy image – and more so now that it was nearby. If Alexandrovsk was the 'world's end' then Viakhtu was a space station – an abandoned one. Miromanov assured me there was 'nothing to see' there, but agreed to take me, as long as the road had not been washed away by the spring floods, and as long as I covered the necessary fuel and drink. At the town's pharmacy, where they knew me by now, I stocked up on bandages.

———

At 5 a.m. a dented red Land Cruiser pulled into Alexandrovsk's main square. Before he introduced me to the man in the back, Miromanov introduced me to Suzanne, who was the car. 'Important to name your vehicle.' He patted the dashboard. 'I knew she was called Suzanne as soon as I drove her.'

The man in the back was his friend Vladimir, the museum's manager. He seldom spoke, but sang quietly all the way to Viakhtu, and doled out the vodka. Both he and Miromanov had dressed in camouflage fishing overalls; in the trunk were their waders and tackle, and next to Vladimir was enough vodka to make the Red Army Choir botch its cue. They were not here on Shternberg's account.

I had looked up Viakhtu in an atlas of Sakhalin, but the modern village was not Shternberg's. His Viakhtu was what Miromanov called 'Old Viakhtu', a mile north on the other side of an estuary, accessible only by boat. And there it was, on the map: Shternberg's 'Russian Palestine', a featureless plain locked between forest and water, labelled *nezhil*: short for 'uninhabited'.

It was the phase of insupportable wetness between winter and summer, when the earth is released from snow only to find itself flooded. *Rasputitsa*. The hares that crossed our path – a sign of bad luck, said Miromanov – were still shucking off their white winter coat. To cross the sagging wooden bridges, over thundering brown water, felt like an act of fatalism. The road rolled through clapperboard fishing villages whose names I knew from Chekhov as well as Shternberg: Mgachi, Tangi, Khoe, Trambaus. I was aware it was an unrepresentative time of year, transitional. Everything was a snow-dozed entropic mess, the light too flat to shake it into beauty.

Miromanov knew the name of none of the plants – 'I do not *know*!' – and was unmoved by a sunrise that caused me to twist in my seat for a better look. His relationship with the natural world was more visceral.

'I have been all around the world. Really, everywhere is the same – Russia, Scotland, America . . . But I could not live in any country where you must release a fish when you have caught it. Why? Why?'

He made a gun of his fingers and shot himself under the chin.

At a fork in the road, we stopped and Vladimir divvied vodka into tin cups, and each of us opened our door and tipped the contents onto the road – for the Nivkh god Bordh, whose domain began there. There was nothing ironic in the act, which in Nivkh terms was more a matter of nourishment than of libation. Vladimir refilled the cups and Englishly I proffered a toast: *to Sakhalin* (spirits make me expansive).

'No!' Miromanov spat. 'Sak-ha-lin! The – hole – of – the – *arse*.'
Another cosmography.

———

Viakhtu – 'New Viakhtu' – stood on the edge of a dune field, a cluster of brightly painted timber houses around a rutted crossroads. Outside his smallholding we met Obet, the fisherman who would ferry us across the estuary to Old Viakhtu, carrying a metre-long frozen salmon over one shoulder.

His fishing camp two miles away at the mouth of the estuary was a breaker's yard of engine blocks and ship's doors. An old orange bus was used as shelter, its window frames caulked with expanding foam against draughts. Welded to its undercarriage, in place of wheels, were sledge-runners made of ten-inch iron pipes with scrolled ends. While we waited for the tide, I dozed inside and watched Miromanov and Vladimir casting their lines into the race. This was why *they* were here.

After two hours the tide turned and Obet deemed the water deep enough. Sighing, Miromanov pulled on an ankle-length oiled cape. The sea was violent and anguished and extremely cold, reeling with half-submerged tree trunks and branches. The boat's outboard worked furiously against the outgoing tide, the bow scooping water. It would have been better to wait; a freak wave might easily fill the hull or throw one of us – *me* – overboard. Sleeves, trousers, hair, the bandage on my leg, all were soon soaked. (Only afterwards, back at the camp, did I understand that it was not a journey Obet would have risked had I not been paying, and that the laughter of Vladimir and Miromanov had been nervous laughter.) Fifteen minutes later, breathless and red-faced, all adrenaline spent, we hefted the boat onto a beach carpeted with driftwood, and clambered up a sandy cliff to the headland.

'Nothing!' Miromanov said triumphantly, looking around at the flat expanse. Just as he had told me.

The headland had been a traditional waystation for semi-nomadic Nivkhi, who had a camp two kilometres away, and, knowing the land better than any incomer, were, like certain Kanak clans in New Caledonia, employed to bring back absconded convicts. Not that most escapees from Alexandrovsk or Dué could hope to survive long in the Sakhalin wilderness, even in the summer. 'If you are anxious to die, you can go anywhere you like,' one old convict warns the new arrivals in Korolenko's 'Sokholinets', the story Shternberg read aboard the *Petersburg*: 'The island is large, a wilderness and a forest.' But escape was not altogether impossible. 'There is but one road for us to follow, and that is to the north, skirting the shore for the entire distance. The sea will be our guide. After travelling some 300 versts [about 200 miles], we shall come to narrow straits, and it is there that we must cross in boats to the Amur shore. Only, let me tell you, my boy,' he adds, 'we shall have trouble in passing the military outposts.'

As well as five houses occupied by freed convicts, a small company of soldiers was based at Viakhtu with Shternberg, since it was a known crossing point for escaped convicts bound for Pogibi, the narrowest point of the Tatar Strait. 'The hope for them as for everyone,' wrote Shternberg, 'was to win the three-rouble prize for each fugitive captured.'

'Nothing!' said Miromanov again, stalking back and forth through the long grass, while Vladimir and Obet stood smoking by the boat. *Next* to nothing: the raised outlines of foundations cloaked by tall dead grass; the scrub-smothered mouth of a well; a few timbers; patches of whortleberries, stunted spruce, a species of thorn bush coming into bud . . . But otherwise only the dark edge of the woods bounding the plain to the north, and the estuary pressing seaward like the outflow from a smelter.

A 'lonely, abandoned grave in the empty taiga,' Shternberg called this place. 'The gloomy sky hung low over the snowy savannah, bordered by a thick fog, and beyond it, apparently, was the end of the world.'

Na krai sveta – the world's end, again – but for him the beginning of another. At first he had only a screened corner of the soldiers' cabin, but eventually he was given his own cabin, where he was able to make a kind of home. On the wall were photos of his friends, including one of Krol (he was not, then, in love); he practised calisthenics, chopped wood, worked on his English. In the summer he even swam. And of course he read: Dante, and Weber (his *History of Greece*), and Engels. 'When I feel the need to see someone, I call the virtuous guard,' he told Krol, 'a big fellow who killed his wife, and talk with him about God and people and lofty matters in general.'

He takes a walk in the taiga, among the drifts of snow, and is cheered by the tentative notes of green; by the 'white flowers' – skunk cabbage, is it? – emerging from the sodden earth; by the aroma of the pines, which perhaps reminded him of his boyhood walks near Zhitomir. Here he finds a small escape, as Louise Michel found her own in the Forest of the West. Back at the settlement, conversation with his few companions keeps him 'tethered to life', but he complains that a 'void' in his head renders him unable to work. He says no more about that 'void' (*pustota*, which might also be translated as 'emptiness' or 'vacuum'), but I'm reminded of the recurrence of the word – *le vide* – in the letters of the Communards in New Caledonia: Johannes Canton, for example, who was confined with Michel on the Ducos Peninsula, and described his despair, his *nostalgie*, as: 'a void which had ballooned'.

He was thirty. Did he remember the advice his mother gave him, back in Odessa? 'You are a kind person and God is just, and He exists everywhere, even on Sakhalin. He will not abandon you.' One day, on the eve of Orthodox Easter, his few Russian cohabitants here in Viakhtu – the former prisoners, the guards and bounty hunters – sought out their educated companion, with a plea: would he conduct

193

the Easter service, since the nearest church was many miles away? No, it does not matter that you are a Jew.

From memory he recited the Sermon on the Mount. The poor in spirit, those who mourned, the hungry and thirsty, the merciful, the wife-killers – his small audience on this remote headland, each man dressed in his cleanest shirt, was spellbound: 'I had not even finished reciting the last verses', he recalled, 'when I began hearing strange sounds. Individual sobs soon gave way to loud sobbing by everyone present.'

———

During the remainder of his sentence, the administration in Alexandrovsk, which had a strategic interest in monitoring the island's indigenous population, granted Shternberg the freedom to mount several 'census-taking' expeditions to settlements in the island's north. Chekhov was by now back home in Moscow, but it was in the authorities' interests to see that the troublesome Jew, with his perpetual complaints, was kept occupied.

His first expedition took place nearly two years after his arrival on the island, eleven months after his removal to Viakhtu. 'On 6 February 1891, on two sledges harnessed with dogs – one for myself with provisions for a month and another for my interpreter – we started on our first voyage.'

The expedition took him into the frozen taiga and swamplands north of Viakhtu, to the winter fishing settlements scattered along the island's north-western coast. Because of his inability to speak Nivkh, Shternberg hired a Russian-speaking Nivkh man named named Obon (until the Soviet era, Nivkh people possessed neither patronymics nor surnames, having no need for them), as well as a Russian sled-driver who was acquainted with the Nivkhi. Though

Obon's Russian was patchy and he had a tendency to impertinence (according to Shternberg), he was 'famous for his intelligence and arts of oratory' and had 'great zeal and an active intelligence'. The trip was aborted after a month because the dried fish to feed the dogs was running out. Shternberg with his sled-driver and Obon returned to Viakhtu, having conducted a census of 1,040 – almost all – of the region's Nivkh population. It seems he was perceived by the headmen as part shaman, because he carried medicines, and part spy, which in essence he was, even if he sought as much independence from his backers in Alexandrovsk as possible. (Despite the radicalism that accounted for his presence on Sakhalin – remember *Politicheskii Terror* – Shternberg never questioned Russia's right to be there, or for that matter the practice of convict labour, though he insisted that 'colonisation . . . ought to be carried out in such a manner so as to minimise the suffering of the aborigines'.)

He had developed a taste for fieldwork, but more than that, the vastness of the taiga promised to fill the 'void' in his head, and a liberty that must have seemed infinite after his years of confinement – in Odessa prison, aboard the *Petersburg*, in the smoky cabins of Alexandrovsk and the almost-island of Viakhtu. He wrote in his diary:

> The beautiful memories, full of poetry as well as very instructive,
> will remain with me forever. Being a nervous person, I found that
> my close contact with the life of [Nivkh people] had a calming effect
> on me and strengthened me . . . How wonderful it is to be lying in
> a small Gilyak boat and going down a scenic and rapid river to the
> sea of Ohkotsk! . . . How wonderful are these nights spent under a
> canopy of the trees lit up by the bright light of the fire or spending
> a rainy day inside a tent, sitting on a bearskin rug and reading the
> latest book!

In June, having written up his notes, he mounted a second expedition, travelling by boat down the River Tym, which rises amid the island's central mountains and meanders to the sea at modern Nogliki on the north-eastern coast. 'The most fantastic legends circulated among the Russians and the Gilyak of the western shore about the Gilyak of the eastern shore. They were called the "black Gilyak" and all kinds of vices were attributed to them.' Chief among these vices, predictably, was cannibalism. It was well known that when the eastern-shore Gilyak captured an unsuspecting stranger they would imprison him in a hut, force-feed him fish, and duly butcher him for the pot. As with most colonist stories of cannibalism among indigenous peoples – for the French in New Caledonia, cannibalism was the most horrifying confirmation of Kanak otherness – the Russians' fears were unfounded. The east-coast Nivkh clans were as hospitable as their west-coast counterparts. Nevertheless: news spread that he had been eaten. 'When I returned to Alexandrovsk, the governor of the island was about to send a detachment to the scene of the crime.'

Shternberg spent a month travelling south down the eastern coast by boat and on reindeer-back. 'I was able to visit all the inhabited parts of the territory and take a detailed census of the population, while continuing my observations on their life and beliefs.' As the salmon began to spawn with the late-summer rains, he returned to the other side of the island, upstream along the Tym – 'Eleven days full of hardship and privation; our provisions were exhausted and the banks of the river were full of bears.' He spent the rest of the year in Viakhtu, writing up his expedition notes and slowly unpicking the intricacies of the Nivkh language, even if 'the grammar and phonetics seemed so difficult that I gave up all hope of ever learning it'.

Nevertheless, over the next two years he became proficient in the west-coast dialect and mounted several further expeditions: to the south of the island and to its northernmost point, Cape Mariia, nearly drowning on the return voyage, before in 1895 he was granted leave to spend several months on the mainland among the Nivkhi of the Amur River delta. Evidently the authorities on Sakhalin did not doubt that he would return. Where would he go if he fled, after all? The land was hardly less hostile than the water. Besides, now he had his vocation.

Our return passage to New Viakhtu was smoother, or at least less frightening. At the fishing encampment, Vladimir built a fire in the lee of the bus and hung a pan of water over it from a crook of driftwood. Potatoes, dill, stock powder, a salmon he had caught, salt, lemon juice, wild onions, a great glug of vodka. Inside the bus as we ate we watched the River Viakhtu, flowing endlessly into the Tatar Strait, and beyond it dimly Old Viakhtu, where none of us would set foot again. There had been nothing there, *pustota*, just as Miromanov said; but it had satisfied my urge for some connection with Shternberg, for whom, in its very bleakness, it had been one of his life's crucial places.

3.

Mikhail was sixty and listened to nothing but early Rammstein, the hard stuff. 'Du Hast' and 'Mutter' on rotation. The only music for the island's spine-fracturing roads. He worked as a driver for Ecoshelf, an emergency oil-spill response firm used by Exxon Neftegas in Nogliki, and he was giving me a ride to Okha, 160 kilometres north, heartland of Sakhalin's oil-and-gas industry.

I had left Alexandrovsk, following the River Tym through the mountains, as Shternberg had, to the oil town of Nogliki on the Sea of Okhotsk. At Nogliki's House of Culture, the day before, the superintendent, Yuri, had put an arm across my shoulders and led me to what he called a 'special exhibit', pulling aside a curtain to reveal a mock-up of a Soviet-era bedroom composed of items donated by

Nogliki's citizens: a gramophone, an accordion, a sewing machine, and hanging above a steel-framed bed a lovingly tapestried portrait of Lenin. Yuri was awaiting my response with the proud but wary expression of someone showing off a consignment of black-market tobacco. It was the museum's most popular exhibit, he said. 'The old people like to come here, and just sit.'

The road north to Okha was flanked by dead firs rising from black swamps. On both sides, the taiga – more larch and spruce here, less birch – extended self-similar to the Sea of Okhotsk on our right and the Tatar Strait on our left. 'Fucking *bullshit*!' Mikhail growled when the road turned rough; 'Fucking *excellent*!' when the tarmac resumed.

Without preamble, he lit a cigarette and told me that his son, aged thirty— and made a *noosed* gesture. Hanged himself, last year. The son of his first marriage. 'Life is hard,' I found myself saying, and he glanced over at me and sniffed. On the flesh of his left thumb was a shark tattoo for his home city, Vladivostok (too cold for sharks off Sakhalin). As we moved further north, the hills were fewer and the mud turned to sand.

———

In Okha – 'Oh-*ha*' – brown bears abounded: in reception (the town has a single hotel for visiting oilmen) was a family of three, like Goldilocks's hosts: Mummy in a bead necklace and Daddy clutching the Russian flag; in the museum nearby, a nine-footer, paws upraised and maw agape, as if beseeching its killer to hold fire. And not only the stuffed kind, real ones: in the woods and around the lagoons, on the logging roads and the oil installations. And as the rivers have been polluted and emptied of salmon, and the forests clear-felled, hunger has made them bold – entering a village to eat someone's mastiff, digging up potatoes from a farmer's field. They had even been seen on the ski slopes above Yuzhno, more than 300 miles south. It was not, I was told, a place where you went hiking alone, and why would you, anyway – go hiking alone?

Shternberg describes the event that lay at the centre of the Nivkh year, the winter bear festival, as 'about the brightest moment[s] in Gilyak life'. An animal caught as a cub is lovingly milk-fed, cosseted and fattened in its pen over several years, until the day comes for its slaughter and consumption by the clan and its guests. In the museum in Yuzhno I had lingered over a miniature mock-up of one such event, meticulous as an architect's maquette: the beloved bear tethered and bleeding out over the course of hours, the people of the village standing and kneeling around it in awe and supplication (and what was perhaps most remarkable, the whole thing – which at first glance appeared to be carved from mahogany – was sculpted, by an unnamed and presumably hungry Alexandrovsk convict, from nothing but bread dough). 'The sacrificial bear, well fed and honoured, will be a daily defender of his clansmen,' Shternberg explains.

When he hiked, sledded and sailed down the north-eastern coast during his second expedition in the summer of 1891, Okha was largely unpopulated, oil having only recently been discovered by prospectors. The town's name comes from the Nivkh 'bad water'. A deer herder comes upon the place one winter, his deer and dogs weak from thirst, but finds the water curdling up from the mires reeking and, where it puddles, filmy and rainbowed. His animals will not touch it and, forcing himself to drink it, he sickens. 'Okha' was a place where life was unsustainable, where the bounty of the world was spoiled.

Today there are some 21,000 people living in the town, almost all of them making a living from oil, directly or indirectly. Outside a single-room English-language school called 'Hakuna Matata', I was persuaded to have my photo taken with its fourteen pupils, the bright children of Exxon's Russian and Ukrainian management, boys

in Reebok hoodies and girls in gingham shirts, all of them immacu-
lately polite. In the town square, under the statue of Lenin, shelves
of bulldozed snow were being corroded by the rain. On each corner:
a woman rubbing her hands against the wind, with bunches of wild
spring onions laid out before her. Okha's ugliness wasn't that of impov-
erishment or neglect or insularity – as well as Hakuna Matata there
was an American-style bistro selling tagliatelle, the indoor market was
busy and the main street had recently been pedestrianised. Ugly was
simply the word that applied to its air of temporariness: nowhere else
on Sakhalin – a far wilder island than the one I called home – had I felt
so viscerally the tenuousness of our lease over nature. At any moment
oil would start belching up from the toilets. The city would awaken to
find bears had trooped out of the forests to avenge their stuffed kinfolk.

———

Among the infractions that will get you sacked by Exxon Neftegas,
Aleksandra told me, are drunkenness and feeding the bears. She was
a 'community co-ordinator' with Exxon, the region's largest employer. What did a community co-ordinator do? She ensured that the
company knew what people were thinking about the company, she
said, good or bad. It was not clear what the company thought about
the people, but it didn't seem that Exxon's dominance of the town,
the region, the island, was questioned. Without oil, Okha would not
exist; without Exxon there would be no employment. The remaining Nivkh communities, scattered about the north, were reliant on
Exxon's grants, even if Aleksandra, who had a degree, was exceptional
among Nivkh people in being employed directly by the company.
Most Nivkh people were insufficiently qualified, she said, even for
the lowliest jobs; but while corruption was endemic (the word 'corruption' caused people to laugh with a sort of agonised delight), there

was no question of racism. It was as if the concept had no translation here; and yet, plainly, the Nivkh communities lived in greater material deprivation than their non-Nivkh neighbours. When Boris Yeltsin, the then president, visited the village of Rybnovsk in 1990, he stepped down from his helicopter, looked around and addressed the murmuring crowd: 'What a nightmare! Do you seriously live here? Places like this make me ashamed to be Russian.'

Aleksandra wore her silver hair cropped short and her spectacles on a string. Her customary expression was a playful smile, the smile of someone who recognised that she was, basically, fortunate. She invited me to come to her home village, Nekrasovka, which lay amid the larch forest fifteen miles to the north-west, on the edge of a giant lagoon. When I met her at her office in Okha at 4 p.m. she was waiting in a gleaming Land Cruiser beside a young man who turned out to be her driver.

A mile west of Okha, on the edge of a Rosneft oil field, Aleksandra had the driver stop beside a power station painted red, white and blue. The denuded hillside was populated by hundreds of nodding pumpjacks, sucking oil out of the earth. I stepped in a puddle slinky with oil, and on the air was the high reek of hydrocarbons. Bad water. A stream had been diverted along raised wooden channels to cool the power station, and where it emerged foamed a sulphurous yellow.

'When I was a child, men fished from this river,' said Aleksandra, who had grown up nearby. 'Now: oil and dust.'

Nekrasovka, half an hour later, was a grid of sandy streets lined with modern housing compounds. As well as being a 'co-ordinator', it turned out, Aleksandra had for sixteen years been a correspondent on Sakhalin's Nivkh-language newspaper, *Nivkh Dif,* and it was in the paper's office (office-cum-anthropology-museum, one room lined with glass cabinets containing salmon-skin tunics and a century-old birch-bark bassinet) that we sat and drank tea, and ate jam and bread and the

201

Nivkh delicacy *mos*, a lardlike aspic of sweetened seal fat and fish skin studded with berries. There had been vestigial ice in the lagoon when we passed, but the afternoon air was warm and through the open windows came the sounds of a dog barking and children shouting.

Aleksandra had grown up in a village outside Okha, a village with only two Nivkh families among 'Tatars' and Ukrainians. Her grandparents spoke fluent Nivkh, and relatives of theirs knew no other language, not even Russian. It was only when she was seventeen, as a student in St Petersburg, that she happened to hear one of her professors speaking the language, and realised, with a start, that she not only recognised his words but somehow understood them, having believed the language lost to her.

'The old life? The old life is gone. This generation knows nothing about Nivkh culture. It is natural. They grew up with the Internet. Only old people speak Nivkh. The young speak only Russian.' But there was empowerment in nostalgia. 'The Soviet era was much better than now. We got free education. We could travel anywhere. We could get a job. Nowadays even with an education you cannot get a job. We can't afford to go anywhere. We try to save money to visit the sanatorium when we are sick; the government will not help.' The customary laugh. As for tomorrow, 'The river is running, everything is changing; policies change, life changes. There is no way to go back.'

For Nivkh poeple it was not the dispersal of their communities that heralded the demise of their language but, on the contrary, collectivisation. A scattered, semi-nomadic population was forced into sedentariness and exile. 'It was very difficult for us,' said Aleksandra. 'After the Soviet era we tried to return, but we had become used to infrastructure, movies, shops, communications. We could no longer live on fish and berries alone.' The past was gone, the homeland was gone; words were vanishing like mist off water. I was reminded of New Caledonia: one people's displacement instigated another's, and on and on in chain reaction: exile begat exile, albeit for the islands' indigenous peoples there was never any possibility of restoration. The old places were synonymous with the past, and as irretrievable.

———

In 1894, when Tsar Nicholas II came to the throne, a decree was issued curtailing the sentences of many political exiles by a third. For some reason Shternberg was excluded, perhaps because of his reputation as a troublemaker. It wasn't until May 1897, just seventeen months short of completing his original ten-year sentence, that he was finally allowed to go home.

What, exactly, had been his achievement on Sakhalin, besides (inadvertently) demonstrating the value of long-term ethnographical field study? As well as recording Nivkh myths and gathering a large body of data about Nivkh religion and language, his most important ethnological feat was to describe the people's notoriously labyrinthine systems of kin relations. In short, he believed that all members of Nivkh society fell strictly into 'wife-giving' lineages and 'wife-taking' lineages, with any man of a given lineage having rights of sexual access to women of his own generation in the wife-giving lineage, including his wife's sisters; and any woman being entitled to the same, *mutatis mutandis*. Furthermore, Nivkh people married only *outside* their own lineage, but *within* an alliance of three given clans. According to Lewis and Engels's taxonomy, therefore, Nivkh society was a living example of 'savagery'. As Shternberg wrote to Krol, 'I have found a kinship terminology and clan system just like that of the Iroquois and Punalua family of the Sandwich Islands [which Morgan had described]; in a word, remains of the marriage form Morgan based his theory on.'

In *The Social Organisation of the Gilyak*, he is more specific: 'The Gilyak system of kinship and marriage fully corroborates Morgan's fundamental hypothesis' – but more than that, 'what in Morgan's case was mere speculation based on terms of relationship, we find fully realised among the Gilyaks'. Shternberg's course was set (the Nivkhi's too), even if he came to realise that terms of kinship among Nivkh people were neither as methodical as he had assumed nor as straightforwardly reflective of reality. 'I took them all for pure-blooded aristocrats,' he admitted later.

If Shternberg had been inspired by his discovery of Engels's description of group marriage, then Engels was no less excited to read, in an October 1892 edition of the newspaper *Russkiye Vedomosti*, Shternberg's first field report from Sakhalin, describing, as Engels put it, 'the right of sexual intercourse between a number of men and a number of women . . . expressly affirmed to be in full force'. As Shternberg wrote, 'When a Gilyak applies the term "wives" to a group of women, they are wives to him in the full sense of the word. When a Gilyak calls a well-known group of men "fathers" they are indeed men who have rights of sexual access to his mother.'

For Engels it corroborated what he had written in *The Origin of the Family, Private Property and the State*, and all that Lewis Henry Morgan had maintained – not only that 'group marriage' was a constant among 'primitive peoples at approximately the same stage of development', supporting the Marxist theory of social evolution, but that it was a crucial element of a 'primitive communism' in which all 'property' was held in common.

Capitalism was inherently monogamous and patrilineal, in Engels's view (and by extension Marx's), because only a system that enshrined female sexual fidelity allowed a father to be confident of his heirs' paternity. 'Democracy in government, brotherhood in society, equality in rights and privileges, and universal education,' writes Engels, 'foreshadow the next higher plane of society.' His final sentence is italicised: '*It will be a revival, in a higher form, of the liberty, equality and fraternity of the ancient gens.*' (Gens being a group of people related through a female ancestor.)

Though he was suspicious of Marxism, Shternberg found his work recruited to the Soviet cause. The Nivkhi themselves, meanwhile, as true 'savages', were cast as proof that communism, communism alone, was humanity's natural state.

———

Over the next two days, as a succession of trains took me back to Yuzhno-Sakhalinsk for my flight to Moscow, I received several WhatsApp messages. The first was from Evgeni, the friendly engineer from the *Sakhalin-8*: 'What book do you create in Russia?' He had been doing more googling. It was a good question, but I didn't reply, partly because of the nature of the message that followed, and partly because I hadn't yet worked out an answer. What I would say now is: 'A book about home.' And if I were to try to explain what I meant by 'home', I might give the Zulu definition: the place where your ancestors are buried.

The second message was from my father. It contained no words at all, just emojis, of flags, black flags:

🏴 🏴 🏴

But when I replied – 'All okay?' – I received no answer, until the next night, in my train bunk again, another of those distressing semaphores arrived from 5,000 miles away:

🏴 🏴 🏴

I cannot bring myself to scroll back to those black flags, but I think of them now as the sails of a ship, or a convoy of ships, moving steadily along a horizon.

III

The Black Flag
Louise Michel

If our understanding of home deepens when we leave, it deepens again when we go back. It's unclear that Louise Michel was eager to return to France. For some exiles, repatriation, when it finally comes, can feel like re-exile, and she seems to have been largely immune to what Johannes Hofer called 'grief for the lost charm of the native land', even if she missed her ailing mother and continued to nurse memories of her childhood idyll of Vroncourt.

In theory, after all, there is no such thing as exile for an anarchist. Peter Kropotkin's 1910 definition remains canonical: 'True progress', he maintains, requires 'free federation from the simple to the compound, in lieu of the present hierarchy from the centre to the periphery.'

Exile forged Michel into a global citizen. Her country became the whole world. Abandoning any notion of centre and periphery, government and governed, home and exile, she returned to Europe and embarked on a life of radical mobility. France, Belgium, Holland, Algeria, London. Political frontiers had always been affronts to her.

'I recognise no borders,' she wrote in her memoirs – that refusal was part of the threat she represented. 'People recognise homelands only to make them a foyer for war,' she told the tribunal after the Commune; and likewise: 'People recognise borders only to make them an object of intrigue. We have a much larger definition of homeland and family: there are our crimes.'

Borders recognised *her*: the United States, which she longed to visit, refused her a visa, and ultimately she would become an exile again, not as a *déportée* but as an *émigrée*.

———

She stopped off in Australia, first Sydney then Melbourne, before boarding a mail barque operated by the Pacific Steam Navigation Company, the *John Elder*. She smuggled aboard five devoted companions, her oldest cats from New Caledonia crammed into a parrot cage. They somehow survived the voyage, spending the 'whole crossing attached like ornaments to the shelf that formed my bed. They never cried out, and were satisfied with fussing over me sadly.'

Nine years before Lev Shternberg passed through the Suez Canal on his way to Sakhalin, Louise Michel looked out from its waters with similar awe, inspired, as Shternberg would be, by the 'endless expanse of the desert'. Among her fellow passengers was an elderly man, an 'amnestied Arab', one of hundreds of Algerians deported to New Caledonia following the uprising against French colonial rule of 1870–1. Since the invasion of Algeria in 1830, French 'pacification' had killed an estimated 825,000 Algerians by 1875, with hundreds more transported to French Guiana and New Caledonia. Freedom came too late for the old man, Michel recalled, for he died at sea.

The *John Elder* arrived in the English Channel on 7 November 1880, some five months after Michel had left New Caledonia, only to spend eight days fogbound and unable to dock. 'The siren wailed constantly,' as they waited there at the mouth of the estuary. 'It was like a dream' – *On eût dit un rêve* – just like her outbound voyage, seven years earlier, aboard that 'dream frigate' the *Virginie*.

As I travelled home from New Caledonia, first to Sydney, then to Singapore, then London, I began to feel that if Michel registered any feeling of absolute freedom in her adult life, it was during those world-crossing transitions, when she was beholden to nobody and untethered from duty as from land. But that week at the mouth of the Thames – that blinded week must have been near intolerable, like being stuck on a plane long after it has touched down. For while she might have been immune to *l'amour du clocher*, she had received word, just before leaving New Caledonia, that her mother, Marianne, was ill, dying even. (Her ageing cats, too, huddling in her bunk against the fog, must have wondered what had happened to their fragrant, sun-dappled lives.)

If that fog, when it dispersed, was a dream-vapour, it was also a curtain lifting on her life's next act. She was fifty years old. I am guilty of viewing her whole life through the prism of her exile, it's true: as if she were no more than a factory item conveyed through a powder-coating unit, her subsequent years indelibly coloured by those six. After-exile was every bit as eventful as before-exile, albeit she left Europe again only once. Her remaining life had its own fulcrums. But if I do tend to see hers as a life of three parts, like this book – I, II, III – it is partly because she herself was inclined to see it that way. It was not so much that she was pining for the time before New Caledonia, but rather that part of her always felt the appeal of that perfect forest, with its lianas and banyans and 'phosphorescent' niaoulis.

When the *John Elder* finally entered the Thames, more than 10,000 miles from New Caledonia, it was greeted by fishing boats containing several of her comrades from the Commune, who were among London's many political exiles from across Europe. Before disembarking, she distributed the five cats temporarily among friends she had made on board, each of whom stepped onto dry land with one squirming under their coat. Those cats. Living souvenirs of New Caledonia, they seemed to be immortal (several were still thriving when she wrote her memoirs six years later). 'Once in London, in front of a fire, with an enormous bowl of milk my friends brought them, they began to stretch out, yawning.' They went with her from London to Paris, where they were intermittently abandoned to the care of her ailing mother. 'I may be used to the smell,' Marianne would complain, 'but the servants aren't so long-suffering.'

'Please,' Michel replied, 'don't let anyone lose my New Caledonian cats.' She adds protectively: 'Let anybody laugh who wants to; they are something alive left from home.'

What did she mean, 'home'?

———

She didn't linger long in London. The next decade would be a period of grief and dissatisfaction for Michel; she seems to have sought some sort of stability, anchoring, only to have to accept that those things were not available to her; she immersed herself in duty, wishing to honour the losses of the Commune – her personal losses, too.

The French State liked to view its penal colonies as institutions of reform, where the savages of the Commune could be civilised through labour and the purifying influence of nature; but even supposing deportation could 'cure' murderers and rapists, exile has seldom had a moderating effect on radicals, and Michel returned from the Forest of the West with a revived sense of mission. She who had once wanted merely to replace the government now demanded nothing less than its abolition.

At Saint-Lazare station, Paris, she was welcomed by a crowd of 20,000, the Red Virgin, homecoming Martyr of the Commune, among whom were several of her old companions-in-exile, including 'the great escapee', as Louis-José Barbançon had called him: Henri Rochefort, who had also returned to France following the amnesty. A confounding figure, Rochefort, in many ways: a strident opponent of authority; a lifelong equivocator; a defender of human freedom; an unashamed anti-Semite. What did he, with his devil's goatee, believe in – other than his own right to influence events? 'I am always instinctively suspicious', he wrote, 'of people who like to dwell on either their loyalty or their patriotism.' In his youth he was involved in what seems like almost weekly duels with those he had defamed in his newspapers or who he believed had defamed him in theirs. (A curious habit for a man averse to the sight of blood and lacking in the martial arts: he took at least one bullet and once managed to stab his own second in the knee.) Rochefort was also perhaps the only figure, other than her mother, to cause Michel herself to equivocate: the man who was her lifelong financial backer and editor, and her valued confidant, had not only been slow to support the Commune back in 1871, but later, from 1895 onwards, was among the fiercest accusers of Alfred Dreyfus, in a case that exposed a deep current of anti-Semitism that ran through French society. Michel's political allies loathed him. And yet how could she disavow her friend who had sent her sweet poems aboard the *Virginie*, who had supported her and her mother, supported them still? She wasn't used to compromise.

On seeing her 'Louisette' after seven years, her mother rallied. Michel walked the boulevards of Paris for the first time since 1871, when the culverts were clogged with blood and the air choked with lime. Over the next two years she established a regimen she would maintain for the rest of her life: near-daily public speaking and campaigning coupled with a literary output – poems, novels, journalism, a memoir – that was extraordinary for its abundance and range. To critique the regime was not enough; only by giving her body up to the cause could she feel her life was being properly spent. This tendency was of a part with her indulgence of the principle of political violence. She would renounce her freedom again and again, as if to be at liberty had ceased to mean anything to her.

In January 1882, her skin resuming its European pallor, she was arrested for insulting a police officer: 'I have already claimed responsibility for much more serious things,' she told the judge. She was sentenced to fifteen days in Saint-Lazare prison, a stretch that hardly inconvenienced her. But beginning in March 1883, less than two years after her return from New Caledonia, a series of events took place that would bring her closer to despair, even breakdown, than either the massacres of Satori twelve years earlier or her banishment to the other side of the planet.

Early that month, the Syndicat des Menuisiers – the carpenters' union – convened a demonstration on the Esplanade des Invalides near Napoleon's tomb (his remains had been brought back from St Helena in 1840). Michel led some 14,000 men and women demanding social reform and employment. She warned the crowd: 'Don't let yourselves be swept away like sheep to a slaughterhouse . . . We are going to march through Paris together, asking for work and bread.'

As the march proceeded along rue des Canettes, two things happened: first, someone passed her a black rag fastened to a stick, the black flag of anarchism, which – dressed in black herself – she wielded for the duration of the march. La Vierge Rouge (the Red Virgin) became la Vierge Noire (the Black Virgin).

Second, the crowd passed a bakery: 'Bread or work!' they roared – 'If you are hungry, take some,' said Michel, 'but do not harm the bakers.'

The bakery was ransacked, then another, before the march was forcibly dispersed by the police.

When the streets had been cleared and the window-glass swept up, an order was issued for the arrest of Mme Michel for inciting trespass and looting.

Fugitive as ever, she'd vanished.

———

When she failed to give a scheduled speech the next day, a police hunt ensued across France and beyond the country's borders. How far could she have travelled in twenty-four hours? A description was distributed:

Abundant black hair
Long nose
Thick lips
High colouring
Large mouth
Black clothing [her lifelong attire]
Hat frequently pushed back from her face

The female Communards had always been deemed traitors to their sex as well as to the republic. It is striking how her physical appearance preoccupied her contemporaries. Her 'mannishness', which her supporters saw as a sign of her integrity, was another mark of 'her rebellious nature' for her enemies.

Rumours: she had been spotted in Saint-Etienne – or, no, Liancourt; she was in Brussels, she was in Switzerland; London? She was seen, bold as brass, on the Bastille–Saint-Ouen tram *and* at the station buffet in Pontarlier. She was on route to Montceau-les-Mines to address the miners; to Lyon for a meeting of the Commission for the Distribution of Relief to the Families of Political Prisoners. 'Others saw me at a pleasure party in the Bois de Boulogne,' she wrote later, 'where I wasn't either.'

A military surgeon who'd known her in New Caledonia, and would recognise her anywhere, swore he had glimpsed her near Neuchâtel – where she wasn't either. For two weeks, now, she had been on the run. 'By virtue of what special privilege does Louise Michel escape being called to account?' demanded *Le Parlement*. Nor was the police's hunt over. Wherever she was, Michel remained at liberty.

Where she was, it turned out, was where she had been since 9 March: 26 rue Censier, the Paris home of Ernest Vaughan, editor of Rochefort's newspaper *L'Intransigeant*. Barely two miles from the Boulevard des Invalides, and in easy reach of her mother, whom she had been visiting regularly, dressed as a man (that 'mannishness' had advantages). Finally she and Vaughan entered the police prefecture: she was at the prefect's disposal, she said; but fearful of being humiliated, he sent her away, despatching agents to follow her and instead arrest her at his discretion. Next day she paid a final visit to her mother before allowing herself to be taken into custody.

More important to her than extending her liberty had been embarrassing her persecutors. She was taken to prison, familiar Saint-Lazare, where she had spent two weeks fifteen months earlier, to be welcomed back by the prisoners and the institution's presiding nuns alike. As a 'first-class miscreant' she had her own room, and was allowed to receive visitors, and even let out under guard to visit Marianne, who was somehow protected from knowledge of her arrest.

If Michel's years on the Ducos Peninsula had made her fearless of confinement, perhaps that brief stop-off in Egypt, on the way back, had also left its mark: 'Prison', she wrote, 'is like the desert. It is the same sensation, whether you are in space where the eye can discern no outer limits or in a tiny enclosure turned in upon itself: the infinite is all-enveloping.' Her monastic streak saved her more than once.

The trial would take place on 21 June. Rochefort sent a lawyer to prepare her, but Michel would speak for herself, just as she had addressed the Council of War in person after the Commune.

The judge: 'Do you take part in every demonstration that occurs?'

Michel: 'Unfortunately, yes. I am always on the side of the wretched.'

It was not long before they came to the question of the black flag. 'Black flags', the judge noted, 'do not drop miraculously into one's hands on the Esplanade des Invalides.'

'All you need to find is a broomstick and a black rag.'

What then was her purpose in crossing Paris with such an item?

'The black flag is the flag of strikes and the flag of famine.' When a flag was shown to her from the table of exhibits, she duly confirmed it was the one she had carried on 9 March.

The judge moved on to the ransacking of the bakeries. Why did she stop in front of the Bouchés' shop? She had not. And what about the Augereau bakery, was it not the case that she had waved her flag to signal her followers to loot the premises? She conceded it was possible that she had moved the flag *involuntarily*; how any such motion was interpreted by the 'children' responsible for the looting was not her concern.

———

What is being done here is a political proceeding. It isn't we who are being prosecuted, but the anarchist party through us.

What is surprising to you, what is appalling you, is that a woman is daring to defend herself. People aren't accustomed to seeing a woman who dares to think.

I've criss-crossed Europe saying that I do not recognise borders, that all humanity has the right to the heritage of humanity.

When we are told that we are enemies of the Republic, we have only one answer: We founded it upon 35,000 of our corpses. That is how we defended the Republic.

———

She expected to be imprisoned, but her sentence when it came – six years' solitary confinement followed by ten years under police surveillance – was a shock. For some, the severity of the punishment was welcome: 'We have wearied of this ostentatious virginity,' wrote *Le National*, 'these displays of fishwife emotions, these appeals to hatred, which, in the name of brotherhood, set one citizen against another.' 'We kill poisonous snakes,' wrote *Le Figaro*, 'we don't leave panthers to roam at will. Moreover, we amnestied the Communards: just see where that has landed us!' The 'savages' of 1871 had returned from the antipodes more savage than ever.

Others viewed the sentence as 'vengeance, not justice', but time and again, from both sides, came the head-shaking assertion that plagued Michel's every deed: the woman should be regarded as insane more than criminal; her proper place was not Mazas prison but Charenton asylum.

In the event, she was sent first back to her home-from-home, Saint-Lazare, and then to Clermont prison in the Massif Central. Just as she had given away her clothes aboard the *Virginie*, she donated her every possession to her fellow prisoners, so that Rochefort when he visited had to stand over her to see she ate the biscuits he'd brought – 'to keep her from dying quite literally of starvation'.

The former castle of Clermont was not the Forest of the West, and six years there was very different from a two-week sojourn with the kind sisters at Saint-Lazare. 'How many prisons!' She counted them off: Satory, Auberive, Numbo, the Bay of the Ladies, Saint-Lazare, now Clermont (to say nothing of the *Virginie*) . . . But something had changed. The infinitude she had perceived during her previous stints had shrunk to stifling darkness. 'Captivity is suddenly more terrifying than ever . . . the walls seem to be gradually contracting, the ceiling to be gradually lowering.'

Her anxiety was compounded by her concern for her mother, who had greeted her after seven long years, only to see her taken away from her again. 'I think you could have served me and others much better,' wrote Marianne, 'had you become a great stage actress . . . I detest that revolution and everything associated with it. Were it not for that, you would still be at my side.' The truth, as Michel knew, was that she was dying. She wrote to the minister of the interior pleading to be allowed to complete her sentence in Paris, so that her mother could 'experience happiness while she is alive and not after she is dead'. She went so far as to propose a deal: 'In exchange for a release or transfer to another prison, just so it be in Paris near my mother, I will go to New Caledonia when she is no longer with us.' She repeated the offer in a subsequent letter, with intensified excitement. The truth was that to be returned to New Caledonia – 'home' – at least once Marianne was dead, would have been no wrench for Michel. On the contrary. She was tired – tired of prison, tired of France. Six days after the first letter her mother wrote to her, urging her not to be troubled, and assuring her that she was 'not getting any worse'. 'I'm sending you some silk thread for your needlework,' she went on. 'Make me the view of the sea I talked to you about.'

Finally, when it was clear that Marianne was gravely ill, Michel was granted leave to visit her in her Paris apartment. So agitated did she become on seeing the reality of her mother's coming death that she suffered a recurring hallucination – a hearse at the door, returning night after night like a black dustcart, ready to remove Marianne even while she was breathing. More than once she had to be restrained by the attending policemen, who seem to have treated her with kindness. On the morning of 3 January 1885 Marianne Michel died. She was buried in Levallois-Perret cemetery two days later, mother of the great Louise, heroine of the barricades, her cortège followed by a crowd of more than 10,000, among them Michel's comrades from the Commune and New Caledonia. But Michel did not complain when she herself was returned to Saint-Lazare and placed on suicide watch, weeping constantly, according to the prison doctor. Even in the depths of Bloody Week, even as her friends were dragged away and shot, one after another, on the plains of Satori: not one tear. Motherless, she felt herself adrift in time, but with none of the sense of possibility she had experienced aboard the *Virginie*. The walls were closing in, the ceiling was crushing her.

——

Her suffering was not merely the self-accounting that is bereavement's usual accompaniment – I should have been more explicit in expressing my love; why did I go away when time was so short? Even her most loyal friends wouldn't have pretended there was no more she could have done to make her mother's life easier. She had turned down the chance to leave New Caledonia and return to Paris *eight months* before the general amnesty. What would those eight months have meant to Marianne? Nor had she been under any obligation to lead the Les Invalides demonstration, or to wave her black flag, when the outcome was hardly unforeseeable. Time and again, ever since she had left Vroncourt, Michel had considered the options thrown up by her politics, and time and again she had come down on the side of her mother's loneliness. The pain of absorbing that truth was nearly intolerable to her.

As before, her friends and supporters campaigned for her pardon, and as before, she insisted she should serve her full sentence. 'Please leave me alone, in my prison cell' – or better yet, return her to exile. Send her back, damn it!

Eight days after the funeral, she wrote to the minister of the interior with a suggestion she had made before: 'I haven't the heroism required to stay in France now that my mother is dead. I am indebted to you for my time with her at the end: I could cancel that debt by running a school for the tribes of New Caledonia . . . I ask you to send me on one of the first boats available.' It is the only one of Michel's letters that makes me pity her. It is as if the words are echoing up, barely audible, from the depths of a cave system in which she is lost.

The minister was not minded to oblige, and she distracted herself by working on her memoirs (they end, aptly, with Marianne's death). In September she was interviewed by Paul Lafargue, Marx's son-in-law, for the journal *Le Socialiste*. She had found a happiness in prison she had never known in freedom, she claimed. She was following the Populist movement in Russia, and had been learning Russian and improving her English. 'Don't feel sorry for me,' she insisted. 'I am really much more liberated than people who are out there walking around under the open sky.' She had felt the same way aboard the *Virginie* more than a decade earlier, she said – liberated in her bondage. 'My being was never so strongly moved by the spectacle of nature as when I sailed on the sombre immensity of the ocean.'

When on 8 January 1886 the president of the Republic yielded to public disquiet and pardoned her, she was livid: *'I declare once again I shall not leave this place until everyone does.'* The same thing she had said when offered early amnesty in New Caledonia. But there was something desperate about her refusal, petulant. She would not go.

She simply refused. The authorities who had spent three weeks trying to apprehend her after the Invalides march were at a loss. 'Extreme urgency,' wrote the minister of the interior to the prison governor, 'liberate Louise Michel immediately.' By force, if necessary. Finally – 'This is turning into a farce' – she surrendered. 'But understand this: I do not consider myself pardoned.'

———

Having finally dragged herself away from Saint-Lazare, she returned immediately to her work. Public speaking, journalism, anarchist meetings. The eye of a storm is a tranquil place to be. But she was furious, sick of her 'friends' and their 'false tenderness', and blamed Rochefort above all for her premature release – Rochefort who in his efforts to have her freed had resorted to claiming she was mad. Interviewed by *Le Figaro*, in her modest sitting room with its walnut piano and tattered trunks, the newly freed Michel told them she would continue to fight for the 'happiness of humanity' – but no longer from France. Where, then? Well, naturally she favoured New Caledonia, the only true home she had known since Vroncourt.

On 12 August she was arrested, again, this time for fomenting unrest, and sentenced to four months in prison, only to be acquitted at a retrial. Then on 22 January 1888, she made a trip to Le Havre, addressing a packed Théâtre de la Gaîté.

The so-called government, she explained, was nothing but a band of thieves, irredeemably corrupt. 'Society must be reborn, and we'd like to see that accomplished through peace and hard work, not bloodshed. But if the bourgeoisie doesn't want to make the Revolution with us, then we'll make it against them.' The threat of violence was ever implicit – she more than most had seen that a desire for peaceful change seldom survives an encounter with reality's fusillades.

Three hours later she was speaking again, this time at the Salle de l'Élysée, to a crowd of 1,500. Near the stage was standing a young man dressed in black like the speaker. A Breton warehouse worker named Pierre Lucas, he had heard her speak earlier at the Théâtre de la Gaîté. He was an easily upset person, but he must have taken care to keep alive his upset over the course of those three or four intervening hours. Coffee, a stranger's kind word, a child's overheard laugh – murderousness is easily derailed.

He came up behind Michel, fifteen hundred pairs of eyes suddenly on him. Stammered out: 'I am not a thief and I am not a murderer. I'm a Breton.' And with that, he made the sign of the cross and shot the 'Red Virgin' in the head, twice.

Lucas was bundled off stage, and attention turned to his victim – who appeared shaken but unharmed. No, no, she insisted, the shots were blanks! She was fine. Fine!

They were not blanks. One bullet had missed, the other had penetrated her mastoid bone behind her left ear.

Two doctors were summoned; both failed to remove the object. 'You could hear steel scraping against bone,' according to Rochefort, to whom she presented the second bullet as a gift (he himself had been wounded by a bullet back in his duelling days). For her part she would not, of course, be making a police complaint against her would-be assassin – a madman to be pitied, very evidently – and boarded the early train to Paris with his bullet still lodged in her head. Could she feel its cool hardness there, I wonder, behind her left ear, as the train rattled towards the rising sun?

For the rest of her life she carried the bullet in her head, a little memento of the death she might have had. As for Lucas, her attitude towards him was as extraordinary as her attitude towards that bullet. It did not occur to her for a second to regard him with anything but pity – but more than pity, respect. It was as if she admired him for attempting to murder her, and would have admired him still more, so to speak, had he succeeded.

To his wife she wrote with words of reassurance: 'It is impossible that your husband was in full command of his wits when he acted; therefore it is also impossible that he will not be returned to you.' She believed he was probably insane, but if he was a 'fanatic, dedicated to his cause', she told *Le Matin*, 'then he was right to act as he did and I would never reproach him for it'. The public had been taught to hate her, she lamented, 'even children'. Hardly surprisingly, she became ill – fever, severe headache, disturbed vision. The bullet appeared to have worked its way deeper into her head. She took comfort in the company of her cats. Finally the Lucas case came to court. On the one hand, Michel claimed, he was not responsible for his actions; on the other, he had not understood the ideas he was acting upon. He was acquitted.

From the moment she was shot, irrespective of its effect on her health, Michel seems to be hastening towards an end, as if having come closer to death than she had even during Bloody Week, she no longer regarded the prospect of her non-existence with the remotest feeling of reluctance.

———

Later in 1888 she was arrested once more, again for fomenting violence, this time in the run-up to a huge demonstration for working-class solidarity. 'The 1 May demonstration must have a revolutionary character,' she had told a meeting in Vienne. 'It must proclaim the coming of the social revolution.'

The evidence that her violent words had real-life implications, apparently, was the police's discovery that anarchists in Paris had been observed buying up a large number of false beards. She had never been afraid of prison, only of being unduly pardoned, and when she was once again informed that she was to be released, while the 1 May demonstrators were left to languish in their cells, the humiliation was too much for her. What effect, if any, Lucas's bullet, still buried in her head, had on her behaviour cannot be known, but for once she was unable to contain herself: she shrieked herself hoarse and destroyed everything in her cell in Vienne prison – the window, the furniture, everything breakable.

'My anger, the lack of air, the lack of food, these things combined to give me a feeling of vertigo . . . I must have suffered from a cerebral fever, for the hallucinations never stopped,' she reflected later. Was she finally succumbing to the *nostalgie* she had been spared in New Caledonia?

I declare that the said Louise Michel, held in the Vienne detention centre, has been stricken with a persecution mania, which makes her behaviour dangerous both to herself and to those around her, thus necessitating her immediate removal to a special asylum for treatment.

She has constantly complained that her friends have abandoned her, that she is weary of the whole struggle and wants to end her life. This disposition to suicide required her immediate admittance to an asylum for the deranged.

Mlle Louise Michel is presently suffering from auditory hallucinations which provoke her to acts of violence. Her ideas are bizarre and, it seems to me, confused as well, as if precocious senile dementia were present. Her confinement seems necessary.

But on 3 June, just a few days after her arrest, she was informed that she was to be 'discharged'. The government was not in the business of making martyrs. This time she did not resist. Prison was one thing, but 'to be thought mad, and shut up with the truly mad, that terrified me'.

She had been shot and nearly killed; her mother was dead; she felt her enemies outnumbered her allies. She knew the government might at any time use the accusation of madness against her, and that, however sane she felt, long-term incarceration in an asylum might prove self-fulfilling.

For Michel remembered something from that episode in Vienne. Those four days of hallucinations were, she wrote, 'like being transported to another world'. What if, next time, she was unable to chart a course home?

———

And so she fled into her own exile, just as her friend Victor Hugo had in 1851. Having returned to France in 1870, Hugo had died in 1885, weeks after Michel's mother. Whether or not (as his diaries imply) they were ever lovers, Hugo the artist, Hugo the campaigner, Hugo her friend, was a lifelong source of energy and optimism for Michel. 'Victor Hugo Crosses the River of Death and Enters the Dark Valley' read a typical newspaper headline from that week. Michel's grief had by necessity been subsumed into the larger cloud of sorrow. Back on the Ducos Peninsula she had left him a small pre-emptive memorial. 'On an enormous rock that opened its petals of granite like a rose . . . I engraved one of Hugo's poems' – the one that ends, rousingly,

Lazare! Lazare! Lazare!
Lève-toi!

'Lazarus! Lazarus! Lazarus! / Rise up!' Is it there, somewhere, that epitaph, amid the tropical dry forest, smothered under lianas or over-grown by the roots of a banyan tree?

At the end of July 1890 she arrived in London, where many of her fellow Communards had ended up, and took a house on Fitzroy Square. 'Yes, I admit it,' she wrote, 'I love this England, where my banished friends are always welcome.' Henri Rochefort, self-exiled in London once again, had a less rosy view: 'All the Frenchmen one meets there resemble stranded vessels, for not one of them resides in England for his pleasure.' But ever since the revolutions of 1848 and 1849, England, with its liberal asylum regulations, had been Europe's polit-ical refuge – indeed the only place in Europe where political refugees of all stripes could expect to find safe haven. (Michel's detested tyrant himself, Louis-Napoléon, had died, in exile, in Chislehurst in 1873.)

For most of her remaining life, Michel would base herself in vari-ous houses across London, from the 'petite France' of Fitzrovia to East Dulwich to Streatham, making a home of sorts among the city's itinerant anarchists and socialists. Far from being a retirement from political life, her years in London had something of the same fortify-ing effect as her years in New Caledonia.

A year after arriving she was able to open a school, the Internation-al Socialist School, for the children of political refugees, on Fitzroy Street, central London. Despite being supported by leading socialists, including Kropotkin (another London exile) and William Morris, it was fated not to survive. It's unclear who was responsible – prob-ably a provocateur-informer who had infiltrated the project – but within months, police raided the premises and found explosives and bomb-making equipment in the basement (planted, we assume). The find came at the height of anarchist violence on the continent – violence Michel was, as ever, reluctant to disavow. 'In the present revolutionary period each must be ready to give his own life without hesitation and to the take the lives of certain adversaries without remorse.'

While she was spared arrest following the police raid, the school was closed down. Her aspirations for it, as she recalled later, had been idealistic, perhaps, but not overwhelmingly ideological: 'By taking on all these little French, English, German children, and teaching them languages,' she told an interviewer, 'I wanted to enable them to know, and later understand, one another, so that eventually, through the communion of ideas, nations might eventually hate one another less and learn to love one another.'

In November 1892 five Paris policemen were killed by an anarchist bomb. 'So much the better,' she responded. 'It's their fault and it will be their fault as long as workers die . . . as long as bodies litter the ground in colonial wars like Dahomey and Tonkin.' If her contempt for colonialism had been sharpened by her time in New Caledonia and the brutality with which the 'Kanak Insurrection' had been suppressed, then perhaps too had her ruthlessness. And yet Michel's belief in the inevitability of political violence coexisted with an instinctive compassion that was violent in its very intensity. She would have died for her ancient reeking cats, let alone for her political allies. There was something self-obliterating about the universality of her empathy, which she extended to those who wanted her dead no less than those she wanted dead. She would have used the word *love*. It was, in some ways, her life's guiding principle, a principle whose geographical analogue I believe she found in the Forest of the West, but before that in Vroncourt.

The place of her childhood never left her. After Bloody Week 1871, awaiting her fate in Arras prison, she had sent a package to her friend Abbé Folley. It included two drawings, one of a sprig of ivy she had found growing in the prison yard; another of a strange building, a large square hangar with a square tower at each corner, set

S. château de Vroncourt HtE marne

in a meadow surrounded by woodland. On my desk is an old post-card, a sepia photo of the same building: *VRONCOURT – L'ancien Château où naquit en 1833 Louise Michel, femme des lettres et révolu-tionnaire.* (*En* 1830, in fact.) When a would-be biographer, Maurice Barrès, visited in 1907 he found the chateau abandoned and close to collapse, but was moved by its 'dark and sombre beauty'. In Michel's drawing, the towers' pyramid roofs are more steeply pitched, and the angle of projection is flatter, but it might be sketched from life.

———

The intensity of the speaking schedule she set herself was bound to make her ill. But exhaustion or sickness had always been prompts to work harder. Since returning from New Caledonia she had rested only when rest was enforced by prison. In 1904, aged seventy-four, Michel was diagnosed with pneumonia while lecturing in France, and almost died – 'It's as if my body became a bundle of rags, and I looked upon it with no more emotion than if I were looking at anything else.' Her response, later that year, was to plan a final great voyage.

She knew by now she could never return to New Caledonia. Across Europe, the concept of the foreign penal colony was increasingly seen as an anachronism, and penal colonialism – making settlers of con-victs – as unsustainable. The final abolition of Europe's penal colonies the following century went hand in hand with general decolonisation, but as early as 1884, the governor of New Caledonia had begun to, as he put it, 'turn off the dirty-water tap', to allow the country to develop without the regular inundation of new convicts. After 1897, all France's deportees were sent to French Guiana, but it wasn't until 1942, when some 48 per cent of *relégués* in the colony died, that its closure began. The last prisoners were finally repatriated in 1953.

In New Caledonia Michel had met several Algerian deportees, resistance fighters from the great insurrection of 1870–1. In November 1904, soon after the French conquest of Algeria was deemed 'complete', she travelled to the colony on a lecture-tour-cum-fact-finding mission. Did she think of her 'dream frigate', the *Virginie*, as they steamed out of Marseilles? Did she see her grieving mother, long dead, waving? With her was her friend – actually better to say she was *his* friend – the anarchist Ernest Girault, who would go on to write the first biography of *La Bonne Louise* in 1906, as well as a lesser-known travelogue in the French orientalist tradition, *Une Colonie d'Enfer* (*A Colony of Hell*).

Much younger than Michel, having been born in the Commune year of 1871, Girault was appalled by the behaviour of his countrymen towards the Algerians but unable to escape his own racialised disgust. It is hard to speak authoritatively while pinching your nose. Towards his travelling companion his attitude, as they travelled from one speaking engagement to another, was that of an antsy custodian taking a famous old artwork on a tour of provincial museums. On the train to the city of Tizi Ouzou, sick of the younger man's entreaties to 'rest', Michel snapped: 'If I was no longer good for anything, I would let myself die!' Not yet. She does not need to be 'taken care of like a child'.

She is no more than a pale essence in Girault's book. Only briefly does she come alive, when he sends her back into her past.

They are on a train again, looking out at the receding lights of Algiers from the rear observation platform, as they trace the Mediterranean east to give another lecture. The surf is loud enough to overwhelm the clamour of the engine. Is she happy to be here, Girault wonders.

Why, 'we are the happiest people in the world.'

But it is true, is it not, that her experience of foreign places has not always been so happy? He is thinking of those years in the South Pacific.

'I do not regret them,' she says, over the crashing waves. Exile gave her the Forest of the West, after all – she has seen Brazil, Australia, icebergs, niaolis; she has been shown the inherent evil of conquest. Who knew what would have become of her had she been kept in France? 'Many people would gladly give up ten years of their life to make such a journey.' Two weeks after her conversation with Girault, Michel left him in Algeria and boarded the last boat back to Europe.

One Who Has Gone Down

Dinuzulu kaCetshwayo

Nearly a month after leaving St Helena, in January 1898, the *Umbilo* dropped anchor off Durban, Natal, carrying Dinuzulu and his enlarged entourage, including Harriette Colenso, who had gone to the island to ensure the party's smooth departure.

It had been a rough crossing. At first the women had been placed by the purser in the forward, second-class cabins, with the men and children together in first class. Colenso hurriedly rearranged the passengers according to custom, with the men left alone in first class, as the outgoing journey was reversed: first the extended calm days of the South Atlantic; then the explosive tumult of the Cape. 'It was a very interesting voyage,' she reflected, 'but one such may last a person for some time.'

The *Umbilo* once at anchor was visited by the Undersecretary for Native Affairs and a magistrate, and Dinuzulu was handed a document in Zulu and English confirming the incorporation of Zululand and Natal under British governance, with the former a province of the latter. He returned to Zululand as 'government induna', as agreed.

233

The following morning the ship steamed into port and began unloading his belongings – including, according to the undersecretary, 'forty tonnes of furniture . . . five donkeys, ten dogs, some rabbits, fowl pens, a canary, a parrot and a monkey'. The party was hastened from Durban, the authorities being reluctant to permit Dinuzulu a grand homecoming of the sort Louise Michel had enjoyed in Paris eighteen years earlier. Only a fraction of the cargo would fit on the small train that would take them from the port to the railhead at Tongathi, thirty miles north, from where they travelled by wagon to Eshowe, to be 'interviewed' by the commissioner of Natal, Charles Saunders.

A four-day wagon journey, hot and cramped and flyblown. Four of the donkeys shipped over from St Helena died, unaccustomed as they were to the humidity. The party was greeted by heavy rain and floods, which destroyed much of the excess cargo left in Durban. It must have seemed an inauspicious homecoming. Furthermore, as Saunders's foremost 'native executive officer', Dinuzulu was told he must live in the furnished house provided for him in Eshowe, a hundred miles from uSuthu land. His promised 'repatriation' was incomplete. One day Harriette Colenso fell painfully from her horse; then the party, one by one, came down with fever. They did not need to be reminded that Eshowe, scene of Dinuzulu's downfall back in 1889, was festering with *ubuthakathi*, or evil machinations. Ndabuko, Dinuzulu's uncle, retreated to the surrounding forests to seek the aid of a traditional healer. Saunders was finally persuaded that Dinuzulu should be allowed to return to the royal homestead, oSuthu, on the banks of the River Vuna fifty miles north of the site where his childhood oNdini had stood. It was a concession Saunders would come to regret. While in the view of the *Times of Natal*, the 'weary years at St Helena had certainly alienated Cetshwayo's son from his people', Colenso saw no such alienation: 'They are as good at heart, and as united as ever,' she assured her sister; what she called Dinu-zulu's 'civilisation' – his top hats and his swagger stick and his lusty hymn-singing – 'will not be a barrier between him and his father's people'. While the authorities had been able to ensure that his arrival in Durban was low-key, his reception as he made his way to oSuthu – a 'triumphal march', in Colenso's words – must have put him at ease. 'His people – including the Government chiefs – from remote quarters, and in vast numbers, met him all along the route, giving him their allegiance and presenting him with money.'

Dinuzulu understood what the British did not, or could not, or had forgotten: that the closer to his land he was allowed to be, the more powerful he grew. Exile, after all, is not just a bid to detach a people from its leader; it is to detach the leader from his source of vitality. Every mile, every minute, empowered him. To return to the centre, to oSuthu and the burial places of his royal ancestors, was to revive a sovereignty that would have remained inert to him had he resigned himself to those wood-panelled rooms in Eshowe.

Nevertheless, the homeland to which an exile returns can never be the one that was left behind. The years that have elapsed cannot be clawed back. Zululand was shattered into bickering chieftaincies and impoverished by a British hut tax that had driven its men into wage labour, often far from home. During the last year on St Helena, furthermore, Dinuzulu received updates about the infectious viral disease that was killing the country's cattle. The reality of the loss must have filled him with dread. It may be that it was neither war nor partition that truly signalled the end of Zulu independence, but the rinderpest epidemic of 1897–8. Some 160,000 cattle had died by the time he returned, and by June around 80 per cent of the entire Zululand herd. Rinderpest precipitated a wholesale disordering of Zulu society, a sundering from the past. For, just as the cattle byre held the central position within every Zulu homestead, so cattle were at the centre of Zulu society and identity. Almost every exchange was valued in head of cattle, including *ilobolo*, or bride price. Since a homestead's oxen were of one community with its people and its dead, rinderpest was a blight upon the home. Only rarely were the animals slaughtered – in famine or to propitiate the ancestors. But by the time Dinuzulu crossed the threshold of oSuthu and entered the royal enclosure again, there were few cattle in Zululand remaining for meat or milk or sacrifice.

His position seemed impossible: the authority vested in him by the British was, like any granted by a usurping power, no real authority. *Government induna*. What was it supposed to mean? Servant, runner, envoi, go-between, lizard-in-the-sand. Yet to most Zulus he remained king by virtue of his blood, with a king's omniscience and powers, a king's wisdom, and a king's duties.

———

In 1902, despite Britain's earlier promises that 'no sale, transfer or alienation of land' would occur, Zululand was annexed to neighbouring Natal, the best of it, about 4,000 square miles, sold to white farmers, while the remainder, rock-strewn, impenetrable, malarial, was doled out to Zulus in the form of 'reserves for Native locations'. After the Boers' expropriation of 5,000 square miles in 1888 (which in turn would be annexed by Natal following the Boer War), the Zulus were left with only a fraction of the land that had been theirs before Dinuzulu's exile. There would be no compensation; those whose homesteads stood outside the reserves could either remove themselves or consider themselves tenants.

The Boer War, between Britain and the independent Boer republics to the north and west of Zululand, was drawing to its end. Unwilling, for the time being, to antagonise the British, Dinuzulu lent his troops to raids on Boer guerrilla camps. His influence among Zulus was cemented when he re-established a royal homestead, kwaNo-bamba ('stronghold of unity'), in the eMakhosini Valley, where his ancestors were buried, and where he himself expected to be buried, unlike his father, far away in Nkandla. Hungry, exhausted, impoverished by the hut tax, alienated from their land and from their past, Zulus were yearning for leadership; the headmen turned to Dinu-zulu, as they had always turned to their king in times of crisis. But he was but a petty chief, he insisted; powerless. You must speak to Natal.

In 1905 a written fiat circulated anonymously among the homesteads of Natal and Zululand: 'All pigs must be destroyed, as also all white fowls. Every European utensil hitherto used for holding food or eating out of must be discarded and thrown away. Anyone failing to comply will have his homestead struck by a thunderbolt.' Associated solely with Europeans, pigs were, like fish and veal, considered taboo by Zulus. Their destruction was an expression of racial autonomy. According to James Stuart, in an official history of the rebellion published in 1913, the message to Zulus was unambiguous. 'It was proposed to rise simultaneously and massacre the whites.' By the colonial authorities and the chiefs of Natal and Zululand alike it was taken for granted that the instigator of the order, if not its actual author, was Dinuzulu, despite his insistence that he'd had no hand in it.

Later Stuart, who had worked as an intelligence officer for the Natal government during the rebellion, conceded that the order was 'more likely to have sprung from the imagination of some Native obsessed with the idea that the conditions of life under European rule were intolerable than from that of Dinuzulu'. Whoever authored the strange directive, that 'obsession' was near ubiquitous among the indigenous people of south-east Africa. And yet when the British announced a new poll tax the following year (the Boer War had been expensive), they seemed to expect it to be accepted, silently, as if it were passing rain.

An extension of the existing hut tax, the new poll tax obligated each headman in Zululand and Natal to collect £1 per annum from every working-age male in his community. It was a moneymaking scheme, but above all a way of pressing Zulus into wage labour. This in a society where a white man's income was twenty times that of a Black man. Dinuzulu himself paid the tax, and encouraged his followers to pay the tax. As far as the government in Natal was concerned he remained as loyal as he was required to be.

On 7 February 1906 a police sub-inspector was murdered with one of his men. A week later two Zulu men accused of the murders were tried, found guilty and shot. Shortly afterwards a further twenty-four men were arrested and twelve of them sentenced to death for the same crimes. The sentence was stayed by the objections of the government in England, but when the prime minister of Natal resigned in protest, the objection was withdrawn and the killings carried out. According to Magema Fuze, 'As they were about to be put to death, they sang songs and clan chants with great gaiety, like people on their way to a festivity; and when ordered to dig their own graves they did so with contentment, like people happy to die.'

This was the immediate setting for the uprising that followed, which became associated with one man – not Dinuzulu, but a minor chief under his putative authority.

The Bhambatha Rebellion, as it became known, was the culmination of decades of theft and displacement, a bid to recover something of what had been forsaken or snatched away. In late February, Bhambatha, a chief of the Zondi clan, was ordered to report with his men to the magistrate in Greytown, Natal, to pay the poll tax. When they did not appear on the appointed date, another summons was issued, which again received no response. On 9 March, 170 Natal police and a troop of mounted rifles were despatched to bring the rebel in. Bhambatha had fled north, to Zululand.

In late March he arrived at uSuthu, with his wife, who was pregnant, and three children, seeking the protection of his king. But Dinuzulu understood that, were word to reach Natal that he was harbouring a fugitive, the authorities there would have the pretext they needed to arrest him. He was right to be wary. By no means an old man, at thirty-eight, Dinuzulu was by now quite unwell, as he was for most of his life after St Helena, virtually bedridden with what seems to have been some form of oedema, and perhaps the early stages of the nephritis that would be the main cause of his death. 'His feet and legs were swollen, his chest was sore, he had difficulty breathing and was unable to pass water,' according to one of his men. In photos of him during these pathetic years, his colonial uniform appears painfully tight-fitting and in his burdened posture it's hard not to read defeat. He cannot, by now, have had much hope of a good or fitting death. The event of his exile cannot be detached from the final destruction of Zululand. With his removal, a keystone of Zulu society was snatched away, and the edifice was bound to topple.

The stranger Bhambatha was told to return to Natal to summon a famous Zulu doctor to attend to Dinuzulu. His family would be allowed to stay, while Dinuzulu considered his request for asylum. It was, of course, as Bhambatha surely knew, a ruse to get rid of him. Clandestinely he returned to his homestead, Mpanza, to prepare for war, having led his supporters to believe they had Dinuzulu's support. On 4 April a detachment of 146 men once again attempted to find and arrest the fugitive. The following day, in a valley near the Mpanza River Drift, the party was ambushed by Bhambatha's men.

The Britons' horses were shot first and their fallen riders shot as they ran. Fifteen horses, four men. All but one of the dead were recovered by the British and taken back to Greytown. When the remaining body, that of a Sergeant Brown, was found on 8 April, it was with its organs torn out and its genitals mutilated. These were not purely acts of degradation, or designed to sow terror, but customary measures to propitiate the spirit of the dead man, which would otherwise seek vengeance on his killer. Of the 150 Zulus, none had been killed in the skirmish, being as they were – as it seemed to them – impervious to the Englishmen's bullets. But any protection they had been afforded by magic or the intervention of the ancestors was temporary.

In early April Bhambatha with his men and hundreds of Zulus from across Natal converged on the Nkandla Forest, with as many as 1,000 camped around the Bhope Ridge where Cetshwayo was buried. Dinuzulu, meanwhile, monitoring the events from Zululand, assured the Chief Commissioner of his innocence: 'I can only say I am perfectly loyal and most anxious to give proof of this in any way the government may wish,' he pleaded, knowing he faced prison or exile once more, even offering to lead his troops to the Nkandla Forest, 'notwithstanding my state of health', to seize 'this dog Bhambatha'.

His acquiescence comforted Natal, temporarily, but it seems to have been inconceivable to the colonial authorities that he was not, somehow, implicated in the unrest, perhaps because they had come to understand that he remained king in practice if not on paper. In response to intelligence that Bhambatha's men were planning to attack Greytown, a large body of men was sent to Nkandla with orders to burn down homesteads, empty grain pits and seize cattle in an effort to flush out the rebels. In early June a detachment of the Natal Field Artillery took up position above Mome Gorge, where Bhambatha and his troops were discovered to be camped. Exits from the valley were blocked. At dawn on 10 June three pistol shots sounded, the sign for the fusillade to begin. It did not cease for sixteen hours. Maxim machine guns, fifteen-pound mortars; shells, shot, dumdum bullets that expand on impact. No quarter was given, no surrender accepted or prisoners taken. Those attempting to flee were shot. Three British soldiers lost their lives. The number of Zulu deaths according to the British was 600, including Bhambatha, though the true figure was far greater. The official historian of the Natal Mounted Police described the event as a massacre – 'It was not a battle.'

Over the coming month of fighting in Natal and Zululand at least 2,000 Zulus were killed against twenty-four British. The stories of mutilations of British dead, particularly ritual disembowelments, that are ubiquitous in British descriptions of the fighting (as they are too of descriptions of the war of 1879) were echoed in reports of what was done to Bhambatha's corpse. The government in Natal, requiring proof of his death, ordered that his body be brought to the town of Nkandla for identification. One Sergeant Calverley had Bhambatha's young mat-carrier, who had seen his chief killed, lead him to the spot in Mome Gorge. A human body is not easily carried by one man and a child across such steep, rocky and densely vegetated terrain, even on horseback, and less still after it has lain unburied for three days. Calverley, who it seems was of a pragmatic bent, cut off the man's head and packed it into his saddlebag.

Yes, said the chiefs summoned to identify the head, that's him, Bhambatha, no question. But among Zulus it was widely believed that those chiefs knew the head was not his. Having escaped unscathed, so the story went, Bhambatha spent the rest of his life sequestered deep in the Nkandla, or perhaps abroad, in quiet anonymity. His king was to find no such sanctuary.

———

The government in Natal found an ally in Anthony Daniels, Dinuzulu's interpreter and secretary on St Helena, who had been subsequently ejected from oSuthu on charges of stealing and so had cause to resent Dinuzulu. He claimed Dinuzulu had supported the rebellion from the start, that guns had been held illegally at oSuthu, and that numerous rebels, besides Bhambatha, had been given refuge there during the uprising. He added that 'war doctoring' – traditional rituals to protect warriors in battle – had taken place at the royal homestead. Dinuzulu was duly charged with high treason and in early December 1907 ordered to give himself up. At this point Harriette Colenso reappears. As she had before, she urged her friend to surrender; and, as he had before, Dinuzulu complied. On 10 December at Nongoma courthouse he was formally arraigned.

The following day oSuthu was raided. As Dinuzulu's daughter, Princes Magogo, later remembered, 'When the soldiers came ostensibly looking for guns, they ransacked our home and looted nearly everything we had.' No rebels were identified and the few guns recovered were legally held. On 14 December, guarded by the Natal Field Artillery, Dinuzulu was taken from Nongoma to Pietermaritzburg. The preliminary examinations opened on 23 December, but the trial itself, in Greytown, did not begin until the following November. In an echo of his 1889 trial, Dinuzulu was charged on twenty-three counts, including high treason, public violence, sedition, contravening the firearms act of 1905, and incitement to murder.

His first barrister resigned in disgust: evidence in his client's favour had been suppressed and any sympathetic witnesses imprisoned. A 'judicial outrage', he complained, before returning to England. His replacement, W. P. Schreiner, was one of the most respected lawyers in southern Africa. But his own fears about the propriety of the trial were quickly confirmed. Witness statements on behalf of the Crown were riddled with 'exaggeration and falsehood' and there was a 'dense atmosphere of intrigue everywhere'. As the prosecution was closing its case, Schreiner received a letter from his client, full of dread for what was coming: 'My sole crime is that I am the son of Cetshwayo.

I am being killed through ill will, there is nothing that I have done.' He feared, with reason, that he was about to be exiled again. The prospect of being shipped back to St Helena, of having to resume that theatrical, impotent, scrutinised existence, must have seized him with despair.

While all but three of the charges against Dinuzulu were thrown out, he was deemed guilty, for the second time in his life, of high treason, for harbouring Bhambatha and other rebels. 'People must understand that they cannot touch pitch without being defiled,' concluded the judge, before issuing a fine of £100 and a four-year prison sentence. The government in Natal, disgusted by the leniency of the verdict, promptly had the royal homestead, oSuthu, destroyed and the uSuthu people 'abolished' – dispersed among three neighbouring chieftaincies.

The Union of South Africa, in 1910, saw the amalgamation of the Cape Colony, the Transvaal, the Orange River Colony and Natal into a self-governing dominion of Britain. Among the new Cape Town government's first acts was one of clemency. Dinuzulu would be released from prison and relocated, with a small staff, to a remote farm in the Transvaal, about 200 miles north-west of oSuthu.

Colenso remained Dinuzulu's 'walking stick', as she had once been her father's. She was despised by colonial Natal as a troublemaker; but few doubted the trust she enjoyed among Zulu people. 'There is none who, should she but exert her power in that direction, could exercise a more pacifying effect on the native mind,' wrote the *Natal Witness*. Although Schreiner agreed to forgo most of his fee, Colenso was almost ruined by the defence costs. Finally, in 1910, with one of Natal's last legislative acts, the bishops in Pietermaritzburg saw an opportunity to avenge themselves upon the daughter of the heretic John Colenso. Under the new Church Properties Act, the land on which he had built Bishopstowe – Colenso's childhood home, where she and her sister, Agnes, still lived after their mother's death – was reverted to the Church of the Province of Natal. Her appeals were unsuccessful, and she and Agnes were evicted. 'It had been done to spite her,' Natal's Attorney General admitted.

Dinuzulu's uncle Ndabuko had died a decade earlier, in 1900, three years after returning from St Helena. A resident of the island reported that the repatriated Shingana, meanwhile, 'has within a month of returning to his kraal, cast off the cumbersome apparel of civilisation'. Nine years later, for his involvement in the 1906 rebellion, he was banished to Amanzimtoti, on the Natal coast. 'They have killed him at last,' wrote Colenso, who was with him in his last days. She had reason to be sorrowful for more than the lonely death of a friend: by then, all that she had worked for – all her father, 'Sobantu', had worked for – lay in ruins: the Zululand she had known was obliterated, and she could not but share some of Britain's shame. She continued to visit and comfort Dinuzulu in his illness, but his second exile was different from his first. He was no longer the energetic young man with 'clear, bright, quick, keen eyes' he had been in 1890, and they both understood the battle for Zululand was finished. She and Agnes died in 1932, months apart, in a cottage in the hills outside Pietermaritzburg.

———

Dinuzulu's place of exile, a 5,000-acre farm officially called 'Uitkyk', he renamed 'KwaThengisa', an abbreviation of the isiZulu 'kwaThengisangaye': 'the place where he was sold'. For what else had been done to him by those Zulus – Daniels, his St Helena secretary, but others too – who had spoken against him? By those who had not spoken *for* him? He lived there quietly with a small entourage, growing sicker. 'My trouble is like that of no one else,' he wrote to

Schreiner, his advocate. 'It beset me when I was a child and my father was taken by the white people and it is still besetting me . . . what is grievous to me is to be killed and yet alive. To die outright is nothing.'

Death in life – the exile's ubiquitous lament. Not only might he just as well be dead, Ovid complained 2,000 years earlier, but in a real sense his life ended when he left Rome. This feeling of having been 'killed and yet alive', also, surely, conceals a secondary anxiety: that as far as your people are concerned – your compatriots, subjects, children – you are to all intents and purposes deceased. Your letters go increasingly unanswered, your face fades day by day from memory and the words of your praise song grow vague with disuse.

But the *Natal Mercury* was still sending its reporters to see the old king: 'If he is well he will play to you on an English organ – and sing to you in the English language. His favourite air is "Home, Sweet Home". He learnt it when in exile, and will never forget it.' Too neatly sentimental to be credible, surely, the exile exiled once more, the sound of an organ, which he learnt to play on St Helena, cast across the static veldt, and a voice, plaintively,

> An exile from home, splendour dazzles in vain,
> Oh give me my lowly thatched cottage again!
> The birds singing gaily that came at my call
> And gave me the peace of mind dearer than all.

When he died, in October 1913, an obituarist, describing the young Dinuzulu's time on St Helena, conceded he had

> learned to wear European clothing, to speak a very little English, and to play the air of the National Anthem with one finger on the piano. It may be doubted whether he picked up anything else of use during his exile, and probably it would have been better for Dinuzulu and

South Africa if, like a man of very different race and calibre, he had
been allowed to end his days on the island.

Examine the photo of him and his party: twenty-three of them,
gathered on the steps of the house called Maldivia, in Jamestown,
in February 1895 – not very far (but what was?) from the shadowy
residence of that man of 'different race and calibre', Napoleon.

In fact, *photos*, since there are two slightly differing shots to be
found in the archives – in both he stands to the right of the frame,
but in one he is wearing his bowler hat, while in the second he is
holding it in his right hand. Princely vanity, perhaps, but not a mean-
ingless gesture, betraying some of his uncertainty as to who he is, or
who he is becoming, or who he is expected to be. Several other figures, besides his slender and imposing one, are identifiable: Ndabuko
(far left) and Shingana (next to Dinuzulu, with his young son), not-
ably displaying their head rings; the interpreter, Daniels (standing,
with the flat cap), who in due course will betray the slender imposing man; and at the centre, matriarchal, regal, imperious, *imperial*,
Harriette Colenso, who is visiting her friends to discuss her efforts in
England to have them released.

Next to her, on the knee of Dinuzulu's companion uMkasilomo,
sits an infant in a floppy-brimmed straw hat, their son, born on the
island a year earlier. The child's name is Solomon Nkayishana Maphumuzana kaDinuzulu Zulu. Maphumuzana: 'the shelter'; 'giver of
rest'. His praise song will style him 'the honeybird that drinks from
deep pools'. His reign will be little happier than his father's, ending
in corruption and debt. But by the time he died, in 1933 (just a year
after Colenso), King Solomon had recognised something Dinuzulu
did not: that power, in this new era, lay in the hands of politicians,
not kings. It was under Solomon that a renewed notion of Zulu
nationhood, and national autonomy, took root in the form of the

political party of which he was an influential patron, named Inkatha, after the sacred grass coil that represented Zulu unity. Some thirty years later, in a more radical incarnation, the party became a decisive force in the battle against apartheid.

——

Some 4,700 Zulus were imprisoned for involvement in the Bhambatha Rebellion. Twenty-five of the supposed ringleaders, whose physical presence was deemed a threat to civil order in Zululand and Natal, were sentenced to exile. Mauritius in the Indian Ocean was earmarked, but when the government there reported an outbreak of beriberi an alternative island destination was proposed, one that had hosted Zulu exiles before, to say nothing of 6,000 POWs from the Boer War between 1900 and 1902. Several of the Bhambatha rebels died on St Helena before their sentence was curtailed a year later in 1910, the same year Dinuzulu was banished to the Transvaal.

The rulers of the new South African republic borrowed several strategies of population control from Britain, including the removal of political opponents. Under apartheid ('apart-hood'), which became law after the National Party won election in 1948, not only were millions of black Africans forcibly collectivised into 'ethnically homogeneous' Bantustans; thousands of local, mostly rural, leaders who refused to acknowledge apartheid laws were subjected to what was known officially as 'banishment'.

Exile was not simply exile: as in other regimes of banishment, a taxonomy evolved. 'Deportation' designated removal, but no particular place of confinement, and applied on a rolling twelve-month basis; 'endorsement' meant removal for an indefinite period to the subject's 'native' region or Bantustan; 'banishment', the most widely used measure, allowed the governor general to order, without trial, the 'removal of any tribe, or portion thereof, or any Native from any place to any other place or to any province or district within the Union upon such conditions as he may determine'.

Now that the British had relinquished power, banishment was usually to some isolated farm within the republic's borders: the Northern Cape; Pietersburg; the Northern Transvaal; Nkandla . . . A journalist visiting the notorious, isolated 'banishment camp' of Frenchdale, near Mafeking in the Northern Cape (today's Mahikeng), noted that there were 'no children's voices, no yipping dogs, none of the murmuring sounds of daily living: there was not even the faraway background hum of passing cars. Nothing.'

For an unco-operative chief, the mere fact of removal to a place hundreds of miles from his people's graves, where his ancestral authority was not recognised, had the same diminishing effect as imprisonment. This had been proven. Some fled into neighbouring countries, while others died in banishment rather than compromise with the white authorities. Cape Town's one-time quarantine station of Robben Island, where Britain had confined Xhosa chiefs during the Wars of Dispossession of the early nineteenth century, became notorious as a prison for apartheid's most powerful enemies, including Nelson Mandela; but it was no longer necessary to ship anyone to some impoverished rock 2,000 miles away.

Nevertheless, St Helena maintained a certain nostalgic status in British diplomatic circles, and not only among its colonial retirees. In 1917 Sultan Sayyid Khalid bin Barghash Al Busaid was sent there following the Anglo-Zanzibar War (another British war of succession). Thirty years later, under the Colonial Prisoners Removal Act, a group of anticolonial activists known as the Bahraini Three was exiled to the island for five years at the request of the ruler of that other British protectorate, Shaykh Salman bin Hamad Al Khalifa. (I'd been shown the Bahrainis' graffiti on the walls of the old battery high above Jamestown. *The quick brown fox jumps over the lazy dog.*)

St Helena's reputation as a dumping ground endures. A few years ago the executive director of an American think tank, writing in the *Washington Post*, nominated it for what he called a 'retirement home for exiled dictators'. He had in mind Ivory Coast's Gbagbo and Libya's Gaddafi, who could live out their days, he imagined, in the island's sparsely populated Blue Hills district. St Helenians, who have never been inclined to see their home as a mere penal colony, a New Caledonia or a Sakhalin, responded with the same scorn they accorded an 1894 proposal from Natal that it send them its 'kaffir stock thieves'.

Sakhalin Fever

Lev Shternberg

Towards the end of his life, having moved for his health to the Black Sea resort of Yalta, Anton Chekhov was asked why he had been reluctant, in later years, to talk about his time on Sakhalin. He paced up and down, as was his habit, and went to a window, perhaps gazed over those inhospitable waters. Finally he spoke: 'Afterwards, everything was *Sakhalinised*, through and through . . .'

Shternberg, who was there for far longer, and under duress, was more deeply Sakhalinised – a sort of frostbite of the soul – and yet of the exiles I have described none was more elevated by the experience. On Sakhalin he discovered his vocation. It's hard to imagine his life unfolding as it did, furthermore, with all its drama and even glory, had he not been exiled *within* exile, to that exposed headland on the Tatar Strait, with its tall white dead grass, its berms of snow, its 'thick fog' – its 'nothing'. If his birthplace, Zhitomir, was the first of his life's poles, then Viakhtu, site of his 'ethnographic baptism', was the second. (My own short time there – an hour, dog-bitten, wet through – endures in my memory with a glow I usually associate with places I love.)

After his release in 1897 he was to return to the 'god-forsaken isolation' of Zhitomir, nowhere else. That was a stipulation of his amnesty – he'd be watched. He had corresponded widely from his exile, he had kept up with the news. Two years earlier he had been given leave to mount an expedition to the Amur River delta. So it was not as if he had been entirely cut off from the world since 1889. But the Amur was still within the geographical realm of exile. Now he was going *back* – not exactly to the Russian heartland (Zhitomir remained within the Pale of Settlement), but to the centre he knew best, and co-ordinates he could call 'home'.

———

Russian ethnography was founded in exile. Shternberg was not the only Populist to carry out seminal ethnographic studies during his confinement in the Russian east. Few of them had been scientists prior to their exile. Among the new generation was Shternberg's People's Will associate and friend Vladimir Bogoraz. Arrested a year after Shternberg, Bogoraz spent his exile, nearly ten years, on the Kolyma river, studying the Chukchi people. The resulting book, a massive volume published after he returned to St Petersburg in 1898, was a landmark in Russian ethnography, and made his reputation. Like Shternberg he did not come home an obedient citizen. In 1905 he was imprisoned for two months for involvement with the Central Bureau of the Farmers' Union; and in 1911 placed in solitary confinement for nine months for the same criminal association. Under a subsequent, far more draconian cycle of deportations, many of the students Shternberg taught in St Petersburg would find themselves forced into the 'field' as deportees.

Shternberg enjoyed no homecoming parade, but someone was pleased to see him. His childhood friend Moisei Krol was the first familiar face he saw after leaving Sakhalin, having received news of his amnesty on 8 May 1897, seventeen months short of completing his original sentence, and long after many of his fellow Sakhalin convicts – those who had survived – had been allowed to leave. The journey back to Ukraine and his family, overland this time, was slow, evidently, because it was November before he reached the city of Irkutsk in south-central Russia. Krol, who had been released in 1895, had returned to the Transbaikal region of his exile, as part of a commission investigating the prospects of agriculture in the region. In his memoirs he describes how he visited Irkutsk on the northern shore of Lake Baikal during a break from his research, only to find that his old friend Lev was passing through on his way back to Zhitomir. Another chance reunion, following their meeting in the political wing of Odessa Central Prison in 1888.

Writing in a newsletter for former political exiles in 1929, Krol suggests the pair felt nothing but optimism for the future when they met again. Their suffering had been fruitful: 'weathered by Siberian frosts and blizzards', they were 'tempered by life's hardships, enriched with new knowledge and strengthened physically and morally'. Was this rehabilitation? Had proscription achieved the authorities' aim of 'curing' dissidents of their dissent? As for his bony, bearded, twitching friend: 'His idealism, so full of enthusiasm, became even deeper, his imagination became even richer, and his faith in humankind and its bright future even more passionate.'

A former revolutionary like Krol would have been cautious in his choice of words, in 1929. But it does seem that Shternberg returned from Sakhalin with a renewed sense of mission, with his energies hardly depleted, even if his excitement about the future was moderated by a sort of chilly fatalism. An old friend who met him in Paris in 1924, after years of separation, noted that he 'was full of the same idealism, the same belief in the power of the human spirit . . . he viewed the events of the present as only a passing moment'.

Soon after returning to Zhitomir he met Sarra Ratner, the brilliant, shy, Jewish director of a women's college, with whom he would spend the rest of his life. Whatever sort of man she had fallen in love with, he was not drained of all hope, like some of his fellow exiles. He was able, evidently, to envision a future. To have lived through exile, when many of his friends had not, reinforced his faith, perhaps even revived it, and he would devote much of the rest of his life to promoting and defending Jewish culture in Russia. The Jews, he believed, were fundamentally a scattered tribe; that was their identity: Zionism was participation in one's own negation. Jewish tradition was the engine of unity: 'Thanks to it,' he wrote, 'the concept of one humankind, which must eventually become a brotherly union, has firmly established itself in the minds and hearts of civilised people.'

In Zhitomir he sought permission to move to St Petersburg, aided by his friends and fellow former exile-ethnographers, including Krol. In 1899, their petitioning succeeded and Shternberg moved to the city, at first lodging with Krol, to write up his research on the Nivkhi. His permit would need to be renewed every three months; but so be it: he was immunised against the humiliations of bureaucracy. After Sarra joined him, he was appointed as senior ethnographer and lecturer at the Museum of Anthropology and Ethnography, largely on the strength of his published papers on Nivkh kinship systems. In freedom, such as it was, he resumed his loves of swimming and cycling, spending summers with Sarra in their dacha outside St Petersburg. A new century. To travel, in the course of five years, from the abject abandonment of Viakhtu – the wind, the icy spume, the dogs – to a marital bed in the capital, and professional esteem. Didn't he have reason to be idealistic?

———

On a snowy day in January 1905, a little over five years after his return to St Petersburg, Shternberg joined some 150,000 striking workers marching to the Winter Palace to demand improved working conditions. He remained, essentially, a Populist, becoming associated with the new Socialist Revolutionary Party, which he saw as the natural successor of Narodnaia Volya. Perhaps scenting danger, perhaps fearing for his career should news of his involvement reach the authorities, Shternberg peeled off before the protestors reached their destination, where 459 of them were killed by soldiers and mounted Cossacks. The Bloody Sunday massacre, as it became known, repulsed much of Russia. 'I cannot think of anything equal to this in the annals of the French Revolution,' Shternberg wrote afterwards.

In early April he was invited to visit America by his friend Franz Boas, the great German-born anthropologist, whom he had first met a year earlier at a conference in Stuttgart. Although it was not published until after his death, *The Social Organisation of the Gilyak*, which Boas commissioned, would become one of the founding works of Russian ethnography. His homeland, meanwhile, was in crisis. At least 400 Jews were murdered in pogroms during his absence, including twenty-nine in his hometown of Zhitomir – where his elderly parents and his sister, Shpritsa, were still living. If Shternberg never entirely rejected political violence himself – despite later supporting political factions that were opposed to terrorism – it was partly because of what his family underwent that spring.

In the days before the attacks, a rumour had been spread that local Jews had used a portrait of the Tsar for target practice. The pogrom was an echo of the anti-Semitic violence that followed the assassination of Aleksander II in 1881. News that Zhitomir's police superintendent had been assassinated prompted a stand-off between the city's Jews and anti-Semitic rioters, who wrongly blamed Jews for the killing, followed by attacks against Jewish property and persons across the city. The focus of the violence was the city's Cathedral Square and the Podol, the poor Jewish district on the banks of the Kamenka. The wealthier streets around Starovilskaya, where the Shternbergs lived, were largely spared. His sister attributed their safety to the effectiveness of the city's Jewish resistance. Krol went to visit them afterwards on behalf of their anxious son, and his parents duly telegrammed him in New York to assure him they were unharmed.

But on the way back to Russia, having stopped off to inspect some Sakhalin artefacts in Vienna's ethnography museum, Shternberg received a telegram. His mother was dead. A 'breakdown' precipitating heart failure. It must have been apparent to him that she was as much a victim of the pogrom as the young man in the Podol, dragged from a bus and clubbed to death.

———

He might be allowed to leave Sakhalin, leave Zhitomir, but he knew there would always be those who deemed him less than wholly Russian. In 1908, the same year he was appointed director of St Petersburg's Jewish Museum, Shternberg was caught up in what became known as the Zhuravskii Affair. Among those who supplied the Museum of Anthropology and Ethnology was a private collector and trustee of the museum named Andrei Zhuravskii, who had founded a research station in Pechora, northern Russia, where he had collected ethnographical items from the region's Nenets and Komi people. His disagreement with the Academy of Sciences, which oversaw the museum, stemmed from the organisation's reneging on an agreement to fund the station, which he claimed resulted in its closure. A series of critical articles he wrote for the right-wing press was taken up by the notoriously anti-Semitic columnist Mikhail Men'shikov, and by the museum's former assistant curator, Bruno Adler, a professional rival of Shternberg's, who told Zhuravskii that artefacts he, Zhuravskii, had supplied to the museum – some of which had been given to him on condition they be retained within the museum – had been sold to a wealthy dealer (a Jew, needless to say), who in turn had sold them on or exchanged them on the museum's behalf for items from other collections.

Zhuravskii publicly accused Shternberg and the museum's director, Radlov, of having benefited financially from the arrangement, and in a letter published in Men'shikov's nationalist newspaper, *Novoe Vremia*, attributed the misappropriations to there being a majority of Jews among the museum's small curatorial staff. Meanwhile Zhuravskii himself, he stressed, was not only a lifelong advocate of the 'ideals of Russian science' but ethnically Russian – unlike 'Khaim-Leib' Shternberg, as he insisted on calling the chief curator, who had been known only as Lev since he graduated from cheder.

In a series of letters to the Academy of Sciences, Shternberg and Radlov rebutted each of Adler's accusations in detail, and finally, in 1911, both were exonerated in a court of arbitration. After two years Shternberg emerged with his professional reputation intact, but he continued to be attacked by both Zhuravskii and his supporters in the nationalist press: the episode must have acted as a reminder, were it needed, that for all his professional success he remained, in the minds of many, an outsider. In a letter to Boas in March 1911, he described the episode as his '*affaire* Dreyfus'. Like Dreyfus, who had been deported for life to French Guiana in 1895, Shternberg had been falsely accused; and like Dreyfus he had been vindicated.

———

Among the main activities of the Museum of Anthropology and Ethnography was staging expeditions, of which the most significant for

Shternberg took place in 1910. After more than ten years, as he was approaching his fiftieth year, he was commissioned by the Academy of Sciences to go back. To return to north-Pacific dusk light, to the scents of larch and snowmelt, to the dawn silhouette of mountains he had seen every day for 3,000 lonely days . . . Perhaps he did not think twice about it, but the expedition came with considerable psychic risks. He had never been ambivalent about his place of exile, as Louise Michel had been about hers (nostalgic, even), despite recognising its significance in his life. He would no more willingly return there for good than chain himself to a wheelbarrow, like the wretched *tachechniki*, and throw away the key.

In mid-May his party crossed Russia on the Trans-Siberian Railway, which had been opened six years earlier, arriving in Vladivostok after two weeks. Just two weeks! They spent the summer navigating the lagoons and tributaries of the lower Amur river on the Siberian mainland, researching the kinship and marriage practices of the region's Nanai people, before finally, in early September, crossing the Tatar Strait.

As they left the mouth of the Amur, their boat was grounded on a sandbank; when they finally reached Alexandrovsk they found that unprecedented spring rainstorms had washed away bridges and roads. Shternberg might have remembered the Nivkh god of thunder, who lives beneath the Tatar Strait. 'And so I am back on Sakhalin,' he wrote to Sarra. 'A great sadness has overcome me. Memories have filled me. Everything here reminds me of the past.'

He stayed for less than three weeks, his anthropological work confined to conversations with a Nivkh man he knew from the 1890s. He seems to have spent those weeks in a state of fearfulness. He made no significant 'discoveries', but perhaps his return to the island should be seen more in the nature of an experiment; a pilgrimage to his own past, and, like every pilgrimage, partly a bid to verify the reality of the place. He did not visit Viakhtu – too much, too far, especially in the season of snowmelt – but in Alexandrovsk he met some of those exiles who had been excluded from the amnesty, and stood over the graves of others. Among Alexandrovsk's visitors only Chekhov was more renowned, and Shternberg was greeted by the island's governor general and all of Alexandrovsk 'society'; but a homecoming it was not. He was frequently doubled over from a stomach ulcer (it would get worse); the rain was unrelenting, the roads indistinguishable from streams. He had 'only one desire', he wrote to Sarra, in faraway St Petersburg – 'to get away from Sakhalin as fast as possible'. Perhaps returning had awakened a pain he had hitherto been able to suppress, like those dark waters rising from the bogs.

The publication of Chekhov's *Sakhalin Island* in 1893 had intensified public disquiet about the Siberian exile system, which was seen as both morally retrograde and ineffective as a tool of settlement. After all, how could any place develop as part of the motherland while continuing to be inundated, year after year, with a new generation of outcasts? It was a fundamental flaw in the system of penal colonialism, one that also complicated French efforts to turn New Caledonia into a functioning overseas territory rather than merely a warring prison island. But while elsewhere in the world the era of penal colonialism was drawing to an end, Siberia was shortly to enter a monstrous new phase in its history as a place of banishment.

With the opening of the Trans-Siberian Railway in 1904, Siberia was no longer the inaccessible Ultima Thule of Russian household mythology, nor was the journey there – which had always constituted a large element of exile's horror – the annihilating marathon it had once been. In 1899 Nicholas II established a commission that limited the use of Siberia as a realm of mass quarantine for common criminals, reserving it for the most serious political cases. With the

1905 revolution, this changed. Whereas in Shternberg's time political exiles in Siberia had numbered in the hundreds, in the early twentieth century exile became not just a weapon against sedition, but a tool of social engineering. But while mass exile quelled the immediate unrest, it created a vast exclave of discontent, and there a new revolution was nurtured.

When Nicholas II was executed following the revolution of 1917, Shternberg the former Populist was hardly sorry – how many years had he devoted to the tsars' overthrow? How many of his friends had died for that cause? – but following the Bolshevik coup that autumn, he would see his own work at the Museum of Anthropology and Ethnography subjected to intensified political scrutiny. In the spring of 1921, when martial law was declared following an uprising of anti-Soviet sailors at Kronstadt, Shternberg was arrested – for the last time – for being a member of the proscribed Socialist Revolutionary Party. It took a week for his colleagues' petitions for his release to succeed. Not a long stretch, then, but nor was Shternberg young, or in good health (he was about to turn sixty and his stomach ulcer had been exacerbated by the city's food shortages). Those days and nights in the 'House of Preliminary Confinement' must have revived memories of Odessa Central Prison more than thirty years earlier.

After 1917 Shternberg continued to combine his work at the Museum of Anthropology and Ethnography with teaching at the Geography Institute and Petrograd Imperial University. He left a deep impression on his students: a stammerer with a facial tic, mouthing haltingly through his black beard while holding an index card up to his glasses. Shternberg's most concise professional and moral statement was his 'Ten Commandments of the Ethnographer', which he shared with each year's cohort. Alongside enjoinders that 'ethnography is the crown of the social sciences' and warnings against 'falsification', plagiarism, drawing 'quick conclusions' and 'bearing false witness', his students were instructed not to 'force your own culture onto those you study' and to treat the society under examination 'with love and attention, no matter what stage of culture' it had attained. That way, 'it will aspire to rise to the level of a higher culture'.

Just as Shternberg remained an unreconstructed evolutionist, like many Russian socialists he remained a supporter, in principle, of Russian imperialism in the far east, at the same time as maintaining that, eventually, 'humanity would become a single brotherly union of cultural and mutual equality and cooperation'.

His students loved this 'thin old man, who seemed to be charred by some internal burning'. Not Sakhalinised: charred, and burning still.

———

As an exercise in penal colonialism, Sakhalin was by now regarded as a failure; as a school of criminal reform it was disastrous, with brutality, extrajudicial murder, squalor and sexual slavery endemic, as Chekhov's book had revealed. After 1894, when 'settled exiles' were allowed to leave, there had been an exodus to the mainland. Since the Russo-Japanese War of 1905, the southern half of the island, below the fiftieth parallel, had been under Japanese control, and Sakhalin had ceased to be 'the final destination of the unshot'. The penal colony had finally been officially closed the following year, with thousands of former convicts simply shipped across the Tatar Strait and dumped on the opposite shore to make their own way 'home', wherever that might be. Sakhalin had become an inconvenience, and its indigenous inhabitants a potential fifth column. In the 1930s as many as a third of all Nivkh men on the island were killed by the NKVD, predecessor of the KGB and FSB, usually on suspicion of spying for Japan. During a secret 1934 campaign, 'the Islanders Affair', the NKVD arrested and shot 115 people from twenty-two North Sakhalin villages, including forty members of indigenous clans. It was enough, in those days, to own a Japanese watch or spectacles, or to be found with a sweet wrapper bearing Japanese characters. People hurriedly buried or burnt silk dresses. One NKVD report of an operation in the village of Grigor'evka describes the 'result of repressive measures undertaken against counterrevolutionary and rebel elements among peoples of the North in 1937–1938': 'Approximately 36 per cent of the adult population was removed, composed mainly of Nivkhi and Evenki [another indigenous group] from forty to sixty years of age, while the remaining 64 per cent expressed their understanding and support for measures undertaken by the Soviet government.'

It was at this time that prisoners including Nivkhi deemed disloyal were put to work building the disastrous tunnel between the mainland and Pogibi. 'When winter comes,' according to a Nivkh story recorded in the 1920s, 'lightning sinks to the bottom of the Tatar Strait, just to the north of Cape Pogibi . . . Lightning lives there like a blind man, not seeing anything.' It is not known exactly how many of the thousands of workers were killed when the tunnel breached the wall of an underground lake.

———

'Each person's life', Shternberg once wrote to a friend, 'should be like a work of literature, regardless of whether it has been completed or not. Thus, it can break off at any moment but still represent a story that is instructive, beautiful, and rich in content.'

He had never been able to bring himself to abandon Morgan and Engels's theory of social evolution – from savagery to barbarism to civilisation – even after it was almost universally discredited, for it was the foundation of his belief in the unity of humankind, innate in both his politics and his Judaism. A tenet of evolutionism, in his conception, was the abandonment of religion; and yet humankind had evolved so far, he maintained, only thanks to the teachings of the prophets.

His legacy to Russian ethnography was not widely recognised until after Stalin's death: he had established the practice of long-term ethnographic fieldwork; he had turned the Museum of Anthropology and Ethnography into one of the world's great ethnographic collections; he had transformed ethnographic education in Russia and inspired a generation of Russian ethnographers. It was perhaps for the best that he did not live to witness the ensuing decades. As Stalinisation hardened, many of his students were exiled to Siberia or shot. His colleague and friend Vladimir Bogoraz escaped persecution by compromising a lifetime's ethnographic work to fit Marxist ideology, dying in 1936. In 1918 Moisei Krol, Shternberg's old friend from Zhitomir, fled Russia for China and then France, where he died in 1942. Sarra Ratner-Shternberg, herself an eminent ethnographer, having battled for years to publicise her husband's work, died from starvation, in 1941, during the siege of Leningrad.

Lev Shternberg's gravestone in St Petersburg's Preobrazhenskoye Jewish Cemetery is crowned with a black marble globe surmounting the epitaph he lived by: 'All Humanity is One'. One of his students, Yurii Kreinovich, heard of his death while carrying out fieldwork on Sakhalin, thirty-six years after Shternberg was there: 'Sleep peacefully, dear *ityk*,' he wrote, using the Nivkh word for father. 'After all, one has to fall asleep some day and find rest from the life of the terrible Sakhalin.' Kreinovich, who himself would be exiled to Kolyma in Siberia ten years later, had already learnt Chekhov's lesson, that certain places, once inhabited, inhabit you in turn.

Epilogue
On Homesickness

These island journeys allowed me to understand that when we are removed from all we know, our greatest hope of orienting ourselves is to look inwards. What we find there, and how we use it, may determine the course of the rest of our life. But as the past draws the memory, so the horizon draws the eye. It can be hard to hold yourself together when your life has been split in two. Long before Shternberg sailed from Sakhalin, the Roman poet Ovid, looking out at the same Black Sea the *Petersburg* crossed, didn't cease to hope he would see the Tiber again, even while in his heart he feared he would die 'unmourned, unhonoured, in a barbarian land'. 'See that my bones / are brought home in a little urn,' he beseeched his wife, 'then I'll not remain exiled / even in death.'

In the winter of AD 17, eight years after leaving Rome, he was buried, as he had feared, beside the Black Sea. He had never been able to admit that Tomis was anything but a cultureless void, without springtime or birdsong or orchards. And yet, reading his poems, you sense that, despite himself, despite his longing, he became acclimatised, even reconciled, to his new domicile: 'I thought to find nothing that pleased me in this Scythian region,' he writes in the *Black Sea Letters*, 'but now the place seems less odious than before'. In the end he seems to have warmed to his hosts, 'ever loyal and hospitable', and, as his native Latin left him, he allowed their language, Getic, to take its place.

It was perhaps natural that, of the forty-plus languages spoken in New Caledonia, Louise Michel the universalist was drawn to Bislama, an Anglo-Melanesian creole: *une langue universelle*. When she returned from Algeria to France in December 1904, energised by Algeria's 'awakening races' and the revolution she anticipated in Russia, her health was deteriorating daily. On 5 January 1905, two weeks before the Bloody Sunday massacre in St Petersburg, she checked into the Hôtel de l'Oasis, Marseilles, after speaking at a series of rallies in the city. Consistent that she, of all people, should die – pneumonia exacerbated by exhaustion – in an unfamiliar room in a nondescript hotel in a city she scarcely knew. When, the previous year, she had almost died of the same condition, she was able to recall a sensation of 'merging with the elements'. It was, she wrote, 'as if infinite love itself became an all-encompassing sense'.

In 2020, when Europe's governments had all but abandoned their duty of care to the stranger, a French naval vessel was bought by activists and refitted as a search-and-rescue boat to assist refugees attempting to cross the Mediterranean from North Africa. The boat was christened the *Louise Michel*. All her life she maintained a commitment to the principle of asylum, that justice and hospitality are indivisible – not, I think, out of a belief that the world is our common home, but, conversely, because she understood that we are *all* strangers. Her dream, following the failure of her school in London, had been to establish a *maison des proscrits*, 'a large refuge-house offering shelter to all exiles'. 'It is to London', she wrote, 'that all those forsaken and exiled by their homelands run for shelter. They find freedom there – but most of them, alas, cannot enjoy it, having nothing to eat.' She had a plot of land in mind; the residents would build greenhouses and practise intensive agriculture (was she thinking of her beloved Chateau Vroncourt, with its stampedes of feral animals, or perhaps her garden on the Ducos Peninsula, her papayas and goats?). 'This international refuge will be open to all those who have been banished or proscribed, for whatever reason. It will operate under the protection of England.'

It was never to be built – the money could not be found – but it remained an aspiration: an ideal co-operative, a House of Outcasts.

By then, the form of exile undergone by Michel, Dinuzulu and Shternberg – political deportation to an imperial outpost – was increasingly seen as outmoded. Between France's first deportations to French Guiana in 1852 and the penal colony's closure a century later, the French empire transported around 100,000 of its subjects to and between its various colonies, including Algeria and New Caledonia. The number of people forcibly expatriated, in one form or another, by the British empire was about 376,000, including the 160,000 who were transported to Australia, and the 6,000 Boer POWs sent to St Helena after the Anglo-Boer War. Under the Russian empire, meanwhile, Lev Shternberg was among nearly two million people sent to Siberia and the Russian far east – a number, it should be said, that was dwarfed during the Soviet period, when as many as twenty-five million were exiled to the same region.

While 'imperial exile' is virtually unheard of today, the idea of the penal colony endures – most conspicuously in America's extrajudicial military prison in Guantanamo Bay, Cuba, where captives from the wars in Iraq and Afghanistan languish after nearly two decades. If penal colonialism contracted alongside empire, the urge to insulate the metropole against 'undesirable' elements of course persists. Most vulnerable, always, are those whose belonging can be questioned. As

I write, a year after the MV *Louise Michel* put to sea, the British government is reported to be planning an 'offshore processing hub' for people seeking asylum, located not in St Helena or any of its other remaining dependencies, but 4,000 miles away in the former German colony of Rwanda.

So if what I feel is a sort of 'nostalgia', it is for a country that has gone, one seen by the world's – or at least Europe's – *proscrits* as a safe harbour; and for a capital city to which those escaping war or revolution could flee without expectation of being sent back or confined to a 'detention centre' or 'offshore processing hub'. From 1823 to the introduction of the Aliens Act of 1905, a period when revolutions were sweeping across Europe, Britain neither refused entry to, nor expelled, a single foreigner, however menacing their political affiliation; it is hard to believe, but not one. As Michel put it, England 'has managed to retain from its sombre past the old virtue of hospitality, of which we have as much need today as ever'.

'The break in my own destiny afforded me a syncopal kick that I would not have missed for worlds,' claimed Vladimir Nabokov, most famous of modern exile-writers, whose family fled Russia after the revolution. And true, had Ovid not been 'relegated', his *Black Sea Letters* and *Tristia* would not exist to console generations of exiles after him. But so be it, he might have said; those were minor works. Instead mourn the glories my exile denied you. Nabokov's 'syncopal kick' can be utterly debilitating, and only someone who has never read a newspaper, or a history book, could believe that the 'barbarian soil' Ovid described was more fertile than that of Rome.

Exile has more often been a collective plight than an individual one. Picture those mountains of life jackets and rucksacks: few exiles are alone in their loneliness. Conquest, after all, is never just a sabre charge or a ship packed with ore; it is a depopulated valley, empty grain pits, embers dimming in an untended hearth. You move these people because coalmines will not dig themselves; these because they'd sooner die, evidently, than live peacefully under you; these because they are a stain upon the very soil; these to keep your expeditionary forces from being ambushed. To be at *home*, you understand, is any people's greatest source of strength. They will die for it, and naturally they will kill for it.

The Zululand Dinuzulu kaCetshwayo was removed from in 1889 was not merely altered by the time he returned, but obliterated, and in a sense he himself with it. When he died, at KwaThengisa, on 18 October 1913, twenty-five years after his first exile, his ailments included gout, nephritis, a haemorrhage and, according to a eulogy, a 'broken heart'. He was not old, but this second exile was irrecoverable. 'The sickness carried him away in great distress,' wrote his friend from St Helena days, Magema Fuze. He was returned to Zululand, at last, to be buried in the eMakhosini Valley, alongside his grandfather, his great-grandfather, and the nation's founding chiefs.

Fourteen years later, a student who visited Lev Shternberg at his dacha in the hills outside St Petersburg, where he and Sarra had retired, detected no failure of the old man's energies: 'Look!' he exclaimed, narrowing his eyes at the setting sun. 'Now look at this pine!' – trees, as the Nivkhi understood, mediate between the world above and the world below.

In August 1927, sixty-six years after he was born, thirty-seven years after he arrived on Sakhalin, thirty years after he left, Lev Shternberg, having lost the power of speech, lifted a finger and moved it through the air to spell:

Я умираю

I'm dying.

A century before Michel's exile, the French Revolutionary politician Jean-Baptiste Carrier invented what he called *déportation verticale*: fettered criminals were loaded onto boats, but rather than being sent to French Guiana were simply drowned, one by one, in the Loire.

But if death is exile, it's unclear to me, now, which party is the exiled one: the person who has died or those left behind. At the end of May, just after I received those dread black-flag emojis from my father, I passed through the Sakhalin oil town of Nogliki on my way back to Yuzhno. Shternberg came this way in 1892, to meet the infamous 'Black Gilyaks', who turned out to be models of hospitality. (Black, in Nivkh terms, is associated with good fortune, while white is the colour of funeral attire.)

If 'oil town' makes Nogliki sound booming, it was not – just a place where the offshore platforms were the main employer. Viewed from the road bridge, the River Tym, which had just thawed, was a stew of timber, whole tree trunks turning silently in the current. The body of the river was ochre with sediment sluiced off the mountains; but a tributary was leaking into it the black water of the bogs. And the black was somehow cleaner than the ochre, the black of an eye's pupil. I was reminded that an old Japanese name for Sakhalin translates as 'Island of the Black River'.

By 1940 the once busy coast, with its dozens of traditional fishing settlements, was all but deserted. Ruins upon ruins. First former convicts had hounded Nivkhi from the best fishing places, then smallpox had almost wiped them out. The first phases of mass resettlement occurred in the 1930s as a result of collectivisation into kolkhozes, collective farms; this was followed in the 1960s with 'centralisation' – the concentration of regional kolkhozes into yet larger agricultural centres. In 1962 the island still had more than 1,000 settlements; by 1986 the number had been reduced to 329.

In Nivkh, 'land', 'homeland' and the island itself are known by a single word: *myf*. Three miles outside Nogliki, on the edge of a vast dark lagoon, two young Nivkh men were feeding a bonfire with sheets of damp plywood. Warming herself by the fire was their mother, Angela. She wore a banana-yellow puffer jacket and large blue-framed glasses. Her family had been living in this quiet corner of the world since before 'the world' existed – before collectivisation, before centralisation, before the arrival of the first settlers from Russia. They were unusual in having returned, rarer in having stayed. The clearing contained a large single-storey timber house, patched with wood, and adjoining lean-tos daubed in pitch, for firewood and fishing tackle. A track sloped through the retarded larches typical of this thin soil – they looked like striplings but were maybe fifty years old – to a seaweed-matted beach cluttered with upturned wooden boats and nets past mending. There was no phone signal, no gas or power. On the horizon, like a contrail, was the mile-long spit that sheltered the lagoon from the swell of the Sea of Okhotsk and, for salmon, made it a refuge from grey whales.

'If there is no fish there is no life,' said Angela. 'You catch fish or you get ill. For our people it is a genetic need.' The bonfire smoke plumed and dissipated scentlessly.

I remembered the condition Chekhov called *febris sachalinensis*, 'Sakhalin fever', a malady peculiar to Sakhalin exiles, which resembled in its symptoms – 'vagueness', headaches and rheumatic pain – the *nostalgie* of the Communards in New Caledonia.

I'd stopped here by chance but it was as if Angela had been expecting me. She was unsurprised by my questions, incurious; she spoke flatly, as if mouthing truths whose sting she had neutralised many years ago. 'We can dance like real Nivkhi, we can sing and catch fish

271

like real Nivkhi. But we have lost the language. A nation without a language is not a nation.'

The peacefulness was that of a very old place settling still deeper into itself. The quiet was intensified, somehow, by a sandpiper's flight call.

The soul is immortal, it abandons the body in the form of a bird.

'We have a house in Nogliki, but we cannot live there. It's better to stay here, where it's cold.'

And the sandpiper's call breaks off, leaving only silence.

Bibliography

Anderson, Clare (ed.), *A Global History of Convicts and Penal Colonies* (London: Bloomsbury, 2018)

Applebaum, Anne, *Gulag: A History* (London: Allen Lane, 2003)

Azzam, A. R., *The Other Exile: The Remarkable Story of Fernão Lopez, the Island of St Helena and a Paradise Lost* (London: Icon, 2017)

Badat, Saleem, *The Forgotten People: Political Banishment Under Apartheid* (Johannesburg: Jacana, 2012)

Bantman, Constance, 'Louise Michel's London Years: A Political Reassessment (1890–1905)', in *Women's History Review*, 26:6, p. 1003

———, *The French Anarchists in London, 1880–1914: Exile and Transnationalism in the First Globalisation* (Liverpool, Liverpool University Press, 2013)

Beer, Daniel, *The House of the Dead: Siberian Exile Under the Tsars* (London: Allen Lane, 2016)

Bensa, Alban and Wittersheim, Eric, 'Jean Guiart and New Caledonia: A Drama of Misrepresentation', *The Journal of Pacific History*, vol. 33, no. 2 (September 1998)

Bell, Bowyer, *Assassin: Theory and Practice of Political Violence* (London: Routledge, 2005)

Berglund, Axel-Ivar, *Zulu Thought-Patterns and Symbolism* (London: Hurst and Company, 1989)

Binns, C. T., *Dinuzulu: The Death of the House of Shaka* (London: Longman, 1968)

——, *The Last Zulu King: The Life and Death of Cetshwayo* (London: Longman, 1963)

Bullard, Alice, *Exile to Paradise: Savagery and Civilization in Paris and the South Pacific, 1790–1900* (Stanford: Stanford University Press, 2000)

Carton, Benedict, et al. (eds), *Zulu Identities: Being Zulu, Past and Present* (London: Hurst, 2009)

Chekhov, Anton, translated by Rosamund Bartlett and Anthony Phillips, *Anton Chekhov: A Life in Letters* (London: Penguin, 2004)

——, translated by Brian Reeve, *Sakhalin Island* (London: Alma, 2013)

Clifford, James, *Person and Myth: Maurice Leenhardt in the Melanesian World* (Durham and London: Duke University Press, 1992)

Colenso, Harriette (ed.), 'Zulu Letters from St Helena' (pamphlet), privately published, London, 1895

Cope, Nicholas, *To Bind the Nation: Solomon kaDinuzulu and Zulu Nationalism 1913–1933* (Pietermaritzburg: University of Natal Press, 1993)

Dlamini, Paulina and H. Filter, translated by S. Bourquin, *Paulina Dlamini: Servant of Two Kings* (Pietermaritzburg: University of Natal Press; and Durban: Killie Campbell Africana Library, 1986)

Doroshevich, Vlas, translated by Andrew A. Gentes, *Russia's Penal Colony in the Far East* (London: Anthem Press, 2011)

Engels, Friedrich, *The Origin of the Family, Private Property and the State* (London: Penguin, 2010)

Figes, Orlando, *A People's Tragedy: The Russian Revolution* (London: Jonathan Cape, 2006)

Fuze, Magema, translated by Harry Lugg, *The Black People and Whence They Came* (Pietermaritzburg: University of Natal Press; and Durban: Killie Campbell Africana Library, 1979). Originally published as *Abantu Abamnyama Lapa Bavela Ngakona*, 1922

Gagen-Torn, Nina I., *Lev Iakovlevich Shternberg* (Leningrad: Vostochnaya Literatura, 1975)

George, Barbara, *St Helena's Zulu Princess* (privately published, St Helena)

Girault, Ernest, ed. Clotilde Chauvin, *Une Colonie d'Enfer* (Toulouse: Les Éditions Libertaires, 2007)

Godwin, Francis, *The Man in the Moone* (London, 1657)

Grant, Bruce, *In the Soviet House of Culture: A Century of Perestroikas* (Princeton: Princeton University Press, 1995)

Guiart, Jean, 'A Drama of Ambiguity: Ouvéa 1988–89', *The Journal of Pacific History*, vol. 32, no. 1 (June 1997) Guy, Jeff, *The View Across the River: Harriette Colenso and the Zulu Struggle Against Imperialism* (Charlottesville: University Press of Virginia, 2001)

Haberer, Erich, *Jews and Revolution in Nineteenth-Century Russia* (Cambridge: Cambridge University Press, 1995)

Hawes, Charles H., *In The Uttermost East: Being an Account of Investigations among the Natives and Russian Convicts of the Island of Sakhalin, with Notes of Travel in Korea, Siberia, and Manchuria* (London and New York: Harper and Brothers, 1904)

Hofer, Johannes, translated by Carolyn Kiser Anspach, 'Medical Dissertation on Nostalgia by Johannes Hofer, 1688', *Bulletin of the Institute of the History of Medicine*, vol. 2, no. 6, August 1934

Holt, H. P., *The Mounted Police of Natal* (London: John Murray, 1913)

Horne, Alistair, *The Fall of Paris: The Siege and the Commune 1870–71* (London: Macmillan, 1965)

Illbruck, Helmut, *Nostalgia: Origins and Ends of an Unenlightened Disease* (Evanston: Northwestern University Press, 2012)

Jackson, E. L., *St Helena: The Historic Island from its Discovery to the Present Date* (London: Ward Lock and Co., 1903)

Kan, Sergei, *Lev Shternberg: Anthropologist, Russian Socialist, Jewish Activist* (Lincoln and London: University of Nebraska Press, 2009)

——, '"My Old Friend in the Dead-end of Empiricism and Skepticism": Bogoras, Boas, and the Politics of Soviet Anthropology of the Late 1920s–Early 1930s', *Histories of Anthropology Annual*, Vol. 2, p. 33 (Lincoln: University of Nebraska Press, 2006)

——, 'Moisei Krol's Return to the Jewish People via Ethnographic Research among the Buryat', unpublished paper

Kauffmann, Jean-Paul, *The Dark Room at Longwood* (London: Harvill, 1999)

Korolenko, Vladimir G., translated by Neil Parsons, *The History of My Contemporary* (London: Oxford University Press, 1972)

————, translated by Aline Delano, *The Vagrant and Other Tales* (New York: Thomas Y. Crowell, 1887)

Krol, M.A., *Stranitsy Moei Zhizni* (New York: Union of Russian Jews, 1944)

————, 'Vospominaniia o L. Ia. Shternberge', *Katorga i ssylka*, 1929

Las Cases, Emmanuel-Auguste-Dieudonné, *Memoirs of the Life, Exile, and Conversations of the Emperor Napoleon*, 1894

Lock, John, *Zulu Conquered: The March of the Red Soldiers, 1822–1888* (London: Frontline, 2010)

Lockwood, Joseph, *A Guide to St Helena: Descriptive and Historical, with a Visit to Longwood, and Napoleon's Tomb* (London: S. Gibb, 1851)

Loos, Jackie, 'The Zulu Exiles on St Helena, 1890–1897', *Quarterly Bulletin of the South African Library*, vol. 53, no. 112 (1998)

Melliss, John Charles, *St Helena: Physical, Historical and Topographical Description of the Island* (London: I. Reeve, 1875)

Merriman, John, *Massacre: The Life and Death of the Paris Commune of 1871* (New Haven: Yale University Press, 2014)

Michel, Louise, *La Commune* (Paris: P.-V. Stock, 1898)

————, *Légendes et Chants de Gestes Canaques* (Paris: Kéva et Co., 1885)

————, *Red Virgin: Memoirs of Louise Michel*, edited and translated by Bullitt Lowry and Elizabeth Ellington Gunter (Tuscaloosa: University of Alabama Press, 1981)

Mokoena, Hlonipha, *Magema Fuze: The Making of a Kholwa Intellectual* (Scottsville: University of KwaZulu-Natal Press, 2011)

Morgan, Lewis H., *Ancient Society* (London: Macmillan, 1877)

Ovid (Ovidius Publius Naso), translated and introduced by Peter Green, *The Poems of Exile:* Tristia *and the* Black Sea Letters (Berkeley: University of California Press, 2005)

Pearson, Andy, et al., *Infernal Traffic: Excavation of a Liberated African Graveyard in Rupert's Valley, St Helena* (York: Council for British Archaeology, 2011)

Piłsudski, Bronisław, ed. Werner Winter and Richard A. Rhodes, *The Collected Works of Bronisław Piłsudski. Volume 1: The Aborigines of Sakhalin* (Berlin: De Gruyter Mouton, 2018)

Rapoport, David C. (ed.), *Terrorism: The First or Anarchist Wave* (London: Routledge, 2006)

Reid, Anna, *The Shaman's Coat: A Native History of Siberia* (London: Weidenfeld and Nicolson, 2002)

Robb, Graham, *Victor Hugo* (London: Picador, 1997)

Rochefort, Henri, *The Adventures of My Life*, vol. II (London: Edward Arnold, 1896)

Saville, John, '1848 – Britain and Europe', in Sabine Freitag (ed.), *Exiles from European Revolutions: Refugees in Mid-Victorian England* (New York, Oxford: Berghahn Books, 2003)

Shternberg, Lev, ed. Bruce Grant, *The Social Organisation of the Gilyak* (New York: American Museum of Natural History, 1999)

Sirina, Anna A., and Tatiana P. Roon, 'Lev Iakovlevich Shternberg: At the Outset of Soviet Ethnography' in *Jochelson, Bogoras and Shternberg: A Scientific Exploration of Northeastern Siberia and the Shaping of Soviet Ethnography* (Fürstenberg, Havel: Verlag der Kulturstiftung Sibirien, 2018)

Stephan, John J., *Sakhalin: A History* (Oxford: Clarendon Press, 1971)

Stuart, J., *A History of the Zulu Rebellion, 1906* (London: Macmillan, 1913)

Thomas, Edith, *Louise Michel*, translated by Penelope Williams (Montreal: Black Rose Books, 1980)

Unwin, Brian, *Terrible Exile: The Last Days of Napoleon on St Helena* (London: I.B. Tauris, 2010)

Waddell, Eric, *Jean-Marie Tjibaou, Kanak Witness to the World: An Intellectual Biography* (Honolulu: University of Hawai'i Press, 2008)

Ward, Alan, *Land and Politics in New Caledonia* (Canberra: Department of Political and Social Change Research School of Pacific Studies, 1982)

Welsh, Frank, *A History of South Africa* (London: HarperCollins, 1998)

Williams, Roger L., *Henri Rochefort: Prince of the Gutter Press* (New York: Charles Scribner's Sons, 1966)

Wolseley, Garnet Joseph, *The Letters of Lord and Lady Wolseley* (London: William Heinemann, 1922)

Wright, Gordon, *Between the Guillotine and Liberty: Two Centuries of the Crime Problem in France* (Oxford: Oxford University Press, 1983)

Yarmolinsky, Avrahm, *Road to Revolution* (Princeton: Princeton University Press, 2014)

Notes

Prologue: On Homesickness

3 'I who lie here': Ovid, *Tristia*, III.3.73
4 'driven off': ibid., III.10.62
5 'troubled frontier post': ibid., IV.1.85
5 'There came to my mind': Hofer, 'Medical Dissertation on Nostalgia'
6 'Neither terrain nor water': *Tristia*, III.8.23
6 'I felt myself': ibid., I.3.73

I

The Red Flag: Louise Michel

11 '*Vive la République!*': Michel, *Red Virgin*, p. 18
11 'between the forest and the plain': ibid., p. 9
11 'I am what is known as a bastard': Thomas, *Louise Michel*, p. 15
13 'My mother was then a blonde': Michel, *Memoirs*, p. 5
13 'In the north tower': Ibid., p. 20
13 'At the tomb': ibid., p. 22
16 'The poor woman': ibid., p. 45
17 'at the heart of affairs': ibid., p. 5
17 'The dominant idea': ibid., p. 25

18 'The peasants sow': ibid., p. 26

18 'And so here is Louise': ibid., p. 52

19 'If the men hang back': Thomas, *Louise Michel*, p. 52

19 'I left her alone': Michel, *Memoirs*, p. 46

19 'Do you hear the brazen thunder': ibid., p. 53

19 'I would have killed my tyrant': ibid., p. 54

20 'It is said to be quite good': quoted in Robb, *Victor Hugo*, p. 454

20 'absolutely devoted to the revolution . . .': Thomas, *Louise Michel*, p. 67

22 'The latter "died well"': ibid., p. 79

22 'On this day': Michel, *Memoirs*, p. 64

22 'People say I'm brave': ibid., p. 65

22 'At the barricade on rue Perronet': Michel, *La Commune*, pp. 290–2

23 'There is an energetic woman'; 'I have never seen her so calm': Thomas, *Louise Michel*, p. 87

23 'a monument to barbarism': *Le Cri du Peuple*, 4 April 1871, quoted in Bullard, *Exile to Paradise*, p. 75

23 'had the effect of an eclipse': the witness was Edmund de Goncourt

24 'totally epileptic': Williams, *Henri Rochefort*, p. 113, quoting Flaubert's correspondence

25 'vast execution squad': Merriman, *Massacre*, p. 147

25 'ran with blood': the Marquis de Compiègne quoted in ibid., p. 166

27 'Just look at her': details of Michel's appearance from the historical archives of the ministry of war, on the Councils of War 1871, quoted in Thomas, *Louise Michel*, p. 130

29 'Louise Michel was an illegitimate child': statement by the Clerk of the Court Martial, quoted in Michel, *Red Virgin*, p. 84

30 'I have finished': testimony, quoted in Michel, *Red Virgin*, pp. 86–7

30 'Take heart': Thomas, *Louise Michel*, p. 128

31 'France had been purging itself of "undesirables"': for details of nineteenth-century French penal policy see Wright, *Between the Guillotine and Liberty*

31 'the best penitentiary system': Édouard Proust: 'La transportation judiciare et les criminels d'habitude ou de profession', 1872, National Archives, Aix-en-Provence, quoted in Bullard, *Exile to Paradise*, p. 121

31 'will be led': d'Haussonville, Vicomte: report on the condition of
deportees to New Caledonia, *Journal officiel de la République française*,
26 July 1872, quoted in Bullard, *Exile to Paradise*, p. 96

Ghost Mountain: Dinuzulu kaCetshwayo

33 'As a baby . . . hold true': Fuze, *The Black People*, p. 122

34 'The most intimate account of daily life': see Dlamini and Filter,
Paulina Dlamini

36 'When Dinuzulu was still a boy': Fuze, *The Black People*, p. 122

36 'By the established church . . . heretical': the offending volume,
published in 1862, was entitled *The Pentateuch and Book of Joshua
Critically Examined*, and showed the absurdity of a literal reading of
the Bible. See Guy, *The View Across the River*, p. 22

36 'The crowd was so great': Lady Wolseley to Lord Wolseley, 13 August
1882, in *The Letters of Lord and Lady Wolseley*, p. 87

37 'Being all fat and big-bellied . . . mat-bearers': Lock, *Zulu Conquered*,
p. 230

38 'The British doctor's report': Some historians of the Anglo-Zulu War
have argued that Cetshwayo's food was poisoned by Zibhebhu's
agents, but given the intense security that surrounded any Zulu
king this interpretation is likely to be based on a misreading of the
isiZulu word for death, *ukufa*, which is routinely used by Zulus in
a metaphorical sense: break a cup, for instance, and you might say
'*ngibulele inkomishi*', 'I have *killed* a cup.' I'm grateful to Hlonipha
Mokoena for this clarification.

38 '*umuntu oshonileyo* . . . one who has gone down': Berglund, *Zulu
Thought-Patterns and Symbolism*, p. 83

38 'As reported by them . . . midst of my army': Ndabuko and Shingana's
version of Cetshwayo's last words in Guy, *The View Across the River*,
p. 6. Fuze's version is in Fuze, *The Black People*, p. 123

39 'trod the earth as if he owned it': Binns, *Dinuzulu*, p. 5

39 'When I die I shall not be altogether dead': Guy, *The View Across the
River*, p. 6

39 'On 5 June 1884 . . . north-west Zululand': Binns, *Dinuzulu*, pp. 35–8

39 'may consider necessary': Guy, *The View Across the River*, p. 99

40 'Dinuzulu's army . . . owed their victory': Binns, *Dinuzulu*, pp. 35–8

42 'Just as your dying in a heap': Guy, *The View Across the River*, p. 245

42 'The knowledge': ibid., p. 260

42 'I have nothing to say to all these lies . . . still a child': ibid., p. 280

43 '"Dinuzulu," announced the judge': Binns, *Dinuzulu*, p. 145

43 'But Osborn . . . Sir Charles Mitchell': ibid., pp. 146–7

43 'The Queen with Her Indunas': Guy, *The View Across the River*, p. 334

44 'What will become of the people': ibid., p. 335

44 'its local position': on Napoleon's exile to St Helena see Las Cases, *Memoirs of the Life, Exile, and Conversations of the Emperor Napoleon*, 1894, p. 37

The Pale of Settlement: Lev Shternberg

45 'Pass a magnifying glass': much of the biographical information about Shternberg in this chapter and elsewhere is drawn from Kan, *Lev Shternberg*

46 'Krol remembered his friend's parents': Krol, 'Vospominaniia o L. Ia. Shternberge'

48 'dilapidated one-storey houses': ibid.

48 'All the residents and frequent visitors to this street': Kan, *Lev Shternberg*, p. 4

48 For Korolenko's memories of Zhitomir see Korolenko, *The History of My Contemporary*

49 'a highly indecent place': Krol, 'Vospominaniia o L. Ia. Shternberge'

49 'Shternberg, who had esteemed Turgenev above almost any of the others': ibid.

49 'and this Jew is a spy and a scoundrel': ibid.

49 'On a hot day . . .': ibid.

50 'I was bereaved of all joys . . . sad and fitting': from Bruce Grant's introduction to Shternberg, *The Social Organisation of the Gilyak*, p. xxix

51 'Society has only one obligation': Bell, *Assassin*, p. 172

51 'Nihilists, my brothers . . .': Thomas, *Louise Michel*, p. 183

52 'Our ultimate political and economic ideal': Yarmolinsky, *Road to Revolution*, p. 211

52 'dull, bourgeois . . . plunder and kill': Krol, *Stranitsy Moei Zhizni*

53 'drained of blood': Krol, 'Vospominaniia o L. Ia. Shternberge'

54 'A "temporary struggle" was required': Ivianski, in Rapoport, *Terrorism*, p. 87

55 'began his career with the terrorist act': Kan, *Lev Shternberg*, p. 318

56 'Preserve the life': ibid. p. 19

57 'It is difficult to reconcile the idea . . .': ibid., p. 19

57 'After two years . . . even that remoteness': for details of their reunion, see Krol, *Stranitsy moei Zhizmi*

58 'such was the squalor': Nikolai Yadrintsev, quoted in Beer, *The House of the Dead*, p. 240

59 'You will see Mount Sinai': Kan, *Lev Shternberg*, p. 22

On Seasickness

64 '*na krai sveta*': *Chekhov: A Life in Letters*, p. 204

65 'One did not feel at all as if one were crossing the sea known as "Black"': Gagen-Torn, *Lev Iakovlevich Shternberg*, translated for me by Lisa Hayden

65 'to transport people': Doroshevich, *Russia's Penal Colony in the Far East*, p. 3

66 'Naval laws are always strict': Korolenko, tr. Delano, 'A Saghalinian: The Tale of a Vagrant' (published in Russian as 'Sokholinets'), in *The Vagrant and Other Tales*, p. 78

67 'He was one "who also sought freedom"': Kan, *Lev Shternberg*, p. 23

68 I'm grateful to Bernard Guinard's genealogy website www.bernard-guinard.com for information about the *Virginie*. Other details, where not attributed, are from Michel, *Red Virgin*.

68 'The *Virginie* reminded her': Michel, *Red Virgin*, p. 90

69 'According to Michel's biographer': Thomas, *Louise Michel*, p.143

70 'The voyage was as likely to take six months as three': Rochefort, *The Adventures of My Life*, p. 47

70 'All my life I had dreamed of sailing': Thomas, *Louise Michel*, p. 140

70 'Her comrades in Paris': Michel, *Red Virgin*, p. 93

71 'After snaring them the sailors hung them': ibid.

71 'I need hardly tell you': Binns, *Dinuzulu*, p. 275

72 'The voyage from Durban to St Helena': I'm indebted to C. C. O'Hanlon for the information on maritime conditions between Durban and St Helena.

72 'Very much alarmed': Dinuzulu to his mother, 21 March 1890, Pietermaritzburg Archives Repository, A. ZGH 727. Z 260

II

Barbarians: New Caledonia

81 'Sequestration leads to dreaming': Rochefort, *The Story of My Life*, p. 93

81 'My lungs are clogged up': Bullard, *Exile to Paradise*, p. 192

81 'Desperate physical pains': ibid., p. 185

83 'Some men kill other men the same way': Michel, *Red Virgin*, p. 93

84 'The uncivilised inhabitants of a country': Ward, *Land and Politics in New Caledonia*, p. 1

84 'a high wooded hill': quoted in Clifford, *Person and Myth*, p. 30

87 'land of eternal springtime': Wright, *Between the Guillotine and Liberty*, p. 140

87 'Antarctic Kerguelen Islands': ibid., p. 148

88 'A Frenchman is not less industrious': quoted in Bullard, *Exile to Paradise*, p. 95

88 'struck by the worst of diseases': ibid., p. 192

88 'that strange and indefinable sensation called home-sickness': Rochefort, *The Adventures of My Life*, p. 219

88 'Another *déporté*, Achille Ballière': Bullard, *Exile to Paradise*, p. 200

89 'We heard the waves beating eternally on the reefs': Michel, *Red Virgin*, p. 96

89 'Her friend Henri Rochefort': Rochefort, *The Adventures of my Life*, pp. 1, 87

90 'The warders were applying': ibid., p. 99

94 'incontestable proof' ibid., p. 135

96 '*maciri*': Clifford, *Person and Myth*, p. 36

96 'I shan't return': Thomas, *Louise Michel*, p. 93

97 'Daoumi had come dressed like a European': Michel, *Red Virgin*, p. 96

97 '*plus canaque que les Canaques*': Michel, *Red Virgin*, p. 112

98 '"Landscape" for Kanak people': Clifford, *Person and Myth*, pp. 40–41

100 'in a perfect state of preservation': *Bulletin de la Société d'Anthropologie de Paris*, 23 October 1879, p. 616

102 For details of Tjibaou, the Hienghène Massacre and its aftermath, see Waddell, *Jean-Marie Tjibaou.*

103 'He rolled down in the ferns': Waddell, *Jean-Marie Tjibaou*, p. 39

104 'Genealogies are rooted in the earth': ibid., p. 100

105 'Nonviolence, yes': ibid. p. 161

107 'When I lost my country': Ovid, *Tristia*, III.3.54

111 'When a comrade was killed': Michel, *Red Virgin*, p. 62

114 'On the morning of 22 April 1988': My account of the Ouvéa hostage crisis draws heavily on Guiart, *The Journal of Pacific History*, pp. 85–102. Guiart's account is disputed: see, particularly, Bensa and Wittersheim, *The Journal of Pacific History*, pp. 221–4

116 'The blood of those who are gone is still with us': quoted in Waddell, *Jean-Marie Tjibaou*, p. 17

120 'It came during the night': Michel, *Red Virgin*, p. 108

121 'The shore of the isthmus . . . in savage silence': Michel, *Légendes et Chants de Gestes Canaques*, pp. 43–4

123 'Deep in a gorge': Michel, *Red Virgin*, p. 105

124 'When her work was mocked': Michel's defender, according to her memoirs, was one M. Locamus; see Michel, *Red Virgin*, p. 119

126 'as though I'd lost a limb': Ovid, *Tristia*, I.3.73

The Man in the Moone: St Helena

128 'According to a British soldier': from 'The Calemma', unnamed author, in *Army and Navy Magazine* annual (London: W.H. Allen and Co., 1881), p. 944

128 'Near to the coast the rough lava': Edith Wollaston, 'Notes on the Lepidoptera of St Helena, with Descriptions of New Species', *Annals and Magazine of Natural History*, 1879

128 'Did you ever see such a town': Lockwood, *A Guide to St Helena*, p. 12

133 'We have negatived proposals': Guy, *The View Across the River*, p. 308

134 Fernão Lopes' story is told in Azzam's *The Other Exile*

134 'I took some 30 to 40 of young ones': Godwin, *The Man in the Moone*, p. 10

136 'he no longer had any preoccupation with the future': Kauffmann, *The Dark Room at Longwood*, p. xviii

136 'Dinuzulu [. . .] evidently came ashore': *St Helena Guardian*, 27 February 1890

136 'He and his party': ibid.

136 'A very large and very nice house': Dinuzulu to his mother, 21 March 1890, Pietermaritzburg Archives Repository, A. ZGH 727. Z 260

138 'In April the *Illustrated London News* caught up': *Illustrated London News*, 26 April 1890

138 'Although an exile': *St Helena Guardian*, 27 February 1890

138 'Nothing can be more deplorable': Melliss, *St Helena*, p. 75

138 'arrival of a steamship': Fuze, *The Black People*, p. 134

139 'few of the inhabitants', Duncan, *A Description of the Island of St Helena*, p. 198

142 'there would be dancing': Fuze, *The Black People*, p. 134

142 'extremely obnoxious': Loos, 'The Zulu Exiles on St Helena', p. 41

142 'We believe we are expressing': ibid.

142 'Miss Cummings and Miss Cressy': Fuze, *The Black People*, p. 134

142 'Now they are old men': ibid., p. 8

143 'the ships of the Portuguese': ibid.

144 'scarcely a hundred tonnes burthen at most': Mellis, *St Helena*, pp. 30–1. For information about the burials and excavations in Rupert's Valley I have relied on Pearson et al., *Infernal Traffic*, and an online talk given by Pearson on 25 November 2020.

146 'Magema Fuze lists the royal offspring': Fuze, *The Black People*, p. 135

147 'the very fact': Binns, *Dinuzulu*, p. 146

148 'My uncles and the girls': Dinuzulu to his mother, 21 March 1890, Pietermaritzburg Archives Repository, A. ZGH 727. Z 260

148 'from one side': the references to 'Habanani' and 'Nenegwa' in this letter are unclear (no such place or person is identifiable), and may

be mistranslations or mistranscriptions on the part of Dinuzulu's
secretary. (Dinuzulu himself was yet to learn to write in English.)

148 'Au-au-au': 'Visiting the Island Princess', *Mail and Guardian*, South
Africa, 27 August 2007 (an unnamed staff reporter visits 'Princess
Dinuzulu')

148 'expressing great pleasure': Loos, 'The Zulu Exiles on St Helena', p. 36

148 'We wish Dr Paul': ibid., p. 36

149 'It is a great pleasure': ibid., p. 37

149 'I greatly desire to learn': ibid., p. 39

149 'I play the "Mariner's Jog"': Garreth van Niekerk, 'The Secret History
of King Dinuzulu', *City Press*, South Africa, 20 September 2015

149 'pride in being well-dressed': Guy, *The View Across the River*, p. 338

150 'uncles were much more unsociable': Jackson, *St Helena*, p. 95

150 'We are too shamefaced': Guy, *The View Across the River*, p. 338

151 'A man grows up': Fuze, *The Black People*, p. 28

151 'The Zulus quite declined': letter of 10 April 1893, St Helena archives,
Jamestown

156 'Here we have a moth never before seen in the world': In his 2022
paper on the discovery ('On two species of *Opogona* Zeller, 1853,
from St Helena Island', *Metamorphosis*, vol. 33), Karisch notes that
'the species is very distinctive among all other known *Opogona* species
on the island in its characteristic bronze-and-black speckled pattern
of the forewings.' Hence the scientific name he gave it: *Opogona
aenea*, from the Latin for bronze, *aeneus*.

157 'Prison Lacks Procedures to Help Young Offenders Back to Work/
School': St Helena *Sentinel*, 5 April 2018

160 'the physical infrastructure of the building': ibid.

161 'My object in coming to England': Guy, *The View Across the River*, p. 313

162 'half a yard of London mud': ibid., p. 307

162 'played a part': ibid., p. 330

162 'We all know': ibid., p. 331

163 'it will be in great measure': ibid., p. 341

163 'Our mother': ibid., p. 354

165 'everyone who remembers my father': ibid., p. 385

165 'that well-known gelding': Loos, 'The Zulu Exiles on St Helena', p. 39

166 'It is now just five years . . . the present aspect of affairs': ibid.,
    pp. 39–40

166 'Loss and suffering': Guy, *The View Across the River*, p. 403

167 'I thought I knew': ibid., p. 388

167 'We are beset with a feverish cold': Colenso (ed.), 'Zulu Letters from
    St Helena' (pamphlet), London, 1895

167 'There is feverishness': ibid.

167 'the English cows': ibid.

168 'a pamphlet published by an island historian': George, *St Helena's Zulu
    Princess*

169 'Hello, sun!': on Napoleon's death, see Unwin, *Terrible Exile*

170 'He must clearly understand . . . Government of Zululand': Guy, *The
    View Across the River*, p. 432

170 'I do not see that you can help him in Zululand': for Colenso's letter
    to Johnstone see ibid., pp. 433–4

The Island of the Black River: Sakhalin

175 'I regret that I am not a sentimental person': Chekhov to Suvorin,
    9 March 1890, *Anton Chekhov: A Life in Letters*, p. 204

175 'the final destination of the unshot': Hawes, *In the Uttermost East*, p. 337

180 'The climate here is marvellous!': Beer, *The House of the Dead*, p. 241

182 'Through the darkness and smoke': Chekhov, *Sakhalin Island*, p. 53

182 'My own privileged position': Kan, *Lev Shternberg*, p. 36

182 'Look at the old shaman . . . I will study them': ibid., p. 41

182 'The Gilyaks never wash': Chekhov, *Sakhalin Island*, p. 165

184 'a dreadful, hideous place': ibid., p. 123

187 'Prokhorov's hair': ibid., p. 293

187 'Hawes tells the story': Hawes, *In The Uttermost East*, p. 341

188 'ethnographic baptism': Shternberg, *Social Organisation*, p. 4

188 'I became interested in this study . . . primitive life': ibid., pp. 3–4

188 'As it is undeniable': Morgan, *Ancient Society*, p. 3

188 'Despite my complete ignorance': Shternberg, *The Social Organisation
    of the Gilyak*, p. 5

189 'children addressed by the common name': ibid.

192 'If you are anxious to die . . . military outposts': Korolenko, 'A Saghalinian', pp. 114–15

192 'The hope for them': ibid., p. xxxiii

192 'lonely, abandoned grave': Shternberg, *Social History* (introduction by Bruce Grant), xxxiii

193 'When I feel the need': Sirina and Roon, 'Lev Iakovlevich Shternberg', p. 212

193 'tethered to life': Gagen-Torn, *Lev Iakovlevich Shternberg*, translated for me by Lisa Hayden, p. 44

193 'a void which had ballooned': see Bullard, *Exile to Paradise*, p. 193

193 'You are a kind person': Kan, *Lev Shternberg*, p. 22

194 'I had not even finished reciting': ibid., p. 101

194 'On 6 February 1891': Shternberg, *Social Organisation*, p. 6

195 'colonisation . . . ought to be carried out': Kan, *Lev Shternberg*, p. 93

195 'The beautiful memories': ibid., p. 48

196 'The most fantastic legends': Shternberg, *Social Organisation*, p. 6

196 'I was able to visit': ibid., p. 7

199 'about the brightest moment[s]': ibid., p. 81

201 'When Boris Yeltsin': Grant, *In the Soviet House of Culture*, pp. 31–2

203 'I have found a kinship terminology': ibid. (introduction by Bruce Grant), p. xxiv

203 'The Gilyak system of kinship': ibid., p. 98

204 'I took them all for': ibid. (introduction by Bruce Grant), p. iv

204 'the right of sexual intercourse': Engels, *The Origin of the Family*, p. 15

204 'When a Gilyak applies the term': Shternberg, *Social Organisation*, p. 98

III

The Black Flag: Louise Michel

209 'True progress': Peter Kropotkin, 'Anarchism', *Encyclopaedia Britannica* (London: 1910), pp. 914–19

210 'I recognise no borders . . . there are our crimes': Michel, *Red Virgin*, p. 169

210 'whole crossing attached like ornaments': ibid., p. 121

210 'amnestied Arab': Michel, *La Commune*, p. 392

211 'The siren wailed': Thomas, *Louise Michel*, p. 165

212 'Once in London': Michel, *Red Virgin*, p. 121

212 'I may be used to the smell': Thomas, *Louise Michel*, p. 232

213 'I am always instinctively suspicious': Williams, *Henri Rochefort*, p. 251

214 'I have already claimed': Thomas, *Louise Michel*, p. 189

214 'Don't let yourselves . . . do not harm the bakers': ibid., p. 207

215 'A description was distributed': ibid., p. 209

216 'Others saw me': Michel, *Red Virgin*, p. 158

216 'By virtue of what special privilege': Thomas, *Louise Michel*, p. 209

216 '"Prison," she wrote': Michel, *Red Virgin*, p. 215

217 'experience happiness': Michel, *Memoirs*, p. 200

217 'I'm sending you some silk thread': ibid., p. 200

217 'Make me the view of the sea': ibid., p. 207

217 'What is being done here is a political proceeding': Michel, *Red Virgin*, pp. 167–9

218 'We have wearied', etc.: Thomas, *Louise Michel*, p. 223

218 'vengeance, not justice': ibid., p. 224

218 'to keep her from dying quite literally of starvation': ibid., p. 229

219 'How many prisons! . . . gradually lowering': ibid., p. 230

219 'I think you could have served': ibid., p. 233

221 'Please leave me alone': ibid., p. 244

221 'Don't feel sorry for me': Paul Lafargue, 'A Visit to Louise Michel', *Le Socialiste*, 26 September 1885

221 '*I declare once again . . . do not consider myself pardoned*': Thomas, *Louise Michel*, p. 250

222 'Society must be reborn': ibid., p. 279

223 'He came up behind Michel': ibid., pp. 280–1

223 'You could hear': ibid.

224 'It is impossible': ibid, p. 282

224 'fanatic, dedicated to his cause': ibid., p. 283

224 'The 1 May demonstration': ibid., p. 305

225 'My anger, the lack of air' and physicians' reports: ibid., pp. 308–11

226 'like being transported to another world' ibid., p. 310

226 'On an enormous rock': Michel, *Red Virgin*, p. 192

227 'Yes, I admit it': ibid., p. 149

227 'In the present revolutionary period': Thomas, *Louise Michel*, p. 322

228 'By taking on': Constance Bantman, 'Louise Michel's London Years: A Political Reassessment (1890–1905)', *Women's History Review*, 26:6, p. 1003

228 'So much the better': Thomas, *Louise Michel*, p. 323

230 'dark and sombre beauty': Barrès, Maurice, *Mes Cahiers*, vol. V, p. 55

230 'It's as if my body became a bundle of rags': Thomas, *Louise Michel*, p. 382

230 'turn off the dirty-water tap': quoted in Anderson, *A Global History of Convicts and Penal Colonies*, p. 137

231 'If I was no longer good for anything': Girault, *Une Colonie d'Enfer*, pp. 61–2

231 'we are the happiest people in the world': ibid., p. 61

One Who Has Gone Down: Dinuzulu kaCetshwayo

233 'It was a very interesting voyage': Guy, *The View Across the River*, p. 436

234 'forty tonnes of furniture': Binns, *Dinuzulu*, p. 161

234 'weary years at St Helena': Guy, *The View Across the River*, p. 441

234 'They are as good at heart': ibid., p. 435

236 'no sale, transfer or alienation of land': Sir Garnet Wolseley, governor of Natal, in an address to Zulu chiefs on 9 October 1879, quoted in Binns, *Dinuzulu*, p. 171

237 'All pigs must be destroyed': Binns, *Dinuzulu*, p. 181

237 'more likely to have sprung': Stuart, *A History of the Zulu Rebellion, 1906*, p. 108

238 'As they were about to be put to death': Fuze, *The Black People and Whence They Came*, p. 143

239 'His feet and legs': Dinuzulu's prime minister, Mankulumana, quoted in Binns, *Dinuzulu*, p. 195

240 'I can only say I am': Stuart, *A History of the Zulu Rebellion, 1906*, p. 214

241 'It was not a battle': Holt, *The Mounted Police of Natal*, p. 209

242 'When the soldiers came': quoted in Binns, *Dinuzulu*, p. 245

242 'exaggeration and falsehood'; 'I am being killed': ibid., p. 249–53

243 'People must understand': ibid., p. 253

243 'There is none': Marks, 'Harriette Colenso and the Zulus', p. 403

244 'It had been done to spite her': ibid., p. 405

244 'has within a month': Jackson, *St Helena*, p. 98

244 'My trouble': Binns, *Dinuzulu*, p. 252

245 'If he is well': *Natal Mercury*, date unknown

245 'learned to wear European clothing': Loos, 'The Zulu Exiles', p. 32

249 'removal of any tribe': quoted in Badat, *The Forgotten People*, p. 29

249 'no children's voices': Cole and Flaherty, *The House of Bondage*, quoted in Badat, *The Forgotten People*, p. xviii

250 'St Helena's reputation as a dumping ground': 'For Gaddafi, a Home on St Helena' by William C. Goodfellow, of the Center for International Policy, *Washington Post*, 2 June 2011

Sakhalin Fever: Lev Shternberg

251 'Afterwards, everything was Sakhalinised': This story was told to me in Alexandrovsk, and may be apocryphal; but see, inter alia, Krestinskaya, T. P., *Motifs of Sakhalin in Chekhov's Works*, vol. xx, p. 111 (Nizhni Novgorod: Nizhni Novgorod Teacher's Training College, 1967)

253 'weathered by Siberian frosts': Krol, 'Vospominaniia o L. Ia. Shternberge'

253 'full of the same idealism': ibid.

254 'Thanks to it': Kan, *Lev Shternberg*, p. 125

255 'I cannot think of anything equal to this': ibid., p. 145

257 'Zhuravskii publicly accused': for details of the Zhuravskii Affair, see ibid.

258 'And so I am back on Sakhalin': ibid., p. 198

259 'only one desire': ibid.

260 For Shternberg's 'Ten Commandments of the Ethnographer' see ibid., pp. 356–7, and Sirina and Roon, 'Lev Iakovlevich Shternberg', p. 243

261 'humanity would become': Kan, *Lev Shternberg*, p. 286

261 'thin old man': ibid., p. 279

262 'result of repressive measures': the account of the 'Islanders Affair'
appears in ibid., p. 103

262 'lightning sinks to the bottom of the Tatar Strait': ibid., p. 117

262 'Each person's life': ibid., p. vii

263 'Sleep peacefully': Kan, *Lev Shternberg*, p. 395

Epilogue: On Homesickness

265 'unmourned, unhonoured': Ovid, *Tristia*, III.3.45

266 'I thought to find nothing that pleased me': Ovid, *Black Sea Letters*,
II.1.3

266 'as if infinite love itself': Thomas, *Louise Michel*, p. 383

266 'a large refuge-house': Bantman, 'Louise Michel's London Years', p. 1006

267 'This international refuge': Thomas, *Louise Michel*, p. 356

267 'By then, the form of exile': figures on global penal expatriation drawn
from Anderson (ed.), *A Global History of Convicts and Penal Colonies*

268 'From 1823 to the introduction of the Aliens Act of 1905': John
Saville, '1848 – Britain and Europe', in Freitag (ed.), *Exiles from
European Revolutions: Refugees in Mid-Victorian England*, p. 19

268 'has managed to retain': Thomas, *Louise Michel*, p. 356

269 'The sickness carried him away': Fuze, *The Black People*, p. 145

269 'Now look at this pine!': Sirina and Roon, 'Lev Iakovlevich
Shternberg', p. 383

A Note on Terminology and Names

Some of the places mentioned in this book are known today by the name given to them by European colonisers. I have attempted to acknowledge these places' earlier names. 'New Caledonia' was the name James Cook coined for a series of islands known by numerous indigenous names, while Kanaky is the name preferred by some modern Kanak independentists. For consistency and clarity, since much of the book is set before the latter term was current, I have referred to the territory as New Caledonia.

The various Nivkh names for the island known as Sakhalin have, with the language itself, fallen out of use. Nivkh is the self-designation preferred by most Nivkhi, and was officially adopted by the Soviet government in the 1920s, replacing Gilyak/Giliak, which is regarded as pejorative. (Nivkhi is the Russian plural noun, Nivkh the singular noun and adjective.)

IsiZulu orthography is inconsistent in historic sources, but I have tended to use the most modern spelling. Prior to colonisation, patronyms were common in Zululand. Dinuzulu kaCetshwayo, meaning 'Dinuzulu, son of Cetshwayo', was universally known as simply Dinuzulu.

Acknowledgements

Edith Thomas's biography, translated by Penelope Williams, was my main source of information about Louise Michel. I have drawn equally heavily on Sergei Kan's *Lev Shternberg: Anthropologist, Russian Socialist and Jewish Activist*, invaluable to a non-Russian reader. I'm also grateful to Professor Kan for his close reading of the typescript of this book. The late Jeff Guy's *The View Across the River: Harriet Colenso and the Zulu Struggle Against Imperialism* was a vital source of information about Dinuzulu's friendship with Colenso and his and his party's time on St Helena.

I am grateful to Clare Anderson for her advice and her work on the global history of penal colonies. Alice Bullard's *Exile to Paradise* was revelatory on the links between exiled subjects of various kinds and indigenous populations. I would also like to thank Constance Bantman, author of *The French Anarchists in London*, for taking the time to read the chapters on Louise Michel, and for her invaluable comments. Claudine Bourcelot was generous in sharing her expertise on Michel's Vroncourt, and Clotilde Chauvin supplied useful information about Michel's time in Algeria.

I would like to thank Carrie Crockett, whose research on Sakhalin exiles, and meticulous reading of the typescript, were invaluable. I am indebted to Emma Wilson for her advice on travelling in Sakhalin, and to Bruce Grant for reviewing part of the manuscript of this book, his essential work on Lev Shternberg, and his studies of Nivkh social and political history.

I am deeply indebted to Hlonipha Mokoena, of the University of the Witwatersrand, Johannesburg, biographer of Magema Fuze, for reading the typescript, and especially her attention to the Dinuzulu chapters. I also thank Dan Yon, St Helena native and anthropologist, for the introduction to Hlonipha and for his own invaluable reading and support. I am also grateful to Thomas Cousins, at the School of Anthropology and Museum Ethnography at the University of Oxford; and to Andy Pearson, for sharing his archaeological work and reflections on St Helena's 'Liberated Africans'.

On St Helena, I owe particular thanks to Basil and Barbara George, Marcos Henry, Edward, Henry and Nick Thorpe, and Michel Dancoisne-Martineau, as well as those others mentioned in the text. I'm also grateful to Lisa Honan, the then governor of St Helena, and to Tracy Buckley, Assistant Custodian of Records at the St Helena Archives. Thanks also to Amy-Jayne Dutton, and to Timm Karisch, for his friendship and expertise. In South Africa, I thank Mbalenhle Zulu at the Killie Campbell Africana Library, University of Kwazulu-Natal; and Pieter Nel and the staff of the Pietermaritzburg Archives Repository. I am also grateful to C. C. O'Hanlon for his help with recreating Dinuzulu's journey from Durban to St Helena.

In New Caledonia I owe thanks to Louis-José Barbançon, and to Ismet Kurtovich and Christophe Dervieux of the New Caledonia Archives, Nicolas Kurtovitch, and Bernard Suprin. I am particularly grateful to Jean Rohleder, for his linguistic expertise, his friendship in Hienghène, and his helpful reading of some early passages.

My trip to Sakhalin was facilitated and enriched by the staff at the Sakhalin Regional Museum in Yuzhno-Sakhalin, including Yuri Alin, Mikhail Prokofiev, Irene Orlova, and particularly Olga Solovyova. I am also grateful to Timur Miromanov, Natalia Kolossova, Yuri Velichko, Denis Aleksandrovich, Dmitry Lisitsyn, Anna Zubko, Tatyana Roon and Anna Babushok. I could not have travelled as freely as I did without the support and kindness of Alisa Kim. I am deeply grateful to her and her family. Some names have been changed.

Thanks to Eva Hoffmann for an invaluable conversation about exile, early in the book's development; to Josh Cohen for his reflections on the psychoanalytical aspects of nostalgia and homesickness; and to Mohit Verma for a psychiatric perspective.

I'm grateful to Sigrid Rausing for publishing a version of the Sakhalin chapter, focussed on Chekhov, in *Granta*. I also thank the Society of Authors for both an Authors' Foundation grant and an Authors' Emergency Contingency Fund grant.

Thanks, Stuart Evers, Lisa Baker, Stephanie Cross and Will Ashon. My agent Patrick Walsh has been a stalwart over the four years of this book's evolution. I am grateful to Lee Brackstone and Ella Griffiths for their early belief in the book (and its predecessors); to my editor Laura Hassan for her commitment and vision; and to Mo Hafeez for his meticulous work on the typescript. At Faber I also owe thanks to Djinn von Noorden, Kate Ward, Jonny Pelham, Kate Burton and John Grindrod.

Exiles is dedicated to my father, Keith Atkins, and to Gillian Atkins, Chloe Atkins, and Katherine Yates.

With love, always, to Bea.

Text Acknowledgements

Every effort has been made to contact the copyright holders of quoted works and images. Lines from Ovid's *Poems of Exile*, translated by Peter Green, © 2005, reproduced by permission of the University of California Press. Lines from *The Red Virgin* by Louise Michel, edited and translated by Bullitt Lowry and Elizabeth Ellington, © 1981, reproduced by permission of the University of Alabama Press. Extracts from *A Life in Letters* by Anton Chekhov, published by Penguin Classics. Translation Copyright © Rosmund Bartlett and Anthony Phillips 2004. Reprinted by permission of Penguin Books Ltd.

Images

Index

Pechora, Russia, 256
penal colonialism: British, 89, 267, 248–9;
  French, 85, 87–8, 230, 267; Russian, 58,
  179–80, 186–7, 259–60, 261; *see also* exile
People's Will organisation (Narodnaia Volya),
  51–3, 252, 255; assassination of Alexander
  II, 51, 53–4; and Shternberg, 54–6
Petersburg (ship), 65, 66–7, 175, 192
Petrograd Imperial University, 260
Pietermaritzburg, South Africa, 33, 41, 42,
  242, 243, 244
Pije (language), 103
Port Alfred, South Africa, 72
Port Elizabeth, South Africa, 72
Port Said, Egypt, 67
Psishchi forest, Ukraine, 49–50, 58
Putin, Vladimir, 173, 174, 176

quicklime, 25–6

Ratner-Shternberg, Sarra, 254, 263, 269
Redon, Louis, 81
Rhodes, Cecil, 162
Richerie, Louis Eugène Gaultier de La,
  85, 91
rinderpest epidemic, Zululand (1897–98),
  235–6
Robben Island, Cape Town, 36, 249
Rochefort, Victor Henri, 15, 19, 21, 187,
  213; exile (London), 227; exile (New
  Caledonia), 68, 81, 88, 89–90; exile
  escape, 91; and Michel, 69, 120, 213, 227;
  and Paris Commune, 68–9
Rome, Ancient, 2, 85, 179
Russia: Academy of Sciences, 256, 257, 258;
  Central Bureau of the Farmers' Union,
  252; Jewish pogroms, 54, 255–6; NKVD,
  261–2; numbers exiled, 58, 267; penal
  system, 58, 179–80, 186–7, 259–60, 261;
  recaptures Sakhalin (1945), 177; revolution
  (1905), 260, 266, 268; revolution (1917),
  260; Socialist Revolutionary Party,
  255, 260; Victory Day, 173–4; *see also*
  Sakhalin Island; Siberia
Russkiye Vedomosti (newspaper), 204
Russo-Japanese War (1905), 261
Rwanda, 268

Rysakov, Nikolay, 53

St Helena: airport, 129–30; Bahraini Three's
  exile on, 249–50; British expatriates/
  citizenship, 133, 140; Colenso visits,
  166–7, 246, *247*; decline after Suez, 138–
  9; Diana's Peak, 166; Dinuzulu's exile
  on, *see under* Dinuzulu kaCetshwayo;
  discovery/colonisation, 132; early
  descriptions, 134, *135*, 139; flora/fauna,
  132, 134, 152–6, *155*, 167–8; Fuze visits,
  138, 142, 145, 146; Half Tree Hollow,
  147, 148, 158, 160; James Valley, 129,
  132, 164; Jamestown, *see* Jamestown;
  Lemon Valley, 143; Longwood House,
  131, 132, 159, 166, 168, 169; Maldivia
  House, *see under* Jamestown; moth
  survey, 152–6, *155*; Napoleon's exile on,
  2, 44, 129, 131, 132, 136; Natal proposal,
  250; National Trust, 153; as place of
  exile, 132, 134, 249–50; Prince Andrew
  School, Francis Plain, 140, 143, 164–5;
  Rosemary Hall, 136, 151, 165; Rupert's
  Valley, 143, 145; St Paul's Cathedral,
  146; and slavery, 142, 143–5; Thompson's
  Wood, 153–4, 168
St Helena, RMS, 129, 153
St Helena Guardian, 136, 138, 142, 148–9,
  166
St Nicholas, 174
St Osyth, 131
St Paul, 146, 148
St Petersburg: Bloody Sunday (1905), 255,
  266; Church of the Saviour on Blood, 51;
  Jewish Museum, 256; Jewish pogroms,
  54, 255–6; Museum of Anthropology
  and Ethnography, 55, 256, 257–8, 260,
  263; Preobrazhenskoye Jewish Cemetery,
  263; Starovilskaya Street, 45, 48, 50, 59,
  256; University, 53, 54, 55, 202; Winter
  Palace, 51, 53, 255
Sakhalin Island: Alexandrovsk-Sakhalinsky,
  174, 181–2, 184, 189, 258, 259; bears,
  196, 198–9; Cape Mariia, 196–7;
  Chekhov Museum, 181, 186; Chekhov
  visits, 64, 174–5, 182, 184, 187, 251,
  259; Dué coal mines, 186; escape route,

ST PETERSBURG,
RUSSIA

PARIS,
FRANCE

VRONCOURT,
FRANCE

JAMESTOWN,
ST HELENA